Yellow Future

WITHDRAWN

D1739362

Yellow Future

Oriental Style in Hollywood Cinema

Jane Chi Hyun Park

University of Minnesota Press
Minneapolis
London

Portions of chapter 6 were previously published in Jane Chi Hyun Park, "Virtual Race," in *Mixed Race Hollywood*, ed. Mary Beltrán and Camilla Fojas (New York: New York University Press, 2008), 182–202; reprinted with permission from New York University Press.

Published by the University of Minnesota Press
111 Third Avenue South, Suite 290
Minneapolis, MN 55401-2520
http://www.upress.umn.edu

Library of Congress Cataloging-in-Publication Data

Park, Jane Chi Hyun.
    Yellow future : oriental style in Hollywood cinema / Jane Chi Hyun Park.
        p. cm.
    Includes bibliographical references and index.
    ISBN 978-0-8166-4979-2 (hc : alk. paper) — ISBN 978-0-8166-4980-8 (pb : alk. paper)
    1. Asians in motion pictures. 2. Asian Americans in motion pictures. 3. Asia—In motion pictures. 4. Motion pictures—United States—History—20th century. I. Title.
    √ PN1995.9.A78P38 2010
        791.43′652995—dc22

                                        2010020852

Printed in the United States of America on acid-free paper

The University of Minnesota is an equal-opportunity educator and employer.

16 15 14 13 12 11 10   10 9 8 7 6 5 4 3 2 1

Contents

Introduction

Race ... has assumed a metaphorical life so completely embedded in daily discourse that it is perhaps more necessary and more on display than ever before.

—Toni Morrison, *Playing in the Dark: Whiteness and the Literary Imagination*

Appropriately enough, the idea for this book came from a movie. Several summers ago I saw the science-fiction classic *Brazil* (1984) on the big screen for the first time. I had seen the film many times on television as a Korean American girl growing up in the American Midwest and Southwest of the 1980s, yet watching it again as a slightly more critical adult I was struck by two startling images in the dream sequences, of which, oddly, I had no memory.

The first image was that of a huge samurailike robot attacking the hero, who had been transformed from a meek, emasculated bureaucrat into a glorious flying knight in shining armor, the second that of hunchbacked Asiatic dwarves dragging the caged heroine, who had also undergone a dramatic makeover from a tough mechanic to a silent, hyperfeminized damsel in distress. In all the sequences the protagonists were centered in the frame and bathed in celestial three-point light, which had the effect of accentuating their whiteness. In stark contrast, the orientalized figures were fragmented and shot in shadow, their presence accompanied by ominous, menacing music. As dehumanized enemies in the hero's escape fantasies, the figures seemed to stand for the oppressive social institutions undergirding director Terry Gilliam's vision of a bleak, technocratic future. As threatening objects that easily blended into the background, they literally embodied the spaces, sounds, and movements used to convey that vision onscreen. I found myself wondering how I could have missed this oriental imagery in *Brazil* and what it was doing in the film.

In *Yellow Future: Oriental Style in Hollywood Cinema* I attempt to answer these questions by looking at similarly fleeting references to East Asia as futuristic and technologized in a range of Hollywood movies since the 1980s, when such references became prevalent in the film industry and in U.S. popular culture more generally. By contextualizing these references within the social, economic, and cultural developments of this period, I consider the ways in which East Asian peoples and places have become closely linked with various forms of technology in recent years to produce a collective fantasy of the futuristic, high-tech Orient—or *East Asia as the future.*

Imprinted in the national consciousness and exported to the rest of the world through media, this fantasy is based on and sustained through imagery, iconography, and modes of performance that conflate East Asia with technology in a global, multicultural context, constituting what I call *oriental style.* Central to my exploration of oriental style is the idea not only of technologized Asiatic bodies and spaces but also of *conditional visibility,* or the ways in which certain bodies, objects, and images are sometimes visible and other times invisible in the dominant culture. As I discuss in more detail later, conditional visibility defines how the Asiatic appears in U.S. commercial media and how people of Asian descent are seen—and just as often not seen—in the public sphere.

It is easy for Asian Americans to condemn images like those I just described as racist stereotypes due to the feelings of anger, disgust, and shame that may arise in us from seeing ourselves distorted in such images. It is also easy to dismiss or dissemble them unconsciously as I did, perhaps to repress those feelings or perhaps because we have grown so accustomed to accepting these flattened racial metaphors as abstract others (i.e., not seeing ourselves in them). On the complementary flip side, it is just as easy to celebrate openly—or to consume secretly with guilty pleasure—the recent proliferation of "cool" Asian tropes that constitute the background and increasingly the foreground of more contemporary Hollywood films such as the *Rush Hour* series (1998, 2001, 2007), the *Kill Bill* dyad (2003, 2004), and *The Forbidden Kingdom* (2008). The challenge lies in examining these representations critically rather than denouncing them as simple stereotypes unworthy of scholarly attention, automatically citing them as evidence of the increasing presence (and implied power) of Asians and Asian Americans in Hollywood, or reclaiming them as subversive tactics that Asian

American artists, critics, and audiences can use to resist the hegemonic Hollywood system.

What ties together the seemingly opposed abject and fabulous depictions of the Asiatic described earlier is the way fans and critics alike acknowledge both for their *style,* not their content, and their *surface,* not their interiority. In other words, both kinds of oriental imagery—the invisible abject and the hypervisible fêted—are reduced to decorative flourishes within the films in which they appear as well as in the popular discourse surrounding them. "Oriental style" describes the process and product of this reduction: the ways in which Hollywood films crystallize and commodify multiple, heterogeneous Asiatic cultures, histories, and aesthetics into a small number of easily recognizable, often interchangeable tropes that help to shape dominant cultural attitudes about Asia and people of Asian descent.

Yellow Future provides a genealogy of this style and its many variations through close, contextualized readings of films in which it appears, from *Blade Runner* (1982), *The Karate Kid* (1984), and *Gung Ho* (1986) to *Rush Hour, The Matrix* (1999), and *Batman Begins* (2005). These readings analyze "oriental style" as part of the ongoing historical *process* of the racialization of East Asians in the United States ("oriental") and as an aesthetic *product* that appeals to multiple audiences due precisely to its seeming lack of depth, subjectivity, and history ("style"). By explicating the relationship between process or context and product or text, I try to show the ways in which oriental style matters culturally, particularly in its reflection and shaping of American popular attitudes toward East Asia in the late twentieth and early twenty-first centuries.

In developing my argument I have been indebted to the work that has been done on film and media in Asian American studies, particularly by Peter Feng, Darrell Hamamoto, L. S. Kim, Russell Leong, Gina Marchetti, Kent Ono, Eugene Franklin Wong, Glen Mimura, Celine Parreñas Shimizu, Jun Xing, and others. Most of this work has focused on representations of East Asian and Asian American characters, on settings and performances in Hollywood films that foreground oriental themes and tropes, or on experimental and feature films, documentaries, and video that were made by, and usually for, Asian Americans. As of yet, no book-length study has appeared that looks closely at what I am calling oriental style: the sometimes unsettling and often quite illuminating ways in which Asian tropes and themes occupy the background of Hollywood movies and how these tropes and themes implicitly structure the primary narratives and characters of these films.

My approach derives from one of the foundational ideas of cultural studies: namely, that style cannot be separated from content, just as aesthetics cannot be separated from ideology. This is not to discount the power of a good story, a tight beat, or an evocative photograph to touch, move, and transform but rather to investigate how they do so and why certain cultural trends, styles, and narratives resonate strongly in certain periods and places for certain groups of people. Lawrence Grossberg calls a coherent, recurring grouping of such resonances a "cultural formation," which Thomas Foster sums up as "a historical articulation of textual practices with 'a variety of other cultural, social, economic, historical and political practices' [that] cannot be reduced to 'a body of texts' but 'has to be read as the articulation of a number of discrete series of events, only some of which are discursive.'"[1] The question that drives this book, then, is this: what factors led to the emergence of oriental style as a cultural formation in the 1980s, its development in the 1990s, and its incorporation into the dominant discourse of Hollywood cinema in the 2000s?

Yellow Future follows a historical trajectory, with each chapter building on previous responses to this question. However, this structure neither assumes nor implies a teleological narrative. As mentioned earlier, at first glance current Asian imagery in Hollywood seems to deviate from earlier, more explicitly stereotypical depictions of East Asians and Asian Americans. High-budget films such as *The Last Samurai* (2003) and *Memoirs of a Geisha* (2005) beautifully showcase Asian landscapes and cultures (albeit from a decidedly Hollywood perspective), while more and more Asian North American actors such as Lucy Liu, Ming Na, Sandra Oh, and Russell Wong grace the big and small screens. The following pages will show further evidence for this shift in the uncannily Asiatic look of cinematic cityscapes and the appearance of a desirable Asiatic masculinity embodied in glamorous action heroes played by stars such as Jet Li, Jackie Chan, and Chow Yun-Fat and performed through martial arts, now de rigueur in Hollywood action sequences. These signs seem to indicate that East Asia, once abject and rejected, has become, or is very much in the process of becoming, attractive and even celebrated in U.S. popular media.

Yet, as the following pages will also show, all of these references to the Asiatic bear the traces of the uniquely orientalist forms of racism that have structured Asian American histories and identities even as some representations, regardless of the time periods and the racial constraints in which they have appeared, have moved beyond expected stereotypes.[2] For instance, Long Duk Dong (Gedde Watanabe), the Japanese exchange student in *Sixteen Candles* (1984), and Mr. Miyagi (Pat Morita), the Japanese American mentor in *The Karate Kid*, are both marked "oriental" through their narrative roles in these movies as well as by the deliberately self-orientalized performances of the actors who play them. However, the former is reduced to a stereotype, whereas the latter is a racialized type that becomes humanized, a process I explore in chapter 3. In other words, although both characters fall broadly under the category of Hollywood oriental stereotype, the differences in how the characters are developed within the narrative, or not, and how this affects the other characters'—and implicitly viewers'—relationship to the Asiatic suggest the need to look more carefully at how stereotypes are deployed in Hollywood.

Along similar lines, an Asian actor's top billing in a film does not at all ensure that the film will not use racist stereotypes or that these stereotypes will be diminished. In fact, as I show in my analyses of recent "Afro-Asian" films in chapter 4, those stereotypes continue to be played to the hilt, often for spectacular and comic effects. Produced and consumed with an ironic, postmodern "wink," such effects detach cultural signifiers of race, gender, and sexuality from the often brutal histories of power and subordination they have traditionally referenced. Played fast and loose on the big screen, these ostensibly emptied signifiers relegate racism, sexism, and homophobia to the past and, in the process, elide their present-day manifestations. Indeed, the role of such stylized racial images in the larger cultural trend that Lisa Nakamura calls "cosmetic multiculturalism"—a trend that characterizes the casts and mise-en-scène of films by younger male American directors such as Quentin Tarantino, Brett Ratner, Robert Rodrigeuz, and Justin Lin—epitomizes the complexities and contradictions of representing racial and ethnic difference in contemporary Hollywood.[3]

The readings of racial imagery that comprise *Yellow Future* offer a preliminary framework for investigating these contradictions by considering oriental images and iconography as *formal, creative conventions* that draw on and influence *sociopolitical representations* of East Asia and Asian America. Using in-depth case studies of *Blade Runner* and *The Matrix* as critical flashpoints, I trace the development of an oriental style that has taken root most deeply and flowered most visibly in Hollywood movies, but that has also begun to permeate U.S. media and popular culture at large. Methodologically I perform what I argue—that is, that background is as important as foreground—by using an interdisciplinary approach that juxtaposes close readings of individual texts with "thick descriptions" of their various and varied contexts.

Chapter 1 provides the theoretical framework for the book, locating the notion of oriental style within contemporary critical discourse on Orientalism, technology, and multiculturalism. I revisit the models of Orientalism and techno-orientalism introduced respectively by Edward Said in literary and postcolonial studies and by David Morley and Kevin Robins in media studies and extended by Lisa Nakamura and Wendy Chun in technocultural studies. I go on to place these models in conversation with the works of cultural theorists such as Etienne Balibar, Homi Bhabha, bell hooks, and Stuart Hall, which focus on the sociopolitical impact of representations of racial difference in popular culture.

Chapter 2 opens with a fairly recent example of oriental style in *Batman Begins,* then historically grounds its materialization within the emergence of the New Hollywood from the mid-1960s to the late 1970s and concurrent shifts in American Orientalism. Centering on the relationship between Pacific Rim discourse and post-1965 Asian immigration, I introduce the concepts of racial triangulation and the model minority from Asian American studies. These concepts play a pivotal role in the film analyses that follow in subsequent chapters, beginning with the science-fiction cult classic *Blade Runner.*

In chapter 3 I perform a close reading of this film, illuminating the ways in which Asiatic imagery appears as an unsettling backdrop that ambivalently reflects and responds to national anxieties about the rising economic power of Japan abroad and the increasing number of Asian immigrants at home. I discuss how in *Blade Runner* oriental style assumes the spectral form of a techno-oriental other that is displaced onto the spaces of the dystopic, futuristic American city and projected through the bodies of secondary Asiatic characters.

Chapter 4 traces the movement of this techno-oriental other from the background to the foreground in three biracial buddy films of the 1980s: *The Karate Kid, Gung Ho,* and *Black Rain* (1989). Weaving together a number of theoretical threads on race and masculinity from African American and Asian American studies, I show the complex ways in which the central relationships between white male characters and their Asiatic friends and nemeses orientalize the former, destabilizing their whiteness and masculinity and subsequently blurring the boundaries between East and West, self and other.

Chapter 5 moves on to the 1990s, when Asia entered an economic recession after Japan's bubble economy burst and Great Britain handed Hong Kong over to the People's Republic of China. At the same time, Hong Kong action and martial arts movies and anime (Japanese animation) entered mainstream media culture in the United States. I give a brief historical overview of the American reception of these Asian popular media, then consider how their orientalized (mis)translations fuse with representations of black style in hip-hop kung fu films such as *Rush Hour* and *Rush Hour 2, Cradle 2 the Grave* (2003), *Ghost Dog: The Way of the Samurai* (1999, hereafter *Ghost Dog*), and the *Kill Bill* movies.

Finally, chapter 6 looks back to *The Matrix,* the sleeper cyberpunk hit that introduced this particular form of Afro-Asian imagery and sensibility to mass audiences. In my close reading of this film I focus on the racialization and masculinization of the passing, mixed-race protagonist played by hapa actor Keanu Reeves and end by discussing the ways in which two key elements of oriental style—techno-orientalism and popular multiculturalism—culminate in the film's metaphoric representations of the Asiatic.

Like *Brazil, The Matrix* presents a depressing picture of the future in which technology plays a major role in turning people into machines—this time, quite actively and literally. However, the racial difference suggested by the "oriental" robot and dwarves in the dream scenes of an otherwise all-white British world have been replaced by a multiracial crew boasting mad martial arts skills: an African American mentor, a tough white woman, and a computer-obsessed, mixed-race hero. This hero passes for All-American as well as white thanks to Reeves's unforgettable early portrayal of one of two clueless California high school students traveling through time to learn world history. Similarly, *The Matrix* passes as a celebration of the once marginal, now stylishly visible elements of multicultural America. In a turn that suggests we have come very far with respect to representing difference in the dominant U.S. culture, we are supposed to identify with these elements and cheer for them against the global threat of an alien enemy technology.

Tellingly, this enemy, which has enslaved all of humanity (most of whose members are nonwhite, as revealed in the sequels), takes the form of expressionless white men in suits called sentinels. Furthermore, in an interesting twist, these sentinels are led by an Australian actor, Hugo Weaving, who was best known in the United States at the time for his role as a drag queen in the successful crossover film *The Adventures of Priscilla, Queen of the Desert* and as the voice of Rex the dog in *Babe*. Much like Weaving and Reeves—Australian and Canadian actors, respectively, who pass splendidly as Anglo-American characters—the film, a product of transnational creative and financial collaboration, passes as Hollywood. Indeed, it *is* Hollywood. As many film historians have pointed out, the assimilation of nonwhite and non-American filmmakers, writers, cinematographers, financiers and distributors, actors and actresses into the melting pot of American film has been and continues to be a defining element of this necessarily transnational national cinema. Most fans know that *The Matrix* was shot in Sydney and Chicago, choreographed by Hong Kong film veteran Yuen Wo Ping, directed by American brothers Larry and Andy Wachowski, and coproduced by Warner Brothers and Village Roadshow Pictures, a subsidiary of the Australian distribution company Village Roadshow.

As much as the oriental imagery in *Brazil*, a British film shot by an American expatriate, initially eluded me, that of *The Matrix* stands out in my memory, and not simply for its innovative combining of Eastern elements such as wire-fu, *manga* and anime styles, and Chinese philosophies with Western ones such as Hollywood three-act structure and poststructuralism—all of which I discuss in more detail in chapter 6. The imagery stands out because I first saw it on the big screen in Seoul, South Korea, where I was born, with my father. It was the last film we saw together. I was mesmerized. He was confused and could not follow the plot. Earlier that week we had visited the spot where his primary school had once been. I remember his nostalgia for a city that had changed almost completely during his lifetime, from a war-torn Third World nation to the most wired country on the planet. Leaving the theater in crowded Shinchon, surrounded by a sea of unsmiling

Koreans, I had the eerie feeling that I was still in *The Matrix;* I was the authentic human being lost in a fake, technologized world: a Korean American ironically trying to pass as Korean in Korea.

Though I was perhaps unconscious of it at the time, the seeds for this study were planted at that moment. I wondered how the difference in me that was Asian, which had been so shameful in 1980s America, had become the template for such a slick, hip Hollywood vision of the future. What follows is the story of how this particular vision has become so commonplace in such a short time in the United States—and some thoughts on why we should care.

1

Style, Visibility, Future

If representational visibility equals power, then almost-naked young white women should be running Western culture.

—Peggy Phelan, *Unmarked: The Politics of Performance*

Yellow Future builds upon and contributes to ongoing conversations in ethnic studies, film and media studies, and cultural studies around Orientalism, technology, and multiculturalism. In the following pages I show how a critical examination of "oriental style" can bring some of these conversations together. I end by focusing on the title of this book, meditating on how *future* might be made to mean something other than the goal of a progressive multicultural narrative or the "positive" representation of a marginal group in the dominant culture. Such a narrative not only falsely equates visibility with power but also assumes that members of marginal groups always and automatically would want to become part of that culture.

Rather than perpetuating this flawed logic by condemning oriental images in Hollywood films for their marginality or celebrating them for their emerging presence in the mainstream, I suggest instead that we look closely and carefully at *how oriental style is marginal* and what kind of cultural work it does in and at the margins. How does this style inhabit the background of popular films? How does it reinforce and critique the ideologies they articulate with regard to gender, sexuality, class, and nation as well as race and ethnicity? Finally, how does it gesture—awkwardly and sometimes poignantly—toward subjects, histories, and experiences that these films cannot and will not recognize? By raising these questions I hope to open up the possibility of imagining different kinds of futures and of imagining our collective future differently.

Reworking Orientalism

In 1978 Edward Said coined the term "Orientalism" to describe a tendency in the West to represent the Middle East as a fantastic, ahistorical space to be occupied and to portray its peoples and cultures as objects to be consumed. Said's book *Orientalism* analyzes the ways in which such representations place the East in a dependent role vis-à-vis the West, reinforcing the power of the latter to speak about and for the former.

Although this power is grounded in the economic disparity between the West and the so-called Rest that is the legacy of European imperialism, Said stresses that it is maintained less directly through intertextual networks that operate at the level of superstructure. Orientalism is thus "a *distribution* of geopolitical awareness into literary, philological, and historical texts . . . a discourse that is by no means in direct, corresponding relationship with political power in the raw, but rather is produced and exists in an uneven exchange with various kinds of power."[1] Instead of confining this colonizing discourse to a particular group of texts or fields, Said treats it as a set of political and cultural strategies that contains and controls the Asiatic through a double movement. Orientalism lumps the plethora of different ethnicities, cultures, and nations that exist on and around the Asian continent into one category: the Orient.[2] At the same time, it fragments this seemingly mono-lithic category into what Lisa Lowe has called "manageable parts," often interchangeable, which are deemed economically, politically, and culturally useful, once again, for and by the West.[3]

The category of the Orient was produced in the period of the Enlighten-ment, the same period to which Michel Foucault has traced the historical origins of the "normalizing gaze" central to the colonization project.[4] Accord-ing to Foucault, the authoritative gaze of the dominant group (rendered as subjects) normalizes and naturalizes marginal groups (rendered as objects) in order to "know" and thus control them through that knowledge. The gaze of the dominant group normalizes by placing members of marginal groups within a teleological narrative of progress in which the goal is to become as much like the de facto normal member of the dominant culture as possible. At the same time, it naturalizes by containing these others within determin-istic scientific laws that preclude them from achieving the goal of normal-ity. The normalizing gaze thus has the effect of distancing the humanized subject (figured as the mind) not only from the objectified other (figured as the body) but also, crucially, from traits of the other within himself, a point to which I will return in later sections.

Said draws parallels between the ways in which the normalizing gaze of the West reduces the Middle East to a racialized object and women to sexualized objects. In other words, Orientalism is gendered: the East is figured as the eroticized, feminized other that exists to be known, penetrated, and subordinated by the masculinized West.[5] A number of scholars in gender studies have since complicated the analogy by revealing the slippery, often ambiguous nature of the power dynamics between self and other with respect to the ways in which performances of gender and sexuality necessarily inform and intersect with those of race, ethnicity, class, and nation.[6] These studies demonstrate that, like the erotic, Orientalism is infinitely nuanced in its myriad articulations and seeming shifts of power, which nonetheless remain grounded in the unequal relationship between one individual or group and another.

In theorizing this paradox Said points out that the durability of Orientalism derives precisely from its productiveness. As he clearly states, "My whole point is to say that we can better understand the persistence and the durability of saturating hegemonic systems like culture when we realize that their internal constraints upon writers and thinkers were *productive,* not unilaterally inhibiting."[7] Said's central project in *Orientalism,* then, was to look at how the ideological forces underlying this particular discourse manage to reproduce themselves horizontally across a wide range of genres and media and vertically from one period to another.

I take up Said's project in *Yellow Future,* extending the questions Said raised along three different axes. First, I analyze popular visual media, specifically contemporary commercial movies, rather than the canonical literary, historical, and philological texts that constituted the objects of Said's study. Second, I consider the sociopolitical context of the United States in the so-called Era of Globalization rather than those of Britain and France in the Age of Empire. Finally, I look at representations of East Asia—predominantly China and Japan—rather than those of the Middle East. To these various axes I apply Said's ideas as well as those of other scholars who have used his work to discuss East Asian Orientalism within the context of U.S. history and culture.[8]

Orientalism was groundbreaking in many ways—not least for inaugurating the field of postcolonial studies. However, its emphasis on European perceptions of the Middle East cannot wholly account for the distinct development of American Orientalism, as Said is quick to note at the beginning of his study.[9] Shaped for the most part by U.S. military conflicts in Asia and by the history of Asian immigrants in the United States, American Orientalism constitutes the starting point for Asian American cultural studies, which expands Said's paradigm by considering how various kinds of racism have impacted and continue to impact the construction of Asiatic communities in the United States.

Until recently, most work in the field has tended to focus on representations of Asian Americans as seen through the lens of American history and culture. This makes sense because one of the primary purposes of the Asian American movement of the 1970s was to empower Asian Americans against institutionalized racism. The most strategic and politically expedient way to work toward this goal was to establish that Asian Americans were indeed American and therefore entitled to the benefits of legal and cultural citizenship due all Americans.

I also take an Americanist approach, not for this explicitly political reason but because such an approach is the most conducive to analyzing representations of difference in Hollywood movies, which reflect, produce, and disseminate dominant national ideologies. A close look at oriental style, however, reveals the significant ways in which not only Hollywood but also Asian America has always already been transnational—a point that David Palumbo Liu elegantly performs when he rewrites "Asian-American" as "Asian/American." The slash or solidus represents a refusal to define Asian American identities in a way that assumes that "American" is the default white national subject while the ethnic marker "Asian" is its supplemental modifier. Palumbo-Liu deploys the solidus to posit "a choice between two terms" wherein the construction "Asian/American" "at once implies both exclusion and inclusion . . . mark[ing] *both* the distinction installed between 'Asian' and 'American' *and* a dynamic, unsettled, and inclusive movement."[10]

This movement refers to two related elements that define the social and political identity of Asian Americans. The first, which I will flesh out later, is the historically ambiguous racial status of Asiatic people in the United States as *unreadable nonwhites.* Neither black (of African descent) nor white (of European descent), Asian Americans are seen as outside or vacillating between the two poles of the so-called black/white binary, which has been the dominant framework for understanding race relations in the United States. Subsequently, Asian Americans have been rendered perpetually foreign, invisible, and suspect. The second element is the increasingly explicit transnationalization of "Asian America" in the past twenty years as immigration patterns have shifted and as national borders have grown ever more fluid and cultural differences ever more hybrid thanks to the increasing availability of new media, communications, and transportation technologies.

In its yoking of the Asiatic with technological imagery, oriental style seems to reflect the diminishing relevance not only of the nation-state but also of the East/West binary of Orientalism in a world gone global through shared media production and consumption. The current position of Hollywood exemplifies these shifts. Even as Hollywood products continue to dominate the world economically, movies and other popular media from Asia have begun to gain international currency and to influence filmmaking styles, trends, and content in Hollywood as well as other national film industries around the world. The growing visibility, accessibility, and popularity of Japanese anime, Hindi film musicals, Hong Kong action flicks, and the Korean Wave or Hallyu reflect the economic development of particular Asian countries in the past thirty years as well as the willingness on the part of their governments and corporations to invest in the production, marketing, and distribution of domestic films targeted toward international markets.

Meanwhile, in conjunction with the rapid ascent of the newly industrialized countries (NICs) (Hong Kong, Taiwan, Singapore, and South Korea) to First World status and their efforts to become global cultural players, a new kind of transnational subject has appeared on the world stage. According to Aiwa Ong, this subject, exemplified by the Hong Kong diasporic elite, plays by and through the rules of an international neoliberal game of identity politics in which "the market is absolutely transcendental" and, in so doing, introduces a new kind of "flexible citizenship . . . [that] respond[s] fluidly and opportunistically to changing political-economic conditions."[11] These cosmopolitan transnational citizens of Ong's study as well as less affluent members of non-Western immigrant communities are forging new kinds of virtual relationships to their homelands and adopted homes through the production and consumption of ethnic movies, television shows, popular music, and web sites.[12]

Yellow Future looks not at these relationships but instead, on the other end of the spectrum, at the production practices that translate and transform non-Western cultural forms into palatable commodities for Western (and Westernized) audiences. Like studies on ethnic and diasporic media, however, it is concerned with how human agency—specifically creative agency—simultaneously shapes and is shaped by larger processes of globalization. How are the dynamics of Orientalism changing in the early twenty-first century as the cybernetic "global village" of transnational capitalism meets the print- and nation-based "imagined community" of industrial capitalism?[13]

This question is central to the book, and I respond to it in various ways in the following chapters. What ties these responses together is the concept of techno-orientalism or high-tech Orientalism, which provides a starting point for examining how and why East Asia has become so closely linked with technology.

Techno-orientalism

David Morley and Kevin Robins coined the term "techno-orientalism" to describe a prevalent form of anti-Japanese and anti–East Asian racism that appeared in the 1980s, when Japan's bubble economy was at its peak.[14] According to Morley and Robins, increasingly ambivalent attitudes toward new technologies such as personal computers, Walkmans, and video games became connected with previous stereotypes of East Asians based on the notion of the yellow peril, a fear of Asiatics taking over Western civilization dating back to Genghis Khan's invasions of Europe in the thirteenth century. William Wu elaborates on the yellow peril thus:

> The fear of this threat focuses on specific issues, including possible military invasion from Asia, perceived competition to the white labor force from Asian workers, the alleged moral degeneracy of Asian people, and the potential genetic mixing of Anglo-Saxons with Asians, who were considered a biologically inferior race by some intellectuals of the nineteenth century.[15]

Richard Thompson traces the modern version of the yellow peril to a painting of Asiatic hordes destroying various signifiers of Western civilization that Kaiser William II commissioned in 1895, prints of which he sent as gifts to other members of European royalty along with President William McKinley. Around this time Social Darwinism, Malthusian population studies, anxieties around the sustainability of imperialism, and social panics around Chinese immigration were coalescing in the United States to produce an American version of the yellow peril. Public intellectuals in the United States, England, and Australia such as Brooks Adams, Charles Pearson, Madison Grant, and Lothrop Stoddard hypothesized that, given limited natural resources, population growth in Asian countries, and the "natural" inclinations for the "primitive" (read non-Western) races to dominate the more recessive, "superior" Nordic race, an unchecked Asia could initiate a world war that would pit people of color against Anglo-Saxons.[16]

This yellow peril narrative appeared at critical junctures in the twentieth century when the West came into military contact with East and Southeast Asia, including the Russo-Japanese War (1905), the Philippine-American War (1899–1913), World War II (1939–45), the Korean War (1950–53), and the Vietnam War (1959–75). Although the narrative was deployed differently to fit the social and political contexts of the periods in which the conflicts occurred and to some extent the cultural specificities of the Asian nation with which the United States was involved, in each case racist assumptions based on the orientalist binary strongly shaped common perceptions of people from that nation as well as those of other Asian nations. Furthermore, the formula of the East as a threatening other to the West—an oriental other that needs to be contained, controlled, and domesticated—continues to be repeated, like so many variations on a tiresome theme, in U.S. encounters with East and Southeast Asia as well as Western Asia or the Middle East highlighted most recently in the second Iraq war and the global war on terrorism.

In the 1980s the oriental other was Japan, and the threat it posed to the United States was economic rather than military, although this economic threat was often represented in and through martial terms. Morley and Robins observe that at that time news and popular media began to depict Tokyo as the quintessential postmodern metropolis while reactivating World War II stereotypes of the Japanese as less human and more machinelike.

Linked with new technologies, Japan, and to a lesser extent the NICs, grew to represent the notion of futurity in the national imaginary.

Techno-orientalism is based on the idea that the West resents the East for its ability to appropriate and improve on Western technology—to beat the West at its own game. Seen as nonwhite appropriators of Western technology, the Japanese become imbued with character traits historically connected with Anglo-Saxon peoples and nations (the British in the nineteenth century and the Americans in the twentieth), including those of rationality, development, and progress, reflecting the West's unconscious hatred for these traits of modernity *within itself.* Japan's success at producing and manipulating technology thus destabilizes the rational foundations of modern Western culture by revealing its power—a power grounded in technological prowess—to be culturally and racially *transferable.*[17]

This fear of a non-Western culture assuming elements of modernity was demonstrated historically in the strong antagonism of the West toward Japan when it defeated Russia in the Russo-Japanese War and emerged as a formidable nonwhite Axis power during World War II. According to Morley and Robins, this antagonism was aimed at the seemingly subversive role of the Japanese as both products and reproducers of Western education and military technology.[18] Similarly, fears of Japan in the 1980s stemmed from its economic success, which was based on the production and trade of new consumer technologies and reached a climax in the late 1980s and early 1990s when Japanese corporations began to buy out important symbols of American culture. At the same time, Japan led research in robotics and cybernetics, high technologies that, in their reproduction of human mental and physiological capabilities, most directly challenged the post-Enlightenment notion of human beings as unique and autonomous subjects.[19]

Through their possession of economic capital, the Japanese appeared to be appropriating American culture while, through their expert manipulation of technology, also questioning what it meant to be human. The combination resulted in new stereotypes of the Japanese as dangerous agents of a new economic and technological yellow peril that threatened to destroy the authenticity and legitimacy of American culture. These stereotypes were often extended to other East Asian groups and expressed through techno-oriental imagery in popular culture.

The Cyberpunk Future

Such techno-oriental imagery was most strikingly present in the near-future settings of cyberpunk narratives, which emerged in the 1980s and spanned a wide variety of media. Examples include *Neuromancer, Blade Runner,* and *Max Headroom,* as well as countless music videos with Asiatic themes and tropes such as those for David Bowie's "China Girl" and the Vapors' "Turning Japanese."

In *The Souls of Cyberfolk: Posthumanism as Vernacular Theory,* Thomas Foster provides a genealogy of cyberpunk as a subgenre of hard science fiction that surfaced in the early 1980s and has since become naturalized as a cultural formation.[20] Pam Rosenthal's description of cyberpunk narratives in the early 1990s as "shockingly recognizable . . . our world, gotten worse, gotten more uncomfortable, inhospitable, dangerous, and thrilling" still resonates, at least in academic circles, perhaps because it so succinctly captures the postmodern blurring of boundaries between diegetic and extradiegetic spaces, reality and fiction, present and future for which these narratives have come to be known.[21] This blurring is epitomized in the commonly held notion that William Gibson predicted the emergence of Internet culture with his fictional description of cyberspace as a "consensual hallucination" in 1984.[22]

Although Gibson did not coin the term *cyberpunk*—it originally appeared in a short story by Bruce Bethke titled "Cyberpunk," written in 1983—his first novel, published a year later, certainly helped to popularize it.[23] Cyberpunk soon grew into a literary movement of young, mostly white male authors writing about young, mostly white male hackers having virtual adventures in a dystopic near future dominated by computers and corporations. In this future, human beings are emotionally alienated due to the mechanization of social relations brought on by postindustrial capitalism. The cyberpunk hero tries to successfully navigate the global network of information that the world has become without losing his (or, more rarely, her) fundamental sense of self. It is no surprise, then, that cyberpunk stories tend to center thematically on what makes human beings "human," interrogating how we differ from advanced forms of artificial intelligence; how we distinguish "real" objects, places, and experiences from their copies; and how traditional ontological categories break down in a society ruled by technology and corporate interests.

In the preface to *Mirrorshades,* one of the first anthologies of cyberpunk fiction, Bruce Sterling, a prominent engineer of the movement, defines the subgenre as a mixture of science-fiction literary traditions, 1970s punk sensibility, and 1980s pop culture:

> The cyberpunks are perhaps the first SF generation to grow up not only within the literary tradition of science fiction but in a truly science-fictional world. . . . Thus, "cyberpunk" . . . captures something crucial . . . to the decade as a whole: a new kind of integration. The overlapping of worlds that were formerly separate: the realm of high tech, and the modern pop underground.[24]

According to Istvan Csicsery-Ronay Jr., it was precisely these allusions to and imitation of media in cyberpunk fiction that led to its demise as a literary movement. As he wryly put it in the 1990s, "[An] interesting question is exactly what cyberpunk literature can offer that video games, hip-hop, and Rejection Front rock cannot."[25] The answer, apparently, was not much more. Yet the same tendencies that made cyberpunk fiction an untenable paradox within a decade of its inception gave its *style* a natural home in the increasingly high-tech aesthetics and technology-oriented themes of visual media, from music videos and performance art to comics, television, movies, and the Internet.

What until recently have gone largely ignored in academic criticism are the ways in which this technophilic style—defined by a global popular multiculturalism and permeated by Asiatic tropes—exoticizes non-Western peoples and cultures. Lisa Nakamura and Wendy Chun, among others, have started to fill this gap with discussions of techno-orientalism in cyberpunk within larger studies of race, gender, and power on the Internet.[26] It is to these discussions that I now turn.

The High-Tech Orient in Cyberpunk and Cyberspace

In *Control and Freedom: Power and Paranoia in the Age of Fiber Optics,* Chun draws a parallel between the virtual landscapes of cyberspace and those of the imagined Orient, arguing that the "high-tech Orientalism" of *Neuromancer,* "like its nontech version, 'defines the Orient as that which can never be a subject.'"[27] Chun describes cyberspace as a distinctly oriental space teeming with Asian trademarks and corporations that exist to be "accessed" by the novel's protagonist, Case, the prototype for the Anglo-American "console cowboy" of subsequent cyberpunk fiction and film.

Chun goes on to note that in its simulation of Japan in the Edo period, the cyberpunk future depicted in *Neuromancer* reactivates the historical moment at which Japan and the United States came into contact, aligning the white male protagonist with the nineteenth-century "imperial subject" whose mission was to "open" Japan to the West. Like the imperialist, Case's power comes from "see[ing] without being seen" as he assumes Foucault's normalizing gaze to conquer and control cyberspace, figured as the virtual Orient.[28] According to Chun, this "high-tech Orientalism" literalizes the inherent virtuality of Orientalism as a Western fantasy of Asia circulated in and through texts.

Taking Chun's argument further, I would suggest that in the process techno-orientalism also changes certain aspects of Orientalism and that these changes are reflected in a couple of significant differences between the "imperialist subject" and the "console cowboy." To start, the latter diverges from the former in *the extent of his dependence* on the Asiatic, specifically the aid of Japanese technology and nonwhite characters. His strong need for these tools (and for people as tools) to express and fulfill his desire for cyberspace effectively destabilizes his subject position.

Let me illustrate what I mean by pointing out what may seem fairly obvious: before Case can use Asiatic technology, he must make it part of his own body. In other words, he must *put on* this technology. Following Chun, the console cowboy puts on aspects of the other when he incorporates technological tools and skills associated with the Asiatic as a kind of prosthetic phallus to penetrate cyberspace. Yet putting on this techno-oriental phallus requires him to *touch* these tools, not simply look at them. Cyberpunk novels and films also represent hackers navigating cyberspace in quite visceral ways, emphasizing the rapid movement of the protagonist in and through architectural networks of information. Introducing touch and movement to the dynamic between self and other brings the two dangerously closer, shortening the distance that vision maintains for an easy objectification of the other.

This physical proximity to Asiatic technology orientalizes the protagonist, who, as a way of dealing with having touched and been touched by this technology, proceeds to put on a particular kind of masculinized performance as the console cowboy. For despite his attempts to master and subdue the other, he ultimately cannot control cyberspace. This is because he is already *part of* cyberspace (that is, he is as much a tool of technology as the tools he manipulates), and, more important, because he *wants* to be part of it. Passages in *Neuromancer* describing Case's physical and emotional need for this "consensual hallucination" make it clear that he is addicted to the act of "jacking in."[29]

Our addictions control us; if we could control them, they would cease to be addictions. The protagonist's addiction to the pleasure he gets from interacting with and in cyberspace—and the ways in which the novel romanticizes this relationship—trouble the notion of a self-contained, self-controlled white male subject who perceives the technologized Orient as his radical other. Instead I would argue that the need and desire for this familiar other constitute his identity as *both a limited subject and a willing object of technology.*

This brings us to the second point of difference between the orientalist and the techno-orientalist. Whereas the latter strives to appear capable, masterful, and virile—all traits associated with traditional forms of masculinity—the former masochistically revels in his impotence. The old cowboy demonstrates his ability to conquer both the frontier and the women through whom he will literally reproduce heirs and metaphorically reproduce the white nation. The console cowboy, meanwhile, plays a passive role in his relationships with technically competent and sexually aggressive women and, overall, comes off as pretty inept when he is not surfing the Internet.

Indeed this nerdy antihero might be said to be queer in the sense that sex with women and its accompanying biological and cultural imperative to reproduce, let alone to reproduce the white nation, simply does not turn him on. What turns him on instead is technology, evidenced in the orgasmic highs he experiences from penetrating cyberspace to access its information with his techno-oriental phallus, which, once again, he must put on, belying his original *lack* of a phallus. Chun describes this "'nerd-cool' form of masculinity" in the following way: "High-tech Orientalism allows one to *enjoy* anxieties about Western impotence. . . . This ecstasy does not obliterate the impotence of the cowboy but rather allows him to live with it. It also reveals the limitations of such sexual fantasies and conquest, for this orgasmic ecstasy constructs cyberspace . . . as a solipsistic space."[30]

In her pioneering studies on representations of race and ethnicity in online communities, Lisa Nakamura looks at how these fantasies from cyberpunk fiction and film are "transcoded" onto the liminal spaces of the Internet.[31] Nakamura argues that stereotypes from these narratives strongly influence how Internet users construct their virtual identities, particularly with regard to racial passing and "identity tourism"—a term she has coined to describe users' performance of these fantasies online.[32] Toward that end, she devotes a chapter in each of her books to tracing the evolution of techno-oriental imagery in popular cyberpunk texts from the 1980s to the 2000s.[33]

Like Chun, Nakamura sees the protagonist of early cyberpunk as an imperialist subject defining himself against and through technological others who are racially coded Asian. She notes that this formula changed a bit in post-1980s cyberpunk narratives such as the novel *Snow Crash* by Neale Stephenson and the *Matrix* movies, which feature racially ambiguous protagonists and nonwhite primary characters. Yet according to Nakamura, the increased visibility of racial difference in these second-generation texts still reaffirms white male privilege by "depicting scenes of white and male users experiencing 'direct' or immediate relations with computer interfaces, while users of color are relegated to the background, depicted with truncated and relatively distant . . . relationships to their hardware and software."[34]

In other words, the power of the protagonist derives from his naturalized connection to and manipulation of digital technologies, which inscribe him as the mind over the body, different parts of which are projected onto the nonwhite characters according to their particular racialized identities as well as their more distanced relationships to these technologies. As in earlier cyberpunk, Asia and Asian Americans are figured as orientalized space and the instruments for accessing that space, whereas people of African descent come to the foreground more in their role as primitive, fetishized bodies that supply the emasculated white male subject with the sexual and cultural mojo he lacks, a point to which I will return in the next section.[35]

In later chapters I draw quite a bit on the significant points that Chun and Nakamura make in technocultural studies about representations of the Asiatic in online spaces. However, by centering on the Hollywood films that they examine peripherally and by using approaches from Asian American studies, ethnic studies, and film and media studies, I build and expand upon their conclusions through historically contextualized readings of similar representations on the big screen. What my readings have in common with their analyses of high-tech Orientalism on and about the Internet (besides the obvious) is the *persistence of race as a signifier for the real* in popular cultural narratives about technology and the virtual. As a number of technocultural feminists have discussed, gender and sexual identities are performed in incredibly queer and often subversive ways through, with, in, and as technology.[36] In contrast, racial and ethnic identities, if performed at all in the same spaces and with the same tools, are played straight and assumed to refer to their "real" counterparts.

Why is this? And what might it have to do with the conditions of racial production and consumption offscreen?

Keeping It Real

This tendency of popular media to represent race as real seems to contradict the idea now commonplace in the academy (at least in the humanities) that racial identities and affiliations, like those of gender and sexuality, are not universal and biologically based but rather socially and culturally constructed. Michael Omi and Howard Winant first articulated this idea in the 1980s through their sociological concept of racial formation, which they define as follows:

> The meaning of race is defined and contested throughout society, in both collective action and personal practice. In the process, racial categories themselves are formed, transformed, destroyed and re-formed. We use the term *racial formation* to refer to the process by which social, economic and political forces determine the content and importance of racial categories, and by which they are in turn shaped by racial meanings.[37]

Omi and Winant point out that in the United States we think of race either as "an *essence* . . . something fixed, concrete and objective" or as "a mere illusion, which an ideal social order would eliminate," with conservatives tending to side with the former notion and liberals the latter.[38] What both viewpoints fail to apprehend is the crucial point of racial formation, which is that race is *a fiction that becomes real* through its acceptance and reiteration by members of both dominant and marginal groups. We experience this most deeply at the level of the body or, more specifically, how we inhabit and move our bodies in different spaces.

As Sara Ahmed notes in *Queer Phenomenology: Orientations, Objects, Others*, "The 'matter' of race is very much about embodied reality; seeing oneself or being seen as white or black or mixed does affect what one 'can do,' or even where one can go, which can be redescribed in terms of *what is and is not within reach*. . . . Race becomes . . . a question of what is within reach, what is available to perceive and to do 'things' with."[39] Following Ahmed, by "race" I mean two things: first, the perception of racial difference based on one's physiognomy and social behavior in certain contexts and second, the attachment of particular cultural values to that perceived difference, which in turn strongly affects one's life quality and chances. How, then, are we taught to see, perform, and treat these differences as such? Put simply, how do we learn to be racist?

According to Etienne Balibar, we learn to see race and to judge accordingly through stereotypes or racial markers that indicate how various forms of racism are deployed and internalized in different social, spatial, and historical contexts. As he puts it,

> Racism . . . organizes affects by conferring upon them a stereotyped form, as regards both their "objects" and "subjects." It is this combination of practices, discourses and representations in a network of affective stereotypes which enable us to give an account of the formation of a racist community and also of the way in which, as a mirror image, individuals and collectivities that are prey to racism find themselves constrained to see themselves as a community.[40]

Like Said, Balibar believes that tracing the formation, circulation, and evolution of stereotypes can reveal the ways in which racist discourses adopt new rhetorical and epistemological models in order to perpetuate existing power hierarchies. In other words, by denaturalizing stereotypes we can expose and challenge the racist attitudes they promulgate.

Before attempting to make this effort, however, we need to understand how stereotypes work to make the fiction of race real. Homi Bhabha defines the stereotype as "a form of knowledge and identification that vacillates between what is always 'in place,' already known and something that must be anxiously repeated."[41] It is the ambivalence implicit in this vacillation that accounts for the durability of the stereotype across space and time and that gives racist discourse its uniquely elliptical and solipsistic qualities. More specifically, what is repeated in the stereotype as the material object and evidence of "common-sense" knowledge (Asians are smart, blacks are athletic, women are bad drivers) is always in excess of what can be proven empirically. Precisely for this reason, the knowledge must be repeated and, through these never-ending repetitions, reified as an inherently unstable form of truth.

According to Bhabha, stereotypes simplify a marginal group by presenting not a necessarily false image of that group but, just as cripplingly, a *fixed and arrested one*.[42] Specific decontextualized traits come to stand in for the entire group, whose members subsequently come to be seen and understood through those traits. This discussion of the stereotype should recall earlier ones of Orientalism and techno-orientalism, particularly the role of the normalizing gaze in *fixing* the other as a static object vis-à-vis the mobile subject. For Bhabha, the stereotype functions as the material trace of the cultural effort to maintain the subject-as-mind/object-as-body split enacted by and through this gaze. Its reiterations sustain the myth of the racial other as a fragmented nonhuman object that can be quantified and categorized and that needs to be dominated and controlled.

Yet a deep, fundamental anxiety also underlies these reiterations because there is always the potential for the racial other to return and resist the normalizing white gaze. As Bhabha points out, "There is always the threatened return of the look; in the identification of the Imaginary relation there is always the alienating other (mirror) which crucially returns its image to the subject; and in that form of substitution and fixation that is fetishism there is always the trace of loss, absence."[43] In other words, if the fetish functions as a substitute for the phallus, which in psychoanalytic discourse defines one's (implicitly male) subjectivity, the stereotype as racialized fetish functions as a substitute for the Western phallus or white (male) subjectivity. The stereotype thus acts simultaneously as a temporary antidote to and constant reminder of "the trace of loss" that impels the white subject to render his or her nonwhite counterpart an other in the first place—that is, either a radical other that needs to be eradicated (xenophobia) or a proximate other that can be assimilated (fetishization).

Richard Dyer further explores this sense of absence in his wonderfully nuanced study of whiteness in visual culture. According to Dyer, *lack* of color, "itself a characteristic of life and presence," is central to the construction of modern white identity as socially privileged yet spiritually impoverished.[44] He describes this lack in the following way: "Whiteness as a race resides in invisible properties and whiteness as power is maintained by being unseen.... True whiteness resides in the non-corporeal.... White is both a colour and, at once, not a colour and the sign of that which is colourless because it cannot be seen: the soul, the mind, and also emptiness, nonexistence and death."[45] Dyer elaborates on the analogy of whiteness to death in the last chapter of *White,* troubling the mind/body split with the following conundrum: "To be positioned as an overseeing subject without [bodily] properties may lead one to wonder if one is a subject at all. If it is spirit not body that makes a person white, then where does this leave the white body which is the vehicle for the reproduction of whiteness, of white power and possession, here on earth?"[46]

It is precisely this anxiety over a materially and culturally privileged white personhood based on the subject's distance from the body that *keeps race real* on the big, small, and terminal screens. More specifically, nonwhite people and their cultures come to represent the body—and traits associated with the body such as sexuality, sensuality, connection, and community— that white people need and desire but must disavow in order to maintain their identities, experiences, and histories as central, universal, and superior.

Such anxiety is intensified in cyberpunk narratives in which proximity to technology gives the white male subject a certain kind of virtual power but distances him even further from his "real" biological body and, indeed, poses the threat of losing that body (read: humanity) altogether to technology, which historically has been gendered female and more recently raced Asiatic.[47] Thomas Foster's close readings of *Robocop* (1987) and Billy Idol's performance in the music video for "Shock to the System" show how white men began to be represented as fragmented and decentered and thus traumatized in the 1980s when the discourses of cybernetics and multiculturalism both became incorporated in the dominant culture. According to Foster, the protagonists played by Peter Weller and Idol, respectively, try to disassociate from the racist history of the United States in which they are implicated but can do so only by assuming a victim position that appropriates and elides the suffering associated with black men at the hands of the white supremacist state.[48] Likewise, Nakamura notes that black masculinity provides the white male with the coolness he needs to distinguish himself from the mechanized white agents in the *Matrix* movies even as black supporting characters "supply the marginal blackness . . . against which whiteness stands in sharp relief."[49] The notion of "black cool" to which Nakamura refers is based on a certain romanticization of black people as the ultimate victims and survivors of white racism. This romanticization, in turn, is based on the dominant model of race relations in the United States, which foregrounds blackness as the racial other and whiteness as the default norm, with other nonwhite groups such as American Indians, Latino/as, Asian Americans, and mixed-race Americans either rendered invisible or pushed to one end of the racial spectrum.

How are these groups represented racially vis-à-vis the black/white binary? What kinds of racial hierarchies exist within and across these different representations? And why is it important to look at these differences comparatively?

Different Differences

This study is premised on the notion that critically interrogating oriental style in Hollywood can provide valuable insight into the widespread fascination not only with East Asian bodies and cultures but also with racial and ethnic difference more generally. Tracing the development of this particular Asiatic style thus entails comparing it to how other nonwhite groups have been perceived and represented in the dominant culture as well as how members of those groups have understood themselves in relation to Asians and Asian Americans and vice versa.

By engaging in this kind of comparative racial analysis I join scholars in ethnic studies such as Gary Okihiro, Vijay Prashad, Bill Mullen, and others whose work compares the histories, cultural representations, and political engagement of and among different racial groups in the United States. These studies demonstrate the ways in which power flows multilaterally, hegemonic ideas are internalized and reproduced within and across marginal groups, and all groups are complicit in varying degrees with the dominant culture.[50] At the same time, a comparative critical lens reveals historical, cultural, and political connections among marginal groups in their struggles to "dismantle the master's house" and to envision more equitable, inclusive structures for recognizing difference.[51] Furthermore, it dislodges whiteness, heterosexuality, and masculinity from the central position these identity categories have occupied legally, socially, and culturally as the standards for humanity and subjectivity in the West.

Likewise, I show the ways in which Asiatic imagery in contemporary Hollywood is forged against and alongside not only whiteness—itself hardly a stable or monolithic racial category—but also racial and cultural identities and experiences other than those of whites. I do this, for instance, by extending the model minority paradigm to members of other nonwhite groups based on their class position, interrogating Afro-Asian collaboration and Afro-Orientalism in contemporary action films and discussing the role of mixed-race and multicultural imagery within oriental style. In the process I start to articulate the complex and often quite contradictory ways we imagine, embody, and perform our racialized identities and relationships, highlighting the deep ambivalence with which we identify both against and through those we consider different from ourselves.

By looking at how East Asian difference is consumed as a curiously deracialized yet still orientalized metaphor, I also join a larger academic discussion around the commodification of racial and ethnic difference. Key questions in this discussion include the following: What kinds of ideological forces drive these modes of consumption through which members of the dominant culture feel they can safely acknowledge and incorporate the racial other? How does this phenomenon materially and psychically affect people of color—those being consumed—as well as the white people who presumably do most of the consuming? Finally, at what moments and under what conditions does this binary of white consumer subject/nonwhite consumed object start to unravel and morph into other kinds of power structures and relationships?

Cultural theorists working across a number of disciplines, including literature, art, anthropology, and film, as well as a number of Asian Americanists whose work I engage in the following pages have traced the presence of non-Western influences in the dominant cultures of Europe and the United States.[52] All of these scholars analyze how various nonwhite peoples and their cultures—reduced to aesthetic abstractions in the Western imaginary—have simultaneously framed *and* permeated, destabilized *and* produced particular constructions of the Western subject.

Perhaps the most influential essay on the topic of consuming racial difference in the United States is bell hooks's "Eating the Other," wherein hooks argues that the "commodification of Otherness has been so successful because it is offered as a new delight, more intense, more satisfying than normal ways of doing and feeling."[53] She equates nonwhite ethnicity in the United States to "spice, seasoning that can liven up the dull dish that is mainstream white culture," and in doing so points out the transparent power of whiteness as the racial norm.[54] In making these assertions hooks draws on two popular metaphors for the American nation: the melting pot and the salad bowl.

The first analogy originated during the first wave of mass immigration from Europe at the turn of the twentieth century and advocated a process of cultural and racial assimilation wherein the immigrant willingly renounced his or her Old World roots to become simultaneously American and white. The second reflects the racial demographic shifts facilitated by mass immigration from Asia and Latin America following the passage of the 1965 Immigration and Naturalization Act and a new kind of racial style politics introduced by the black cultural movement, which tried to decolonize the political consciousness of African Americans through the celebration of black culture and aesthetics. Modeling themselves after the black cultural movement, cultural nationalist movements within the Chicano/a, American Indian, and Asian American communities soon developed their own forms of racialized ethnic styles.[55]

Being white quickly became unpopular in the period of ethnic resurgence that followed, which conflated ethnicity with race in problematic ways. Within the pluralistic framework promoted by this sudden national interest in racial and ethnic difference, white and nonwhite ethnicities grew to be seen as equivalent, a move that ironically depoliticized the struggles of black and other nonwhite groups for political recognition in the white supremacist system that had been implicitly promulgated by the melting-pot notion of nation.

At the same time, the nonhyphenated, ahistorical white citizen celebrated in the melting-pot metaphor became a bland, colorless dish in need of colorful ethnic spice. In other words, whites and nonwhites alike increasingly came to see whiteness as a more general and problematic *lack*, not only of physicality, sexuality, or spirituality but also, after the cultural nationalist movements of the 1970s, of identity. Here whiteness—once the aspiration of new Americans—was destabilized and dehistoricized at the same time that identity was equated with the styles and (stereo)types of non-Western peoples created by whites and nonwhites.

The observation of hooks that Anglo-Americans want to cast off the burdensome legacy of U.S. imperialism and racism and to deny their own racial privilege comes out of this particular historical and cultural moment. According to hooks, white people celebrate and desire people of color because they feel that the life/styles of their nonwhite counterparts are somehow more real or authentic than their own. Consequently, nonwhite identities and experiences gain cultural value as commodities in the marketplace through the reductive terms of postindustrial capitalism and a white middle class that sees itself as culturally bankrupt and lacking a legitimate history.[56]

In "New Ethnicities" Stuart Hall complicates this binary of resistance versus consumption in his attempt to make sense of the increased visibility of black bodies and the emergence of rich, multifaceted narratives about black experience that were appearing in British popular culture during the 1990s. Hall notes that films such as *Territories, Sammy and Rosie Get Laid,* and *My Beautiful Laundrette* highlight the multiple differences that constitute black British identity with respect to gender, sexuality, class, and ethnicity. And he goes on to argue that the nuanced and often ambiguous representations of blackness in these films question its construction as a homogenous racial category defined primarily through and against whiteness. Hall calls for new ways to analyze these representations that can go beyond positive/negative image criticism:

> You can no longer conduct black politics through the strategy of a simple set of reversals, putting in the place of the bad old essential white subject, the new essentially good black subject. Now, that formulation may seem to threaten the collapse of an entire political world. Alternatively, it may be greeted with extraordinary relief at

the passing away of what at one time seemed to be a necessary
fiction. Namely, either that all black people are good or indeed that
all black people are the *same*.[57]

Ellis Hanson levels a similar critique in his terrific introduction to *Out Takes:
Essays on Queer Theory and Film* when he asks, "Why valorize verisimilitude
over fantasy in works of art? Why suppose that anyone would like homo-
sexuals more if they could see them the way they really are? Does the reality
of gay people's lives necessarily make for good cinema? If someone made a
movie about *my* life, I doubt I would see it."[58] Hanson points out that the
representational approach to making and theorizing gay and lesbian cinema
often reproduces the very normative, static notions of gender and sexuality
that this approach purports to resist.

In its place Hanson suggests a queer approach to cinematic depictions
of difference to question the reified categories of difference that we have
internalized and are afraid to critique for fear of being called racists, sexists,
homophobes, or, even worse, sellouts. In this instance he defines *queer* not
only as "a rejection of the compulsory heterosexual code of masculine men
desiring feminine women . . . but also as . . . a resistance to normalization as
conceived more generally as a sort of divide-and-conquer mentality by which
cultural difference—racial, ethnic, sexual, socioeconomic—is pathologized
and atomized as disparate forms of deviance."[59] In an oblique way, I respond
to Hanson's call in *Yellow Future* by queering not only the representational
strategies that have been used to imagine the Asiatic in U.S. cinema but also
the critical modes that have been used to analyze those strategies.

Drawing on hooks's still relevant critique of racial exoticization and Hall
and Hanson's important injunctions to look at the ambivalences and differences within representations of marginal groups, in the readings of the stylized Orient in Hollywood that follow I have attempted to develop a nuanced
and multilayered theoretical approach with which to analyze the recent proliferation of Asiatic images in U.S. popular media. Ideally such an approach
would complicate the easy critical move to see these images simply as orientalist stereotypes while continuing to take into account the often implicitly
racist frameworks in and through which they are produced.

This approach is difficult to implement because it must come to terms
with the idea that the marginality of a subordinate group is in some ways a

necessary condition for the representation of that group in the dominant culture. This is, of course, historically the primary mode through which Anglo-Americans have recognized nonwhites and through which nonwhites have learned to recognize themselves, whether by unwittingly internalizing those racialized constructions or stridently reclaiming them. The success of social movements such as the civil rights, feminist, and gay rights movements, all of which have drawn heavily on the "strategy of a simple set of reversals" to represent historically oppressed social groups, demonstrates the political necessity and efficacy of activating those constructions at certain moments and in certain contexts.

Yet as Hall points out, this model of normative visibility also reifies differences across and within various groups, entrapping them in the zero-sum game of identity politics that continues to define those in the margins through the values and standards of those in the center and subsequently reduces all people to static one-dimensional stereotypes. The same legal system that recognizes particular kinds of identities and experiences as seen by and through the perspective of the dominant group can neither account for nor address the continuation of deeper socially and culturally embedded modes of unconscious discrimination.[60] Feelings of aversion, attraction, and ambivalence toward those different from ourselves, which cannot be explained or understood using positivist logic, reside not only in our individual psyches but also in our local, national, and global cultures. These cultures are shaped more and more by the mediated images and stories that we consume together, for the most part uncritically.

The entertainment industry, of course, produces and disseminates many of these images, which reflect and mold our mass fantasies through an interrelated network of media. In feature-length films these fantasies are usually communicated indirectly through spectacle and mise-en-scène rather than directly through plot and dialogue. As Geoff King notes, these two forms of narrative are implicitly connected in the driving force of Hollywood movies, which is to draw the sustained attention (and disposable income) of as many viewers/consumers as possible: "Profitability has usually been more important than unity or homogeneity. The desire to appeal to a mass market is likely to produce a degree of built-in *in*coherence and conflicting demands. Spectacle is often just as much a core aspect of Hollywood cinema as coherent narrative and should not necessarily be seen as a disruptive intrusion from some place outside."[61] Yet the overriding tendency among film and media scholars who examine the ideological dimensions of cinema has been to privilege narrative over spectacle. That may be why the films discussed in this scholarship are almost always *explicitly* about race, that is, they are films that foreground the stories of nonwhite characters and usually contain some kind of progressive political message condemning racism. I queer this approach by looking at how racial difference structures the ideological messages of films that seem to have nothing to do with race. I do this by focusing on the ways in which nonwhite bodies and cultures are rendered as spectacle in these predominantly white films—both as hypervisible performances that rupture the narrative proper and as invisible alien presences that seem to sustain it.

Much like covert forms of discrimination in the social world, subtle forms of racism, sexism, and homophobia embedded in the backdrop of popular-media narratives often are ignored or dismissed. The fact that these messages have become so utterly normalized and naturalized—to the point that they are even able to elude the relentless critical radar of academics—would seem to demonstrate the incredible hold they have over us. In the next and final section I discuss the power of this taken-for-granted presence as it relates specifically to oriental style.

Yellow Future as Conditional Present

Yellow future obviously plays on the phrase *yellow peril.* The title of this book thus recalls the violent legacy of racism and imperialism that grounds Asian American history even as it alludes to more complicated forms of East Asian exoticism that are becoming increasingly prominent as the term *peril* is replaced with *future.*

Yellow future describes the mediated milieu in which people of Asian descent find themselves in the United States, rendered white by default or relegated to the background vis-à-vis not only white but also other non-white groups. As highlighted in the coverage of events such as the 1992 Los Angeles uprising, the 1999 Wen Ho Lee case, and the 2007 Virginia Tech shootings, news media situate Asian Americans in the national imaginary as perpetual foreigners at worst, honorary whites at best, and usually liminal figures that lie somewhere between these two polarized roles.[62]

Tellingly, most references to East Asia on the big screen appear in a similarly in-between space. Asiatic difference is sometimes hypervisible, as in the martial arts sequences of action movies starring Steven Seagal, Claude Van Damme, Jackie Chan, and Jet Li or the breathtaking landscapes and opulent costumes of such period films as *Empire of the Sun* (1987), *The Last Emperor* (1987), and *Crouching Tiger, Hidden Dragon,* (2000). At other times it is hardly visible at all, as in the bit role that Steve Park plays as the female protagonist's awkward former classmate in *Fargo* (1996); the Shanghai cityscape dotted with inscrutable Chinese faces, which amplifies the protagonist's sense of disorientation in *Mission Impossible III* (2006); or the consistently Asian meals consumed with chopsticks in the apocalyptic near-future world of *Children of Men* (2007).

In its invisibility and hypervisibility this imagery literally marginalizes Asiatic peoples and cultures on the big screen, the effects of which we feel in the sociopolitical realm. At the same time it underscores the *conditional presence* of Asia and Asians in the United States as simultaneously foreign and familiar. Indeed, oriental style encapsulates the curious paradox of the domesticated other we think we know, the other we admire and love and occasionally accept as one of our own; the other we do not realize that we fear and perhaps even hate.

Oriental style does not refer to the static, abstracted representations of East Asia as radical other to the West that we find in so much popular discourse as well as in seminal critical work by Roland Barthes, Julia Kristeva, and many other Western thinkers. Instead it refers to moving images on the screen, which are visceral as well as visual. The imagery that interests me is contained within the frame of the shot, but it also *moves* within that frame and in so doing unsettles and changes it. In the moment of disruption opened through that movement, we encounter the Asiatic not as pure, fixed exteriority but instead as virtual space situated in an alternate time in which subjects temporarily become objects and objects become subjects, where we suddenly and unexpectedly meet the other and experience ourselves as othered.

"Yellow future" is this alternate space and time that oriental style opens up. It is the critical space between visibility and invisibility, reality and potential that Teresa de Lauretis calls the "space-off" in *Technologies of Gender: Essays on Theory, Film, and Fiction*. De Lauretis borrows the term from film theory, where it is defined as "the space not visible in the frame but inferable from what the frame makes visible," and applies it to her discussion of how we might acknowledge and construct feminist subjectivities that are not defined by and through patriarchy.[63]

The space-off disrupts the binary of inside/outside, which situates women either inside or outside patriarchy and the teleology of linear time and places them on the progressive path toward gender equality, against and away from what are presumed to be the sexist roles and attitudes of the past. Rather than an actual space or time, de Lauretis theorizes the space-off as "a *movement* from the space represented by/in a representation, by/in a discourse, by/in a sex-gender system, to the space not represented yet implied (unseen) in them."[64] This movement occurs in and through "the spaces in the *margins* of hegemonic discourses, social spaces carved in the interstices of institutions."[65] The "elsewhere" that de Lauretis describes, then, is not located in "some mythic distant past or some utopian future history: it is the elsewhere of discourse here and now, the *blind spots, or the space-off,* of its representations."[66]

For de Lauretis the space-off presents a way of imagining something new by looking closely at what is in front of us and asking not just what is missing but what are *we* missing, *what are we failing to see?* When we really look, what we find in the blind spots are neither reflective of a wholly injurious past nor harbingers of a bright and certain future but instead moments of possibility in the present that show the ways in which the past and the future are always intertwined and under construction.

Along similar lines, Elspeth Probyn suggests using a new tense—the conditional present or anterior future—to reconceptualize the self as continually changing and growing as it touches and is touched by others. In "Technologizing the Self: A Future Anterior for Cultural Studies" she urges academics who work on issues of power, identity, and representation "instead of standing on our differences and wearing our identities as slogans . . . to put the images of our selves to work epistemologically and ontologically."[67] In other words, Probyn advocates a transformative politics that starts with an understanding of ourselves as works in process—flawed people with historical baggage who can try to make the world a more equitable place by learning from the past while living in the "as if" of potential.[68]

The notions of the space-off and the conditional present are particularly relevant to the project of *Yellow Future* because the future of its title is in so many ways already here and has always been here. It lies in the traces of the racisms that have shaped and continue to shape American history and identity. Yet, as I hope to show in the following pages, this future also points toward ways in which we can acknowledge these traces and, by seeing and working through them, move collectively toward imagining something new and possibly different.

2

An Oriental Past

Yellow peril and model minority are best understood as two aspects of the same, long-running racial form . . . whose most salient feature, whether it has been made the basis for exclusion or assimilation, is the trope of economic efficiency.

—Colleen Lye, *America's Asia: Racial Form and American Literature, 1893–1945*

Rave reviews and huge box office returns for *The Dark Knight* (2008), the most recent installation of the Hollywood comic franchise, underscore the relevance of Batman as a superhero for our age. Unlike most of his counterparts, who are aliens (Superman) or mutants (Spiderman), Batman has no supernatural powers. Instead, his existence is a testament to the powers of Western science and a celebration of the technological prostheses that constitute the cyborg. In addition, his motivations and actions are less clear-cut, more complex and ambiguous. Batman thus blurs the lines between good and evil, human and machine, and, as I will argue shortly, West and East.

This blurring is made most apparent in allusions to technology and the Orient in *Batman Begins,* which provides the backstory for Gotham's troubled vigilante-hero. Oriental style—the representation of Asiatic tropes through the discourses of technological advancement and racial progressivism—undergirds the primary ideological conflicts in the film, returning in even more obvious, almost ironically caricaturized forms in *The Dark Knight.*

Directed by Christopher Nolan, *Batman Begins* opens with an ominous image of a swarm of bats flying across and darkening the screen. This image transitions into one of young Bruce Wayne (Gus Lewis) running away from his childhood playmate (Emma Lockhart), from whom he has filched an arrowhead discovered on the grounds of his family's mansion. In the midst of running, Bruce falls through a hidden hole in the garden where, after a moment of stillness, a dark cloud of bats surrounds and overwhelms him with their frenetic movements and high-pitched shrieking.

The adult Bruce (Christian Bale) wakes from this nightmarish memory to the equally nightmarish reality of a rough Bhutanese jail where he is the only non-Asiatic prisoner. When a burly inmate attacks him, Bruce fights back until the police arrive to throw him in a cell where he is greeted by a mysterious European named Ducard (Liam Neeson) who invites him to join a vigilante organization called the League of Shadows. Ducard offers him a "new path" if he can find a "rare blue flower that grows on the Eastern slopes." Bruce completes the mission and arrives at the League's headquarters, a Buddhist temple perched in the Himalayas, where he meets its leader, Ra's Al Ghul (Ken Watanabe), an imposing East Asian man in the trappings of a Tibetan monk. He undergoes training in *ninjitsu,* scenes of which are intercut with flashbacks to his childhood and adolescence in Gotham.

In these flashbacks the bats are coded demonic and oriental as exemplified in two key scenes: the murder of Bruce's parents and his initiation into the League. In the first scene young Bruce experiences a panic attack at the opera as he watches *Mefistofele* with his parents. In the sequence that triggers Bruce's attack, the stage is overrun with silhouettes of dark, demonic figures scaling black wires and singing in harsh, dissonant tones. The drumbeats become more pronounced, and the singing turns into chanting as medium close-ups of the figures are spliced with quick shots of the bats from the opening, conflating them with the devilish bodies onstage. Bruce asks to leave, and Thomas Wayne (Linus Roache) promptly ushers his family out of the opera house. Almost immediately they are accosted by a mugger (Richard Brake), who kills Thomas and his wife as their son watches helplessly. Indirectly then, Bruce's bat phobia leads to his parents' death, which becomes the catalyst for his departure from Gotham several years later.

Unable to bear the guilt he feels for their murder, a young adult Bruce leaves his privileged life to learn about criminality as an anonymous sojourner in the Third World. We see him first in Africa, stealing fruit and sharing it with a hungry black boy; then in China, where ironically he is caught stealing shipments for Wayne Enterprises; and finally in Tibet, where he is orientalized—transformed into a ninja to serve the League of Shadows.

This sequence leads us to the second scene in which bat imagery figures prominently. Drugged on fumes from the blue flower he has found, Bruce faces a line of ninjas that comes forward to block him from his goal, a lacquered chest in front of a temple shrine. The action sequence that ensues is crosscut with sharp flashbacks to the bats in motion from the opening as well as the demonic bodies in the opera scene. These previous images are linked to the syncopated, ritualistic movements of the ninjas as they deftly move in out of formation and of Bruce himself, who evades them precisely by blending in. The initiation ends when he maneuvers his way to the chest and opens it to let out a swarm of bats.

At this point Ducard places his sword against the neck of the ninja he (and we) believe to be Bruce, who instead appears unexpectedly behind his teacher, demonstrating that he has mastered the art of oriental stealth. Ra's Al Ghul applauds from above as the camera cuts to the last step of the initiation, in which he orders Bruce to execute a prisoner. When the initiate hesitates, R'as chastises him for his compassion, a weakness unacceptable in the leader of a future mission to destroy Gotham. Bruce responds by letting the prisoner go, setting fire to the temple, and saving Ducard, the only other visibly white person in the League, after which he returns, via the Wayne Enterprises helicopter, to the United States.

Back home, Bruce creates a dramatic alter ego to rid his hometown of crime and corruption. Meanwhile, the previously orientalized bats become

Christian Bale in Batman Begins *(2005). Bruce Wayne battles ninjas as part of the rite for his initiation into the League of Shadows.*

associated with blackness—through the bat cave, which Alfred (Michael Caine), the British butler, informs Bruce was once connected to the Underground Railroad, and through the African American character Lucius Fox (Morgan Freeman), Thomas Wayne's former chief engineer, who becomes technological adviser to his son. Paralleling the initiation scene with the ninjas, Bruce finally conquers his fear of bats when he becomes "Batman," standing calmly among the bats and reclaiming the site of his childhood trauma as his new secret headquarters. In the process, he also reclaims the heritage of his paternal ancestors, extraordinarily rich white men committed to social justice movements.

Bruce learns, for instance, that his great grandfather was an abolitionist who built the subterranean wing of the house to aid the passage of black slaves to freedom during the antebellum period. And later Fox tells Bruce that he had helped his father construct another, more literal railroad, the train that Thomas Wayne had hoped would narrow the increasing gap between rich and poor by connecting the different neighborhoods of the city. While Alfred constantly reminds Bruce of his responsibility to continue the work of his father, Fox helps him to act on that responsibility by providing him with the sophisticated mechanical technologies to fight crime and, later, the medical technology to save Gotham from the League's unique style of chemical warfare. Fox plays Q to Bruce's James Bond, supplying him with all the accoutrements—costume, gadgets, weapons, and the requisite Batmobile—crucial to the creation of the Batman image.

In contrast to the first half of the film, the second half lacks explicit Asiatic imagery. However, the specter of the Orient implicitly continues to drive the narrative. Specifically, the technologies used by the League to attempt its destruction of Gotham and by Bruce to protect it are linked to East Asia and the Middle East. Although Fox has designed Batman's weapons and gadgets, the raw materials used to construct them are made in and shipped (cheaply) from China and Singapore. The League's terrorist plot also requires two key technologies associated with the Orient: a poisonous hallucinogenic derived from the Tibetan blue flower and a "microwave emitter" that Wayne Industries has developed as a war weapon for the U.S. military to use in the Middle East.

In much the same way that the bats are domesticated in the second half of the film, blackness is domesticated in the service of reviving postwar liberal values as a solution for class conflict. Furthermore, the bats, now associated with this domesticated racial other, are also used, literally and figuratively, to defend Gotham (read the United States) against foreign invasion by an invisible, insidious, and technologized Orient in the film's climatic revelation of R'as Al Ghul's true identity as Ducard, an amalgam of East and West gone horribly wrong.

The double identity of R'as/Ducard, of course, mirrors that of Bruce/Batman, which underscores the doubling already inherent in their mentor/student, surrogate father/son relationship. More to the point here is the fact that both are also orientalized white men who appropriate Asiatic skills and philosophy, combining them with new technologies to fight injustice in seemingly opposed ways. Whereas the latter advocates a policy of domestic reform based on his father's idealistic liberalism, the former deploys a strategy of international terrorism. Yet the vigilante methods used by Batman/Bruce to realize his father's dream are based in the same violence and Asiatic technology used by R'as/Ducard.

Although the oriental style structuring *Batman Begins* may be relatively new, its roots lie in the histories of Hollywood and American Orientalism in the 1960s and 1970s. The demise of the studio system led to different kinds of filmmaking in Hollywood during this period, exemplified by rebellious, socially critical films by then-young directors such as Martin Scorcese, Arthur Penn, and Francis Ford Coppola. Meanwhile, the Immigration and Naturalization Act of 1965, which ended the quota system for immigration from Asia, challenged the black/white binary and brought major demographic shifts to the Asian American community. These two concurrent historical shifts paved the way for the emergence of oriental style in the 1980s, and it is to an overview of these shifts that I now turn.

The New Hollywood

As Geoff King observes, "the New Hollywood" has come to describe two seemingly different kinds of filmmaking and product. The first, experimental and auteur-focused, was aligned with what has also been called the Hollywood Renaissance, a brief period of filmmaking from the late 1960s to the mid-1970s that saw the debut of unconventional, self-consciously artistic, and socially critical films such as *Bonnie and Clyde* (1967), *Easy Rider* (1969), and *The Godfather* (1972). The second model, which followed the first, was explicitly commercial and spectacle-focused, typified by ideologically and formally conservative films such as *Jaws* (1975), *Jurassic Park* (1993), and *Titanic* (1997).

At first glance, the two strains of the New Hollywood seem widely divergent. However, a closer look reveals a few common points. To begin with, both were and continue to be closely associated with the first generation of film school–educated American directors such as Francis Ford Coppola, Martin Scorsese, Robert Altman, Steven Spielberg, and George Lucas, among many others who incorporated avant-garde elements of foreign and grade-B films into the Hollywood feature. Both forms of New Hollywood cinema were also responses to the decline of the film industry after World War II due to factors such as the 1948 Paramount decree that ended the practice of vertical integration that had characterized the studio system (explained later); the steady erosion and eventual abolishment of the 1930 Production Code; suburbanization and the advent of television as an entertainment alternative; a better-educated, more politically progressive youth market (the "baby boomers"); and the growing U.S. market for foreign films and art cinema.

With the disintegration of the studio system, independent film production became the norm rather than the exception. Studios scaled down their operations and found alternative sources of funding by merging with better-diversified companies. As a result, producers and agents acquired more power and movie production generally grew cheaper, allowing for more creative freedom and experimentation on the part of young filmmakers. Meanwhile, the target audience also grew more fragmented during the late 1960s, a trend that had begun in the previous decade with the emergence of the teen market. Audience fragmentation was accompanied by revisions to the Production Code, which led to the ratings system that replaced the Code in 1968. This allowed for more explicit depictions of sexuality and violence onscreen, paving the way for movies such as *Rosemary's Baby* (1968), *Harold and Maude* (1971), and *Taxi Driver* (1976), which dealt with morally ambiguous topics in ways that often precluded easy audience identification.

These films, like many from the Hollywood Renaissance, drew a great deal from the work of foreign auteurs such as Jean-Luc Godard and François Truffaut in France, Sergio Leone and Michelangelo Antonioni in Italy, and Akira Kurosawa and Yasujiro Ozu in Japan. Devices that young American filmmakers commonly borrowed from these directors included violations of continuity editing and the "180-degree rule" through devices such as jump cuts, flashbacks, flash forwards, and use of the zoom lens.[1] According to Thomas Schatz, such "directorial winks," along with opaque characters and difficult, unclear endings, broadly situate the earlier New Hollywood cinema in the modernist camp.

Although modernist tendencies had existed previously in Hollywood, particularly in the detective and musical genres, they had remained ornamental to or been subsumed by the invisible narration frame typical of the classical Hollywood film, described as follows:

> A "good" classical film—that is, one with well-developed characters with whom viewers identify and whose conflicting goals, stakes, and capacities generate a series of causally-related events that build to a crisis and necessary resolution—this good film is one which seems to flow effortlessly from shot to shot, from scene to scene, carrying its audience along as steadily as the film winds through the projector. A good classical story *seems to tell itself.*[2]

In contrast, Schatz defines the modernist style as a preoccupation with "the *how* over the *what* . . . a realization that in certain texts the how actually *is* the what."[3] Whereas classical films aim for universal appeal by eliding the aesthetic and rhetorical techniques used to tell the story, modernist films self-consciously expose and thus denaturalize the mechanisms of the cinematic apparatus. Bertolt Brecht's notion of *Verfremudungs effekt* (alienation effect) encapsulates the modernist belief that revealing the process of narrative construction in this way can have radical effects on viewers, shocking them out of false consciousness. In other words, modernists believe that it is possible to make a difference through the production and consumption of art, including cinema. Indeed, even at their most baroque and self-indulgent, they tend to believe in and romanticize the idea of resistance. As the products of a young generation expressing its discontent with American hegemonic institutions at home and abroad, the movies of the Hollywood Renaissance qualify as modernist in this sense.

The modernist revolution envisioned in Hollywood during the 1960s and the 1970s was quickly contained and commodified in the highly corporate

New Hollywood of the 1980s. Justin Wyatt's seminal study of the New Hollywood blockbuster in *High Concept: Movies and Marketing in Hollywood* discusses this shift, focusing on the postmodern elements of the contemporary blockbuster, which became standardized in the late 1970s through films such as *Jaws* and *Star Wars* (1977).[4] The assumption behind the production of such movies is that spectacular vehicles such as fast-paced action sequences, cutting-edge special effects, stars, and soundtracks will sell films more effectively at the box office than will character development and complex story lines, not only at home but, just as important (if not more so), abroad. In addition, profits can be reaped by repackaging and selling these non-narrative elements after, and increasingly concurrent with, the release of the film. Viewers can experience a film over and over again by consuming a number of ancillary products derived from it, including the soundtrack, video games, fiction works, comics, toys, and web sites as well as through pilgrimages to amusement parks such as Universal Studios, Disneyworld, and Disneyland.[5]

The reception practices thus encouraged by the production, marketing, and distribution practices of the high-concept film fit Fredric Jameson's notion of the postmodern text.[6] The film-viewing experience is fragmented in the sense that the primary narrative is explicitly commodified and obsessively repeated in various related forms. Likewise, changes in production practices since the 1980s can also be defined as postmodern, summed up in the shift from the vertical studio system of the Old Hollywood, in which the film was conceived of as a finished, unified *product,* to the horizontal financing strategies of the New Hollywood, in which the film functions as a media event—one *process* of experience within a larger constellation of commodified experiences. The move from an emphasis on vertical production to one on horizontal consumption through audience targeting demonstrates the growing power of media corporations and reflects the increasingly connected networks of media production and distribution to which I alluded in the introduction.

The New Hollywood blockbuster provides an excellent example of the paradoxical nature of flexible accumulation in the post-Fordist system of entertainment production. Socioeconomic shifts since the 1980s, such as deindustrialization and the rapid expansion of transnational corporations (TNCs), have helped place the film industry within a complex international web of distribution outlets and delivery systems owned by an ever-diminishing number of huge media conglomerates.

Every year the studios release a handful of blockbuster movies to finance the rest of their films and to maintain general operations. These so-called tent-pole movies have exorbitant budgets, not only due to their high production values but also due to the cost of the promotional strategies required to draw a large, diverse audience—strategies such as saturation advertising, simultaneous national and international theatrical release, and commercial tie-ins.[7] Costs are recouped through profits from ancillary markets as well as from theatrical and distribution sales in foreign markets.[8]

Such synergistic marketing and distribution tactics address an increasingly fragmented and market-segmented audience. However, they do so in the sense of the postmodern articulated by David Harvey, which, "eschewing the idea of progress . . . abandons all sense of historical continuity and memory, while simultaneously developing an incredible ability to plunder history and absorb whatever it finds there as some aspect of the present."[9] If the fundamental tone of modernism was nostalgia for a lost unified subject accompanied by an ambivalent appropriation of difference, the tone of postmodernism is a nihilistic giddiness accompanied by the playful symbolic cannibalism of various racial, sexual, and gendered others.

The relatively recent shift in how the center positions itself vis-à-vis the margins is discernible in how racial, sexual, and class differences appear in contemporary Hollywood cinema. By *the center* I mean those who economically and culturally control the production of media images and stories, mainly white, middle- and upper-class men. Although their position obviously does not translate directly to stories that feature only wealthy, educated, Anglo-American men (which most viewers, including white men, would probably find quite dull), the mainstream media continue to privilege the perspectives and fantasies of whiteness, heterosexuality, and the middle to the upper middle class, primarily because their stories are directed at those who can afford the products they sell.

Because of political gains by marginal groups and recent mass immigration from Asia and Latin America, more women, people of color, gays, and lesbians are being interpellated into that consumer category. So far, however, the differences they have brought to the historical construction of the consumer have been mostly cosmetic and have usually been contained within narrative structures and themes that uphold the social and cultural norm as straight, white, and, most important, middle class. In other words, difference is allowed into the national imaginary only if it can enhance, at best, and affirm, at worst, the prevailing ideologies of the dominant culture.

We see the same pattern in the historical processes through which Asian Americans have become publicly visible as potential legal and cultural citizens in the United States. These processes are circumscribed by the narratives of American Orientalism and Pacific Rim discourse.

American Orientalism

As noted in the introduction, scholars in various fields have taken up Said's theoretical model to examine the origins and maintenance of American Orientalism. Constituting the backdrop of these studies are the intertwined histories of colonization and modernization and their effects. These histories connect dominant representations of Asians to Africans, Latino/as, and indigenous peoples because all these peoples have been forced at some point to enter the world order of Western industrial capitalism as nonhuman objects (slaves) and/or not quite human subjects (aliens ineligible for citizenship and marginal citizens).[10]

While acknowledging this shared history of oppression, it is important to consider the unique characteristics of an orientalist Western gaze focused on East Asia. In what ways have East Asian peoples and cultures been seen as similar to those of other nonwhite groups? And, just as important, when, how, and on whose terms have they been regarded as different from these groups—as conditionally white or racially uncategorizable? By looking at the specific ways in which East Asia and people of East Asian descent have been acknowledged in the United States, we can get a sense of the role that the Asiatic has played in the racial landscape of the real and imagined nation.

Divergences between American and European Orientalisms stem primarily from the fact that historically the United States and European nations have defined and asserted themselves differently as colonial powers. Unlike the latter, which seized and directly ruled territories in Asia from the early sixteenth century to the middle of the twentieth, the former, itself once a British colony, began to consolidate an informal empire in China and Japan only in the late nineteenth century through unequal trade policies and practices, most notably the Open Door Policy. This less direct, neocolonial form of U.S. empire-building in East Asia was accompanied by more explicit forms of colonization and military engagement in the Asian Pacific, specifically the Philippines, Gaum, and Hawaii.

As John Kuo-wei Tchen describes in *New York before Chinatown: Orientalism and the Shaping of American Culture, 1776–1882,* East Asia already was present in the national imaginary before this period: for most of the eighteenth century, the Far East existed in the minds of the newly independent American upper bourgeoisie as an exotic fantasy land defined by luxury objects from the China trade. According to Tchen, this "patrician Orientalism" gave way to a larger middle- and working-class "commercial Orientalism" in the mid–nineteenth century when the country expanded westward even as racial tensions were rising over the institution of slavery in the North and the South. With the arrival of more actual Chinese during this period in California and the West, attitudes toward East Asia shifted from an admiration of exotic oriental goods to a hatred of dangerously proximate oriental bodies.[11]

At this time, California represented the last vestiges of the U.S. frontier and its associations with certain physical, economic, and legal freedoms. The white business elites needed cheap labor to sustain California's booming economic growth, but within the parameters of their recent entry into the Union as a free state. They were able to meet this need by denying legal and cultural citizenship to Chinese immigrants who were willing to work for lower wages than their white, working-class counterparts. The result, as Claire Jean Kim puts it, was "a labor force that would fulfill a temporary economic purpose without making any enduring claims upon the polity."[12]

White nativists responded to the increased presence of Chinese laborers by associating them with then new technologies and framing anti-Asian sentiments in nostalgic rhetoric for the frontier, as Robert Lee notes in *Orientals: Asian Americans in Popular Culture.* The Chinese thus became dehumanized physical markers of the mass industrialization that threatened the livelihoods of a mostly white ethnic (primarily Irish), male, and immigrant working class.[13] The perception of mechanistic so-called coolie labor as an economic menace lay behind coeval representations of the Chinese, which highlighted their radical difference from Anglo-Americans. Images of vermin-eating, idol-worshipping, opium-smoking, asexual Chinese bachelors and hypersexual Chinese prostitutes constructed the Asiatic body as both alien and pollutant: inassimilable, dangerous, deviant, and dirty.[14]

"Bachelor society" was a misnomer, because most of the men in these communities had wives and families in China who were not able to join them due to stringent immigration laws such as the 1870 Page Act, which prohibited the entrance of "Chinese, Japanese and Mongolian women" on the pretext of eliminating the Asian prostitution trade. Later, the 1922 Cable Act, which stripped of citizenship any female U.S. citizen who married a foreign national, made it difficult for Chinese men to marry white women. These laws served to keep the Chinese population disproportionately male and single and precluded the development of permanent Chinese American communities.[15]

Perilist fears that these nonnormative male Asiatic bodies would take over the white nation led to the Chinese Exclusion Act of 1882 and to subsequent legislation that banned other Asian immigrants from entering the country. In 1888 the act was broadened to include Chinese of all occupations, and in 1892 it was extended for another fourteen years, followed by exclusionary legislation against South Asians in 1917, Japanese and Koreans in 1924, and Filipinos in 1934.[16] In the cultural arena, anti-Asian sentiment was reflected and reinforced in popular songs, fiction, theater, art, and eventually cinema. In other words, orientalist attitudes toward the Chinese in the nineteenth century became the template for constructing, containing, and excluding all Asian immigrant groups in the twentieth century.

That template is based on the concept of racial triangulation, which Claire Jean Kim introduced to describe the racial role of Asian Americans with respect to the black/white binary.[17] According to Kim, racial triangulation occurs through two related processes: "relative valorization," in which whites valorize Asians over blacks to dominate both subordinate groups, especially the latter, and "civic ostracism," in which whites construct Asians as "immutably foreign and unassimilable" to exclude them from the public sphere. Racial triangulation is thus based on essentialized notions of racial and/or cultural difference for African Americans and Asian Americans and fails to distinguish among Asian American subgroups as well as between Asian Americans and Asians. As Kim points out, this double Orientalism is glaringly apparent in similarities between how Chinese and Japanese were seen and treated during the anti-Chinese movement of the mid–nineteenth century, the anti-Japanese movement of the early twentieth century, and Japanese American internment during World War II.[18]

After the war, traces of Tchen's patrician Orientalism resurfaced in the sentimental rhetoric used to establish the United States as a new global superpower, targeting Asian nations such as Japan, Korea, and Vietnam, which the United States needed as allies in the Cold War. As Christina Klein elaborates, whereas in European Orientalism the Occident was masculinized through structures of "hard" knowledge, in Cold War American Orientalism it was feminized through structures of "soft" affect.[19] This diplomatic gendering makes sense given the strategic nature of America's international presence in a period of nuclear threat and rapid decolonization. The United States could assert itself as the "good cop" and distance itself from both the Communist powers and the old European colonial guard only by appearing to embrace the racial, ethnic, and cultural differences of the Third World while trying to assimilate those differences in its own terms.

At the same time, yellow perilism became linked with fears of Communist takeover in Asia, framing popular and public discourse on China, North Korea, and North Vietnam even as it orientalized the Soviet Union as the threatening and alien "East" to America's "West." During the Vietnam War, at the height of disenchantment with the U.S. government's containment policy abroad and the escalation of racial tensions at home, the People's Republic of China (PRC) and the Viet Cong, as examples of anti-Western and anti-capitalist "bad subjects," became rallying points for American activists and intellectuals of color, especially those in the Asian American community and some segments of the African American.[20] These movements were contained in the conservative 1980s when government policies favoring deindustrialization and privatization took center stage, ushering in the neoliberal attitudes and practices that currently characterize American society.

A dual mode of representing East Asia persisted throughout all these sociohistorical shifts. From the 1982 murder of Chinese American autoworker Vincent Chin by white coworkers who mistook him for Japanese, fears of Japan buying out America, and false allegations that Taiwanese American scientist Wen Ho Lee had been spying for the PRC in 1999 to the concurrent celebration of the Asian American model minority, "Asian chic," and Asian foodways and spiritual practices, notions of East Asia and Asian America in the dominant culture were defined in what appear to have been oppositional terms.[21] Yet these seemingly paradoxical attitudes were based on the same fundamental association of the Far East with capital, labor, and economic progress that had lain behind the fantasies of China in the minds of America's founding fathers and the xenophobia toward "cheap coolie labor" in those of white, working-class immigrants a century later. Whether contemporary representations of East Asians and Asian Americans have veered toward those of "model minority" or "yellow peril," they have all stemmed from the conflation of Asiatic difference with the liberating *and* dehumanizing mechanisms of capitalism and the technologies that have fueled it.[22] As Colleen Lye points out, "yellow peril and model minority are best understood as two aspects of the same, long-running racial form . . . whose most salient feature, whether it has been made the basis for exclusion or assimilation, is the trope of economic efficiency."[23]

The trope of economic efficiency that structured representations of Asians in the mid-nineteenth century to the mid-twentieth also figured strongly in technologized stereotypes of Asians and Asian Americans that began to appear in the 1980s. News stories consistently lumped together foreign and domestic people of Asian descent, using the suprahuman traits associated with Japan at the time to highlight the achievements of second-generation Asian Americans. These were the children of post-1965 immigrants, who ostensibly were invading the bastions of higher education, the health and science sectors, and corporate America.[24] The group they constituted grew as immigration from countries such as China, South Korea, Vietnam, and India increased and immigration from Japan dwindled.[25]

National anxiety, then, not only about Japan's increasing influence over American capital and culture but also about the rising number of Asian Americans, helped shape dominant cultural representations of the Asiatic. Asian America, Japan, and the newly industrialized countries (NICs) became the new faces of transnational postcapitalism during this period, limning a global frontier of information and ushering in a particular form of techno-orientalism that draws on and promulgates key aspects of Pacific Rim discourse.

Pacific Rim Discourse

Christopher Connery traces the etymological origin of the term *Pacific Rim* to U.S. national security discourse in the 1960s, which was concerned with containing Communism in East and Southeast Asia. Originally referring to geological formations in the Pacific Ocean, including the Bering Strait, China, Japan, Southeast Asia, and the western coasts of the Americas, in the early 1970s *Pacific Rim* came to refer to the relationship between the United States and East Asia, centering on the economic roles of Japan, the NICs, and China.[26]

Several factors led to this shift in Pacific Rim discourse from a military to an economic meaning, including the U.S.–China rapprochement and the end of the Vietnam War, the meteoric rise of Japan to First World status, and, most important, the worldwide economic depression following the 1973 oil crisis.[27] This depression facilitated the emergence of contemporary postindustrial capitalism defined by the notion of flexible accumulation, which David Harvey summarizes thus:

[Flexible accumulation] is characterized by the emergence of entirely new sectors of production, new ways of providing financial services, new markets, and, above all, greatly intensified rates of commercial, technological, and organizational innovation. It has entrained rapid shifts in the patterning of uneven development, both between sectors and between geographical regions, giving rise . . . to a vast surge in so-called "service-sector" employment as well as to entirely new industrial ensembles in hitherto underdeveloped regions.[28]

The movement from a Fordist, managerial, mass production–oriented capitalist system to a post-Fordist, entrepreneurial, batch production–oriented one occurred in large part due to the growing rates of structural unemployment and the weakening power of labor groups and movements in the 1970s. The period also saw the decline of U.S. hegemonic power inside and outside the country's borders and the global erosion of the core-periphery model.

In particular, according to Connery, the economic escalation of Japan and the NICs demonstrate the need for a "new spatial imaginary" that can take into account the fact that "cores and peripheries coexist in former cores and peripheries."[29] Connery locates this new imaginary in Pacific Rim discourse, which positions East Asian countries (led by Japan and China) as a group of successful First World or soon-to-be First World powers whose economic and cultural strategies the United States can use to improve its own declining international status. In so doing, it advocates a "*non*-othering discourse" in which East and West assume a kind of "metonymic equivalence."[30]

On its surface, then, Pacific Rim discourse appears to be the diametric opposite of Orientalism, which is based on the West's othering of the East. Yet I would argue that this discourse actually resurrects an aspect of Orientalism that has been undertheorized in postcolonial studies, namely, the West's identification with the East as its projected self rather than its radical other—an identification that occurs more and more through the mediation of various old and new technologies. Linked to the simultaneously exoticizing and assimilationist aspects of Cold War American Orientalism, Pacific Rim discourse informs Asian immigration to the United States after 1965.

Post-1965 Immigration

The Immigration and Naturalization Act of 1965, also known as the Hart-Cellars Bill, was pivotal in changing Asian arrival and settlement patterns in the country. According to Min Zhou and James Gatewood, the number of Asian immigrants grew from 5 percent in the 1950s to 35 percent in the 1980s where it stabilized. Between 1971 and 1995, approximately 17.1 million immigrants—90 percent from Asia and the Americas—entered the United States, almost equaling the 17.2 million, mostly from Europe, that had arrived at the peak of U.S. immigration during the first quarter of the century. Consequently, at present Asians comprise approximately 4 percent of the total U.S. population and are estimated to become 8 percent of the national body by 2050.[31]

The 1965 Immigration Act was the culmination of legislation passed between 1943 and 1952 to repeal the anti-Asian immigration laws initiated in 1882. That legislation had consisted of the 1943 Magnuson Act, which granted Chinese Americans naturalization rights and extended them to Filipinos and Asian Indians in 1946; the 1945 War Brides Act, which granted nonquota immigration status to Chinese wives of citizens and then to Japanese and Korean wives in 1947; and the 1952 McCarran Walters Act, which lifted the 1917 ban on immigration from the Asian continent and the Pacific Islands (formerly known as the Asiatic Barred Zone and renamed the Asia Pacific Triangle) and repealed a clause in the 1924 Immigration Act that had blocked all Asians from naturalization except Filipinos (because the Philippines were an American territory at the time).

The McCarran Walters Act continued to place quotas on Asian immigration, however, by restricting the number of visas granted annually to people from the Asia Pacific Triangle.[32] Presidents Harry Truman and Dwight Eisenhower both opposed this quota system because it exposed a crack in the image of the United States as a racially liberal nation-state qualified to lead the capitalist world against Communism. Following passage of the Civil Rights and Voting Rights acts, the 1965 Immigration Act was proposed to seal that crack and passed easily under the dominant assumption that the elimination of the Asia Pacific Triangle would not lead to significant immigration from Asia.[33]

This assumption was quickly disproved by the dramatic increase in the number of Asian immigrants as the Asian American population grew from 1.4 million to 8.8 million between 1970 and 1994.[34] The act allowed 20,000 visas to be issued to people from all non-Western countries regardless of the size of the host nation, highly favored family reunification, and encouraged immigration by the professional middle class (PMC).[35] It also covered refugees fleeing Communist regimes, with dislocated Southeast Asians dominating this category from 1981 to 1988.[36]

Post-1965 Asian immigration to the United States differed from preceding immigration waves in terms of class, national, and gender composition. The act reflected the national demand in the mid-1960s for foreign labor to fill positions in engineering, science, and health. The United States needed topnotch researchers in science and technology to win the international arms race, while at home the privatization of health care required more doctors and nurses. Due to government cuts in education, however, few citizens were qualified to fill these positions. The possibility of educating members of the U.S. working class for jobs in these fields was ignored in favor of hiring foreign-trained immigrants—mostly from India, China, and the NICs.

Unlike earlier Asian immigrants of whom the majority had been working-class, this new group of immigrants, with the exception of war refugees, arrived with considerable economic and cultural capital. Its members constituted the "brain drain" that occurred in developing nonwestern countries during the 1970s.[37] For the most part, the PMC already had been exposed to U.S. culture and ideology in their home nations through the presence of

American TNCs, military forces, and mass media. Many had also participated in educational programs in the United States. They were thus familiar
with and often desirous of the economic opportunities and individualistic lifestyle offered by the United States in contrast to their still developing
home countries.[38]

By the 1980s, when the second generation of the PMC was entering the
upper echelons of the American educational system, working-class, immigrant women—mostly from Latin America and Asia—replaced the PMC as
the primary group entering. Since then, as Lisa Lowe notes in *Immigrant
Acts*, "proletarianized female labor" has comprised the majority of immigrants from Asia. Once in the United States, these women are hired in the
garment, custodial, and high-tech industries to perform menial labor, often
in subhuman conditions for low pay.[39] Their labor, crucial to the service-
oriented economy of flexible accommodation, has led to a resurgence in
anti-immigrant nativism and spurred the passage of legislation restricting
immigration, echoing nativist sentiment against Chinese male laborers in
the nineteenth century.[40]

Post-1965 immigration patterns from Asia, then, have made an already
diverse racialized group in the United States even more so. At present, Asian
Americans run the gamut in terms of national, racial, and ethnic backgrounds, generations, and classes as well as sexual, religious, and political
affiliations. These divisions are evident within a single ethnic group; when
one tries to draw connections among different Asian ethnic groups, the
picture grows even more complex. Unlike African Americans, who have a
longer, shared history of oppression in the United States, and Latino/as,
who speak the same language (albeit with different dialects and accents),
Asian Americans have little in common except for the similar ways in which
they have been perceived and represented in the dominant culture. Even in
this instance, there are differences in how those of South Asian, Southeast
Asian, and East Asian descent are seen and treated in various parts of the
country, and in all instances, issues of class, gender, and sexuality play an
important role in how different Asian American groups are coded in the
dominant culture. Additionally, the same ethnic and national groups that
may bond under the umbrella of an imagined Asian American community
in the United States sometimes have long histories of conflict in their home
countries.

Yet when members of these ethnic and national groups arrive in the United States, they all fall in the same racial category, "Asian." The dichotomy here is interesting. Socially and politically, "Asian American" is a collective identity that is neither clearly defined nor easily recognizable. Culturally, however, certain popular stereotypes continue to reproduce and perpetuate a monolithic image of Asian Americans as East (and increasingly South) Asian, foreign, wealthy, and highly educated. That hegemonic image draws strongly on the idea of the model minority.

The Model Minority and the Gook

Despite the many differences sketched here within the Asian American community, first-generation Asian Americans tend to share a conception of the United States as a less class- and gender-stratified land of opportunity than their home countries—an image they gleaned from mediated encounters with American culture in their respective homelands. As Lowe puts it, for many first-generation Korean, Filipino, Vietnamese, and Cambodian Americans U.S. immigration comprises a "'return' to the imperial center"—a kind of "return of the repressed" in which the repressed element is the history of U.S. war, violence, and colonialism in Asia.[41] As the schizophrenic link between Asia and America, Asian Americans operate within the representational boundaries of what Robert Lee calls the "model minority as gook," a phenomenon he describes as follows: "The rapid growth of the Asian American population and its apparent success render the model minority . . . everywhere invisible and powerful. In the narrative of American decline, Asian Americans are represented as the agents of foreign or multinational capital. . . . The model minority is revealed to be a simulacrum, a copy for which no original exists."[42]

First articulated in 1966 by social demographer William Peterson in a *New York Times Magazine* article to explain the economic success of Japanese Americans interned during World War II, the model minority thesis was soon extended to other Asian American groups. In his cogent analysis of this thesis, David Palumbo-Liu points out its contradictions, which still shape popular discourse on Asiatic peoples in the United States.[43] As Palumbo-Liu notes, Peterson attributes Japanese Americans' "superiority," vis-à-vis not only blacks and other minorities but also whites, to traditional Japanese "core values" such as "proud independence, stoic fortitude, group and family loyalties, and community cohesion," which are instilled in them in relatively segregated Japanese American communities.[44]

Yet because these values and the excessive forms of success they engender threaten to destabilize the white nation-state, the model minority thesis also needs a way to eradicate the overly successful Asian American, and to do so from a position of Anglo-American strength rather than weakness. This is accomplished through the trope of assimilation as Palumbo-Liu explains:

> Ironically, the journey to recovery [of a nation "weakened" by social movements within and the Cold War and decolonization movements without] was to be led by a people who, once that mission was accomplished, would literally self-destruct by virtue of the fact that they would have become *too* successful. That is, they had become *Americans,* but as such they were contaminated with exactly the weaknesses and complacency from which their marginal status had protected them. Asian Americans could show America how to be "great" again, but after doing so they were either remarginalized as "Asian" or brought down to more a pedestrian sphere: that of "normal" Americans. It was left to white Americans to be inspired by, but ultimately to surpass, Japanese Americans, aided by the resuscitation of "America" as an inherently white nation.[45]

As Palumbo-Liu goes on to stress, this logic renders untenable the category of "Asian American," which either comes to describe the perpetually foreign members of an exemplary subnation seen simply as an extension of or as the thoroughly assimilated members of the U.S. nation-state. Touted as the highest form of national belonging to which a nonwhite person can and should aspire, assimilation grants the model minority a limited form of inclusion in the national body. This inclusion is limited because it requires the Asian American subject to perform an anxious form of whiteface in which the subject must reject his or her racial and ethnic difference to align with the white norm against other groups of color and the black underclass in particular.[46]

Once again racial triangulation comes into play here. Whereas before and during World War II it was used to construct Asian Americans as alien foreigners who needed to be excluded or exterminated, after the war the same ideological framework was used to construct them as model minorities that could be assimilated, keeping other nonwhite groups "in their place." In this way the myth of the model minority upholds a neoconservative individualist ethos even as it elides the diversity among Asian Americans and underemphasizes the persistence of anti-Asian racism in the United States.

Lee points out a flip side to the figure of the model minority, which he dubs the "gook," drawing on a racial slur for people of East and Southeast Asian descent that targets the Asiatic national power that happens to pose the biggest military threat to the U.S. at a given point in time.[47] And so we see the term used to refer to Filipinos in the Philippine–American War, North Koreans in the Korean War, and the North Vietnamese in the Vietnam War. This figure embodies the racial trace of historical anti-Asian sentiment in the United States and, like various strains of the "yellow peril," appears markedly in times of national crisis such as war and economic depression. Since the 1990s, the threat of the "gook" has surfaced in media representations of Korean American entrepreneurs defending their stores during the Los Angeles uprising, Chinese American lobbyists seeking policy favors with large contributions to the Clinton campaign, and, more recently, Korean American English major Seung Cho's massacre of fellow students at Virginia Tech University. Media coverage of these events depicted the Asian Americans engaged in disloyal, non–model minority behavior as *foreigners* rather than Americans, that is, as expendable scapegoats or treacherous threats to the nation.

Yet the line between "gook" and "model minority" is a thin one, as demonstrated by the easy transposition of traits used to represent one Asiatic group onto another. The "gook"—almost always gendered male—is dehumanized through his nonlegitimate legal and cultural status, which is reinforced through orientalized stereotypes of sexual and emotional absence, excess, and perversity. In short, this indistinguishable representative of the yellow peril is depicted as the radical other of the Western subject insofar as he or she seems to lack an original, modulated core self—that is, as *inauthentic.*

Significantly, the figure of the Asian American as model minority—usually gendered female or feminized—is also characterized as inauthentic.

As a useful nonwhite sidekick or token, this figure performs a necessary but potentially dangerous prosthetic role vis-à-vis the Western subject, necessary in triangulating American racial dynamics and thus upholding white privilege and dangerous precisely in his or her ability to *imitate* the Western subject and thus question its humanity. Paradoxically, then, it is the potential for these model minorities to become "human" (i.e., to inhabit the categorical space of cultural, economic, and political privilege historically reserved for the West) that serves to maintain their nonhuman position.

It is precisely these anxieties over whiteness, humanness, and authenticity, articulated through oriental style, that permeate the central questions in *Blade Runner,* the science-fiction film classic to which I now turn.

3

American Anxiety and the Oriental City

By 1990, Frank Gehry's architecture is praised in a mainstream review as "post-apocalyptic," having a "Blade Runner inventiveness." The term "Blade Runner" is also applied to police tactics—Operation Hammer, the gang "sweeps" of 1991, and the watchful waiting (promotional campaign by LAPD) after the Rodney King beating. And, most of all, by 1994, it is applied to the widening gulf in real-estate values—"Blade Runner neighborhoods"—the middle-class panic about crime that is helping to spin many poor communities in Los Angeles further into the problems that this fantasy suggests. One myth builds another.

—Norman Klein, *The History of Forgetting: Los Angeles and the Erasure of Memory*

Blade Runner opens in the year 2019 with a bird's-eye view of nighttime Los Angeles, belching fire and glittering neon. A surveillance car whooshes out from the darkness, then plunges back into the city toward a golden pyramid-shaped ziggurat. A huge unblinking eye is superimposed on the façade of the building before the camera takes the viewer into one of its rooms. Holden (Morgan Paull), a middle-aged bureaucrat, languidly smokes a cigarette as he administers a Voigt-Kampf test, similar to a polygraph, to Leon (Brion James), a nervous, wide-eyed sanitation worker. When Leon asks him questions about the test, Holden tells him the scenarios he has been using are hypothetical, designed merely to elicit an emotional response in the subject. Leon grows more agitated, responding with shorter, jerkier answers until he is asked to describe his mother, at which point he shoots his interrogator from under the table. The camera cuts to the large digital face of a coyly smiling geisha before it sweeps down into the streets to settle on Deckard (Harrison Ford), a haggard, middle-aged man in a trench coat reading a newspaper in the rain.

With its compelling juxtaposition of film noir elements, the artificial human, and lush, techno-oriental imagery, this evocative opening of *Blade Runner* provides an unforgettable vision of the near future that continues to resonate in popular culture. Since its release in theaters over twenty years ago to an underwhelming response, British director Ridley Scott's second attempt at the science-fiction film genre has become a Hollywood staple and a cult classic, not just among science-fiction fans but among many members of the North American intelligentsia as well. The film has spawned a huge following: a recent search for web sites offering *Blade Runner* material returned 4.5 million hits.[1] Meanwhile, the look of *Blade Runner* continues to be reproduced in a wide range of media, including cinema, fiction, animation, video games, advertisements, and comics. Much like the cyberpunk style it helped to spawn, the depiction of urban dystopia in *Blade Runner* has become clichéd—so thoroughly embedded in the American popular consciousness that it is hard to remember when and how we could have

Harrison Ford in *Blade Runner* (1982). Rick Deckard reads a newspaper before ducking into the sushi bar.

experienced the future otherwise. Future noir or tech noir settings have characterized most science-fiction films from the 1980s to the present, including the *Terminator* series (1984, 1991, 2003), *Strange Days* (1995), *Judge Dredd* (1995), *Dark City* (1998), *eXistenZ* (1999), and the *Matrix* series (1999, 2003), among many others.

At the same time, Ridley Scott's vision of Los Angeles has managed to seep into the real world, as Norman Klein's observations in the epigraph make clear. The film depicts in exaggerated form contemporary problems that plague postindustrial cities, including increasing levels of pollution, overpopulation, media saturation, racism, and classism. In this sense, it can be argued that *Blade Runner*, like much science fiction, has proven eerily prescient, blurring the lines between cinematic fantasy and sociopolitical reality. What is forgotten in this narrative of science fiction turned fact, however, is how these stories also reflect and refract the prevailing attitudes of the social, political, and historical contexts in which they are told. To understand the impact of cultural texts like *Blade Runner*, then, we must identify the ideologies at work in these texts and examine how they are reproduced, repudiated, and negotiated, not only through primary narratives that focus on plot and character development but also through secondary narratives that evoke the texture, tone, and spaces of their stories.

One form of ideology that played an important role in shaping the futuristic world of *Blade Runner* was a kind of casual, taken-for-granted Orientalism on the part of its director and production crew. These Americans and Europeans saw Asia as the unfamiliar opposite of the familiar West and hence the logical other with which to depict a future gone wrong. Their allusions to a mostly East Asian Orient in the film struck a strong chord in viewers. Since its release, many critics and scholars have commented on the Asiatic signifiers in *Blade Runner*, and some have suggested connections between those signifiers and the film's allusions to slavery.[2] However, only a few have considered how the ornamental Orientalism of the film *implicitly structures* its central thematic question, that is, what makes some entities human and others not quite human or "more human than human?"[3]

This chapter centers on that issue through a close examination of the relationship between the oriental imagery in the film and its representations of race, class, and gender. My reading of *Blade Runner* juxtaposes the ideological dynamics of the world it presents against those of the industrial and sociopolitical contexts in which it was made and continues to be interpreted. Appropriately enough, then, it opens with a section called "Contexts," which provides an overview of the adaptation, production, and reception of *Blade Runner*. "Visions," the second section, takes a more in-depth look at the cultural and aesthetic influences behind the film's oriental tropes, drawing on interviews with director Ridley Scott and members of the art crew. The final section, "Implications," discusses the narrative and ideological roles of these tropes through analyses of specific scenes.

Contexts

Adaptation

Blade Runner was based on Philip K. Dick's novel *Do Androids Dream of Electric Sheep?* (hereafter, *Androids*). A highly prolific writer, Dick produced a total of thirty-three novels, winning the prestigious Hugo Award in 1962 and the John W. Campbell Memorial Award in 1974. He also gained a strong fan base in the 1960s counterculture with psychedelic novels such as *The Three Stigmata of Palmer Eldritch* and *Ubik*. At the time of his death in 1982 (right before the opening of *Blade Runner*), Dick's work was widely acclaimed throughout Europe and the United States.[4] Since then his fame has grown with the rapid integration of cyberpunk sensibilities into popular culture. In the past few years, retrospectives of Dick's life and work have appeared in the *New York Times* and the *New Republic*; his autobiography, *Valis*, has been turned into an opera; and high-end publishers Ballantine Books and Gollancz have reissued his books. Once relegated to the pulp shelves, Dick's work is now being taught as part of the U.S. literary canon. Indeed, *Maus* author Art Spiegelman summed up the extent of Dick's posthumous influence thus: "What Franz Kafka was to the first half of the 20th century Philip Dick is to the second half."[5]

The strong relevance of Dick's idiosyncratic vision to the early twenty-first century is best demonstrated by his continued popularity in Hollywood, which is ironic given the author's antagonism toward the entertainment industry. Since the release of *Blade Runner*, his work has become a favorite of those seeking material to adapt into the science-fiction action genre. Several of his novels and short stories have been produced as Hollywood films, including, in addition to *Blade Runner*, *Total Recall* (1990), *Screamers* (1995),

Impostor (2002), *Minority Report* (2002), *Paycheck* (2003), and *A Scanner Darkly* (2006).

Set in 1992, *Androids* concerns the exploits of bounty hunter Rick Deckard after he accepts an assignment from his boss to kill six androids ("andys") recently escaped from a Martian colony. Deckard takes the job to buy the object of his heart's desire, a real pet sheep to replace his artificial one. Along the way he falls in love with one of his targets, a female android named Rachael who betrays him. The world Deckard inhabits is coated with radioactive dust, nuclear residue from World War Terminus, which has killed most life on earth and left the majority of human survivors sterile or mentally deficient. Those with means have fled the planet to make their homes on distant, unpolluted worlds, while those who remain raise animals as status symbols, with biologically natural beasts outranking mechanical ones. Like the radioactive dust that has turned the planet into an environmental wasteland, the "andys" are carryovers from and reminders of the war. Created initially as war weapons, these former "Synthetic Freedom Fighters" are used as slave labor in peacetime to develop colonies on neighboring planets.

Hampton Fancher and David Peoples made several changes in their adaptation of *Androids*, among them omitting the pseudoreligious subtext of the novel as well as its emphasis on the artificial animal trade, diminishing the roles of the female characters, and taking the action outside the deserted office buildings of the novel into the teeming metropolis that has become the hallmark of the movie. However, like the book on which it is based, *Blade Runner* focuses on the protagonist's growing sense of self-alienation in a postapocalyptic, hypermediated society. Because the film engages with this theme through a combination of the science-fiction, hard-boiled detective, and action genres, its formal focus lies in the physical spaces where characters interact rather than in the development of their interpersonal relationships. This focus has the effect not so much of erasing the metaphysical concerns of the novel, as Robin Wood has suggested, as of embodying them in the relationship between the characters and their environment.[6]

Dick himself noted this connection after seeing shots from the film in postproduction. A few months before his death, he described the symbiotic adaptation process in the following way: "The book and the movie do *not* fight each other. . . . They reinforce each other, but they are different. [The production crew] concentrated on the main theme . . . the attrition on him [Deckard] of killing creatures, which although technically [they] are not human . . . are official humans. . . . He sees in them a certain beauty and a certain nobility. And . . . he begins really to question . . . what he's doing.[7]

Release

Dick was convinced that the film adaptation of his book would be a success, but it would take a decade for his prediction to come true. As Paul Sammon chronicles in *Future Noir: The Making of Blade Runner,* the process of getting the story to the screen was not an easy one. The crew hit a major obstacle in December 1981, when the film's primary financer, Filmway, pulled out of the project because Scott had gone over schedule and over budget. Fortunately, working at breakneck speed, producer Michael Deeley was able to find new sponsors: the Ladd Company, an independent production house run by Alan Ladd Jr., who had produced *Star Wars* and *Alien* (1979); the Shaw Brothers Studio in Hong Kong, run by Singaporean mogul Sir Run-Run Shaw and famous for its martial arts movies; and Tandem Productions, run by writer-producers Bud Yorkin, Jerry Perenchio, and Norman Lear and known for its television productions.[8] This three-way international deal, which provided ancillary distribution and exhibition venues through television, video rentals, and foreign markets, contributed to the film's slow and steady success, which crystallized in the theatrical release of the director's cut in 1992.[9]

When it opened at theaters on June 25, 1982, however, *Blade Runner* met with dismal returns at the box office and mixed response from the critics. A few months before its release, producers had screened a rough cut (later known as the director's cut) for focus groups in Dallas and Denver. Frightened by the negative audience response, executives ordered a recut to make the film more intelligible to the American public. The resulting domestic cut featured Ford's monotone voice-over and a "happy ending" in which Deckard and Rachael escape to a countryside composed of outtakes from Stanley Kubrick's horror film *The Shining* (1980). Unfortunately, these cosmetic changes failed to bolster the film's popularity and sales. Despite heavy promotion of *Androids* as a tie-in to the movie, *Blade Runner*'s opening box office gross was $6.15 million; by the end of its first week it had grossed only $8.7 million—a fraction of its $28 million budget.[10]

Meanwhile, another more upbeat and kid-friendly science-fiction movie had become the summer hit. Shot for $10.5 million, Steven Spielberg's *E.T.: The Extraterrestrial* opened on June 11 and made back its budget in the opening weekend with a gross of over $11 million.[11] Unable to compete, Warner Bros. withdrew *Blade Runner* from theatrical distribution and released it on television through its cable affiliate, the Movie Channel, and on video through its Home Video outlets.[12] Consequently, the film achieved its cult status through the exhibition and distribution venues of cable television and video rentals and sales, which became increasingly important in the 1980s. Most people became fans through repeated viewings on the small screen, which proved more conducive to an appreciation of the film's rich set design and textured narrative.

Reception

Critics who wrote about *Blade Runner* immediately after its release failed to see the complementary relationship between its visual and narrative elements. Richard Meyers summed up the popular opinion of the time when he elevated the latter over the former: "*Blade Runner* was a collection of film sets in search of a movie."[13] Those who praised the film likewise focused on the prominence of the set design, comparing *Blade Runner* to other "adult" (read "art house") science-fiction films such as *Metropolis* (1927) and *2001: A Space Odyssey* (1968). In particular they emphasized the credibility of its futuristic city: "The *Blade Runner* setting fascinates because it is plausible. Los Angeles 40 years from now could easily look much like it does in this movie."[14] And as Douglas Pratt pointed out, it was the *style* in which that urban vision was rendered that lent the movie to repeated viewings: "Why is the film so popular on home video? . . . It is drenched in action and special effects, but more importantly, it drips with style, and viewers, desperate for anything which is unique and imaginative, lap it up."[15]

Ironically, Scott had not marketed the film toward these "arty" fans. Instead he had hoped to attract the male adolescent market by incorporating the visual style of adult comic books in the film's set design, especially that of Jean "Moebius" Giraud's work in *Metal Hurlant* (translated in the United

States as *Heavy Metal*). In an interview shortly after the film's release he stated, "The films that have fascinated me the most in the last couple of years tend to have been films, which are derived from comic strips. . . . Therefore there is [sic] a lot of broad strokes, fast bold action, and colorful characters."[16] Scott's description of his idea for the movie fits the model of the New Hollywood blockbuster, which had been the template for his previous hit film *Alien*. With a production design bearing the artistic marks of H. R. Giger and Moebius and technological villains in the form of the "Mother" ship and the android Ash, *Alien* bore some of the superficial tropes of cyberpunk with its dystopic look and themes, but ultimately remained contained within the formula of the Hollywood space opera with its distinct three-act structure, its clearly delineated themes, and a goal-oriented protagonist with whom the audience strongly identifies.

In contrast, the formal qualities of *Blade Runner*—namely, its pastiche of film noir, popular culture, and science fiction; its ambivalent stance on technology; and its lack of closure—proved incompatible with the narrative requisites of a box office hit. Such elements led Franklin Bruce to herald *Blade Runner* as the forerunner of what might be called cyberpunk cinema: "The new films—drawing on the common urban experience of much of their audience, drawing on a dystopian consensus, if you will—don't have to explain themselves. . . . *Blade Runner* . . . is one of the first films to avail itself of this new consensus."[17] Although most suburban audiences had not participated in the "common urban experience" on which this "dystopian consensus" was based, nonetheless the film heralded a way of viewing the future as an extreme version of the present.[18] To learn where this style came from and why its fusion of technology with the Orient still resonates with audiences, we now turn to look at the director and design team of *Blade Runner*.

Visions

Imaging the Future

Trained at the London School of Art and described by Deeley as "having the best eye of anyone in Hollywood," Ridley Scott has emphasized the importance of mise-en-scène in his films with aphorisms such as "A film is a seven-hundred-layer cake" and "Sometimes the design is the statement."[19] According to Scott, "There should be a total integration on a film, a complete synthesis running through the hands of a director who is involved in everything. . . . Certainly, there are moments in movies when the background of a shot can be as important as the foregrounded actor, whether that background be a figure or a landscape."[20]

Instead of replicating the classical Hollywood style, which subordinates mise-en-scène to montage and stresses a linear, character-driven narrative, the director views filmmaking as a carefully orchestrated visual and aural performance. Scott believes in creating "total environments" for his films that play as much of a role in the narrative as do its plot and characters. Drawing on his art background and his experience in advertising, Scott designed *Blade Runner* through a method he calls "pictorial referencing" in which he and his production assistants scour a wide variety of sources for illustrations that evoke the central moods and themes of the film. Important visual foundations for *Blade Runner* included paintings by Rembrandt, Vermeer, Hogarth, and Hopper; various styles of Western and non-Western architecture, underground French comics, and German expressionist and noir films, especially *Metropolis, Citizen Kane* (1941), and *Chinatown* (1974).

Scott and the art team layered the various artistic concepts in these found images to create a densely textured, intricately detailed world for their film. They used this technique to construct a dark, dirty, crowded, and mechanized city that would carry and complement the primary themes of *Blade Runner*—loss, alienation, and dehumanization. Along with mixing different visual styles, Scott combined three time periods in the film: the 1940s (past), 1980s (present), and 2020s (future). The aim was to imagine the future nostalgically as old, worn, and somewhat decrepit. Scott and his production crew achieved this by evoking film noir, the signature cinematic style of 1940s Hollywood, through the pop commercial aesthetic of the 1980s.[21]

Examples of film noir, from *Double Indemnity* (1944) and *The Big Sleep* (1946) to *Body Heat* (1981) and *L.A. Confidential* (1997), contain themes and motifs similar to those in *Blade Runner*. Film noir originated from hard-boiled detective novels by such authors as Raymond Chandler, Dashiell Hammett, and James M. Cain, which were serialized in France in the category "Serie Noire." Films resembling these narratives began to fall under the "noir" label as well.[22] In these tales the American city typified by Los Angeles became the consummate symbol of urban hell, the American dream gone wrong.[23] Film noir externalized the unease, fear, and despair of characters through lighting and design techniques derived from German expressionism, a style brought to Hollywood in the 1940s by Fritz Lang, Max Ophuls, Billy Wilder, Otto Preminger, and many others.[24]

The appeal of film noir lies in the viewer's identification with the usually male protagonist as he makes a series of bad choices that pull him into psychological states of paranoia, cynicism, and emotional numbness not unlike those experienced by war veterans suffering from shell shock. This internal landscape is manifested outwardly in two tropes that define the genre: the cold, indifferent city and the dangerous female love interest. Both function as instruments of industrial capitalism at its worst, drawing an attraction/repulsion response from the protagonist and, by extension, the audience. Supplying the social dimension to this aesthetic, Silver and Ward suggest that film noir functioned as a black slate upon which national anxieties were cathected when veterans returned home to their newly prosperous country.[25] In other words, these films provided a fantastic space for working through insecurities around postwar American masculinity, which stemmed from the threat of Communism abroad and that of increasingly independent women and people of color at home.

The two threats converged in representations of the Orient and the femme fatale in film noir. Referencing Asian allusions in classic examples of noir such as *The Shanghai Gesture* (1940), *Lady from Shanghai* (1947), and *The Manchurian Candidate* (1962) as well as contemporary ones such as *Chinatown, Year of the Dragon* (1985), and *Black Rain* (1989), James Naremore notes, "If the Far East was repeatedly associated in film noir with enigmatic and criminal behavior, it was also depicted as a kind of aestheticized bordello, where one could experience all sorts of forbidden pleasures."[26] This dual role of East Asia resembles that of the femme fatale, the smart, sensual, treacherous love interest who must be extinguished for her evil, boundary-crossing ways or converted into an honest woman. For example, *Lady from Shanghai* has a white female protagonist associated with—and presumably contaminated by—the exotic perversities of that Chinese port city. The link between the mythologized image of East Asia and the figure of the femme fatale neatly follows the gendered logic of Orientalism.

Before considering how that connection relates to the role of oriental imagery in *Blade Runner*, we need to get a sense of how the design crew envisioned its futuristic backdrop. According to William Lightman and Owen Patterson, "The starting point [of the production design] is the desire to create a certain aesthetic and emotional texture—the nitty-gritty, funky world of a hard-boiled private eye; and the sociology is conjured up in order to give the design a logic and steadiness."[27] This view, namely, that the film's creative vision *precedes* the sociohistorical referents used to express it, privileges the aesthetic over the cultural elements of cinema, failing to note the inherently dialectical relationship between the two.

Conceptual artist Syd Mead takes a small step in acknowledging this relationship with his notion of "in-head memory," which he defines in the following way: "People will believe something is real only if it is done right and compared to what they think it should be."[28] The idea of in-head memory raises a compelling point, namely, that one must draw on existing social and cultural referents to construct convincing fantastic worlds. Without such reference points, the audience would have no idea how to comprehend or navigate these worlds.

The *Blade Runner* production crew used certain reference points to create a retrofitted city, which Mead describes thus: "The street sets were going to show this accumulated progress. The buildings would just become surfaces on which you'd mount retrofitted electrical conduits, air conditioning ducts and all kinds of other things."[29] Trained in urban design and city planning, Lawrence Paull, the production designer, explains the social rationale behind "retrofitting": "You go back to the script, and the middle classes have left the earth.... And who's left in the center of the city but the working class, the unemployed, and the homeless. These people do not have ... the skills to fix what breaks in the city.... They discard what isn't really working; they take other generators and machinery and retrofit it to the buildings."[30] Here the notion of "accumulated progress" is integral to the visualization of a future society built literally on those of the past and the present. Paull points out that certain social and cultural referents are necessary to create recognizable fantasies. And these referents—whether they are trench coats or images of geishas—must be accompanied by common ideological codes that make sense of those objects in the social world. To a large extent, these cultural codes are shaped and disseminated through images and narratives produced by the media industry, which are understood and accepted in varying degrees by the audiences that consume them.

Although a psychoanalytic examination of the unconscious racial, gender, and class assumptions behind filmmakers' technical choices lies beyond the scope of this study, we can look at the choices themselves and at the explanations that the producers lent them. For instance, at the same time that Scott drew on the 1940s, he drew on the 1980s—the "present" at the time of filmmaking—to build a credible future city. According to Scott, his goal was a magnified version of "New York on a bad day."[31] This required projecting an experience of urban density, tension, dirtiness, and dislocation on the screen. What images, then, along with those of rainy streets at night and expressive lighting, did Scott and his crew members cull from their collective cultural memories to simulate this experience?

The final set design and comments from members of the art department point to mental pictures of the overdeveloped modern Asian city. In *Blade Runner* the non-Western streets of Tokyo, Hong Kong, and Calcutta combine with the mythic streets of 1940s Los Angeles to produce an uncanny aura of familiarity—how one might remember a city from a bad dream. Giuliana Bruno describes this city as an intensification of present-day racial and cultural mixing, which culminates in a "China(in)town": "In the postindustrial city the explosion of urbanization, melting the futuristic high-tech look into an intercultural scenario, recreates the Third World inside the first. One travels almost without moving, for the Orient occupies the next block."[32]

In Hollywood cinema Asian cities usually have been depicted as densely packed areas that typify the negative effects of overdevelopment. Early examples can be found in films such as *Shanghai Express* (1932) and *Casablanca* (1942), where the psychological dramas of white principal characters are set against a backdrop of nonwhite "oriental" people for whom "life is cheap." Later Akira Kurosawa, with his modern crime thrillers *The Bad Sleep Well* (1960) and *High and Low* (1963), introduced Western art-house audiences to views of the postwar Tokyo cityscape. Meanwhile, Seijun Suzuki brought a similar urban aesthetic to the Japanese grade-B film in *Tokyo Drifter* (1966) and *Branded to Kill* (1967) even as the *Gojira* movies provided a simplified version of densely populated, rapidly modernizing Tokyo for mainstream audiences. From here it is not a big stretch to speculate that celluloid fantasies of the East Asian metropolis might have been in the heads of the *Blade Runner* production crew when they were creating their futuristic city.

Indeed, according to Mead, Scott envisioned the future as distinctly Asian, highly technological, and overcrowded. Mead also makes it clear that for artistic inspiration he drew on his own experiences as a Western foreigner in Tokyo:

> There is a kind of Hong Kong or Calcutta kind of density that Ridley was after. The graphics on the streets contribute to that density without being as distracting as English language signs would be for an American audience. . . . I had noticed that myself in Tokyo on the Ginza where the signs look incredibly jumbled, but I was not distracted by being able to read them so I could enjoy the pure visual composite they created.[33]

This mythic Orient of opaque signs looms large in the *Blade Runner* city, exemplified by the neon signs in Chinese and Japanese script that light up the darkness and the flashing virtual geisha hawking pills and Coca Cola. A link between these flickering signs—constantly moving yet still—and the bodies of the Asian and non-Asian extras that make up the background, which makeup supervisor Marvin Westmore named "'Asian Blade Runner Blue' . . . sort of a greasepaint with a light blue cast to it,"[34] is suggested in the following comment by cinematographer Jorden Cronenweth: "The streets were depicted as terribly overcrowded, giving the audience a future time frame to relate to, we had street scenes just packed with people . . . like ants. So we made them look like ants—all the same. They were all the same in the sense that they were all part of the flow. It was like going in circles . . . like going nowhere."[35] Like the Asian script flashing in neon above, the bodies on the streets below take on a compressed and unintelligible quality meant to dislocate the presumed Western viewer. That the signs and bodies heaving in the mise-en-scène were put there deliberately to alienate this audience appears, at first glance, to support the perilist aspects of Orientalism.[36]

Yet these alien signs and bodies also *fascinate,* as indicated by viewers' continued obsession with a fantastic Los Angeles rendered indistinctly Eastern. Given this fascination, how might we begin to account for the strong appeal of the film's production design? Rather than consigning the discomfiting specter of the Orient to the extreme background of the film, I suggest that it occupies its visual *middle* ground, between the blue-black base of the night palette and the luminously lit white bodies of the principal characters. East Asian iconography and Asiatic bodies as iconography are definitely distorted and relegated to the mise-en-scène. Nonetheless, they are visibly *present*, in stark contrast to the conspicuous *absence* of black iconography and bodies. This conditional presence in the *visual* middle space of the film summons the idea of Asian Americans as model minorities who occupy a *social* middle ground between dominant white culture and other racial others. We can start addressing the ambivalence of this middle space by considering the relationship between space and power in the film.

Race, Space, and Power

As in many cities in science-fiction cinema, in the city of *Blade Runner* class division is depicted in spatial terms. High, interior, well-lit, and open spaces are privileged over low, exterior, dark, and crowded ones. The rich occupy the former and the poor the latter, while the middle class is situated somewhere between the two. The penthouse occupied by Tyrell (Joe Turkel), CEO of the Tyrell Corporation, which produces the replicants, is located high above the rest of the city. Deckard lives below Tyrell, but still above the street rabble in his ninety-seventh-floor apartment, while J. F. Sebastian (William Sanderson), the mild-mannered, socially obtuse genetics designer, lives below Deckard in a huge, gorgeously decaying house at street level. Both Deckard's and Sebastian's homes are based on prominent historical buildings in Los Angeles. Deckard's apartment is modeled after the Ennis House, built for Charles Ennis by Frank Lloyd Wright in 1924, and Sebastian's house after the Bradbury office building, designed by George H. Wyman for Louis Bradbury in 1893. Regarding the former, Kevin McNamara observes, "The Ennis House (1924) sits on a ridge above the city, an appropriate setting for a design by a strident champion of 'extreme individualism' and bitter opponent of urbanism and machine culture." Both Wright's legacy as "bitter opponent of urbanism and machine culture" and the Mayan design of the Ennis House, which stylistically links Deckard's home with Tyrell's, associate Deckard with the same lineage of Enlightenment values and aesthetics that Tyrell embodies more explicitly. In the film this lineage is threatened by the presence of the hard, industrial aesthetic that characterizes the streets and by the poor mechanized inhabitants who live and work in them.

Sebastian is the only white human male in *Blade Runner* (with the exception of extras whose homes we never see) who lives near street level. According to McNamara, the Bradbury building, the architectural basis for Sebastian's home, was itself inspired by a description of a futuristic department store in Edward Bellamy's influential utopic novel *Looking Backward*. McNamara points out that in *Blade Runner* this vision of a space for commodity fetishism and exchange has crumbled into the cluttered, warehouselike laboratory digs of a lonely "chickenhead."[37] Sebastian's ailment is Methuselah's complex, a disease that ages him prematurely. Like the "old technology" that constitutes the lower city in the form of recycled architecture and machinery, his body is in a state of "accelerated decrepitude." As unnatural, diseased, and retrofitted Sebastian embodies the very qualities of the city in which he lives.

The streets of this city are crowded with freaks, people of color, and the poor and working class, who are constantly assaulted by the presence of the commercial corporate state in the form of advertisements, surveillance cameras, lights, and patrolling helicopters. This hybrid mass of subaltern people takes on a distinctly East Asian tenor. As Bruno puts it, "The film is populated by eclectic crowds of faceless people, merchants, punks, Hare Krishnas.... The city is a large market; an intrigue of underground networks pervades all relations. The explosive Orient dominates, the Orient of yesterday incorporating the Orient of today."[38] Both the Orient of yesterday and the Orient of today are defined through postcapitalist production and consumption. It is no coincidence, then, that this presence "dominates" a city whose various spaces and citizens are linked primarily through the exchange of commodities, which includes artificial humans.

As mentioned in the last chapter, the historical encounters of Anglo-Americans with East Asia via objects and people as objects gave American Orientalism two seemingly contradictory faces. The first, associated with luxury items from distant mythic lands, symbolized elegance, wealth, and power, or the Orient as consumable style. The second, associated with uncomfortably close Asiatic bodies, signified an unwanted, dangerous, and potentially contagious kind of cultural difference, or the Orient as invisible worker. Both manifestations of Orientalism, the first rooted in desire and fascination and the second in fear and disgust, yoked Asiatic difference with industrial capitalism. Regardless of the increased numbers of Asian

Americans in the United States, this double-faced Orientalism has not disappeared in the era of postindustrial capitalism. To the contrary, it remains and, in some ways, has intensified under high-tech conditions.

Implications

In 1982 Ridley Scott displayed the beginnings of this high-tech Orient in the backdrop of *Blade Runner* even as he referenced the invisible service industry that keeps the orientalized city running through its working-class Asiatic merchants. This final section discusses how the film's representations of the Orient as style and body, product and producer, merge in the racially fluid bodies of the replicants.[39]

I argue that three forms of the Orient exist in *Blade Runner*. The first is embodied in the secondary characters of East Asian descent, who signify the socially undesired but economically necessary Asian American subject. The second can be found in the images and iconography of the city, which allude to East Asia as foreign, corporate, and dangerously feminine. The third collapses these elements of the oriental other in the roles of the replicants. As slave laborers, they are invisible workers like the Asiatic characters. Yet as forms of cutting-edge technology produced by the Tyrell Corporation, they also constitute the consumable style that defines the city.

The Orient as Invisible Worker

One character refers to Asians, Latinos, and their multiracial progeny as "little people," second-class citizens who claim the new, multicultural landscape of Los Angeles in 2019. Woven into the next few pages are readings of three secondary Asian American characters who fall in this category, focusing on their roles vis-à-vis the primary white male characters.

As noted at the beginning of this chapter, we first encounter Deckard reading a newspaper before ducking into the White Dragon, an open-air fast-food stand much like those in many Asian countries. A blade runner, or bounty hunter, Deckard is clearly displaced in this environment. Surrounding him are young punks and commuters washed in blue tint and placed in shadow. Their fast-moving bodies blend in with the neon signs and television screens that clutter the frame. They wear different kinds of futuristic industrial clothing, carry plastic umbrellas with lighted tips, and are absorbed in the images that constantly flash around them. In contrast, Deckard wears a rumpled trench coat, his movements are slow, and he reads a newspaper. Terribly archaic in this setting, he is the focus of the camera and clearly is the figure with whom the viewer is supposed to identify.

Howie Lee, or the "Sushi Master" (Robert Okazaki), the unnamed purveyor at the White Dragon, wears what looks to be a sushi chef uniform and speaks rapidly in "cityspeak," the multilingual pidgin of the working class, which sounds predominantly Japanese and Cantonese. His speech is as incomprehensible as the Chinese and Japanese neon signage is to Western viewers. He and Deckard argue over how many pieces of sushi Deckard should order. When Lee tells him he can order only two, Deckard is visibly annoyed. His face reflects the disgusted resignation that American tourists so often express in Hollywood movies when they are forced to confront the cultures and customs of the Third World. Indeed Ford displays the same

Robert Okazaki in *Blade Runner.* "The Sushi Master" haggles with an annoyed Deckard in cityspeak.

expression here as he does in *Raiders of the Lost Ark* (1981) when he casually confirms the notion of American supremacy in the Middle East by shooting the Arab character who has just impressed the audience with his elaborate swordplay.

As Deckard is chewing his rubbery sushi, slurping his *udon* noodles, and reflecting on his failed marriage, Gaff (Edward James Olmos), a nonwhite blade runner, arrives on the scene with a Korean police officer. Like Deckard, Gaff sports a 1940s detective look, complete with trench coat and fedora hat, but exudes a more foppish air. Gaff tells Deckard that their superior, Captain Bryant (M. Emmett Walsh), has sent him to take Deckard to police head-quarters. After a terse exchange in which we learn that Deckard wants to renounce blade running, Deckard reluctantly leaves with Gaff. Lee plays a significant role in this brief interaction, which paradoxically renders him invisible. Gaff uses cityspeak, which Deckard claims he cannot understand. Lee becomes Deckard's translator, and the audience's as well, because no subtitles are provided in the scene. As translator, he is placed between the two men, his face positioned to directly address the audience. Yet he is not the focus of our gaze. The camera instead spotlights the adversarial relation-ship between Deckard and Gaff through shot reverse shots in which they grunt their lines, followed by Lee's high, squeaky voice translating.

This scene resembles the second turning point in John Ford's classic west-ern *The Searchers* (1956), in which an old Mexican guide (Nacho Galindo) is also placed between two differently raced adversaries as he translates the words of Indian chief Scar (Henry Brandon) for the protagonist Ethan (John Wayne), who later reveals that he understands the language. Here, too, we suspect that Deckard understands cityspeak but feigns ignorance to keep his racial and class identity distinct from those of Lee and Gaff. Gaff, in turn, refuses to speak in proper English. Again, the viewer is meant to identify with Deckard, the disoriented white man. Gaff plays the role of the mysteri-ous and potentially dangerous racial other, while Lee, the Asian American male, provides comic relief as he proffers a useful service to both characters and the audience.

The same representation of the Asian worker as valuable but dispos-able aid appears in the scene between Chew (James Hong), a synthetic eye engineer, and the replicant leader, Roy Batty (Rutger Hauer). When Roy enters Chew's laboratory, the Eyeworks, with Leon, Chew is fiddling with lab instruments, muttering and giggling while dipping artificial eyes in bubbling chemical mixtures—a depiction that recalls orientalist images of ancient herbalists in Chinatown. He wears a gray, fur-fringed uniform to keep warm in the freezing temperatures of the laboratory and is hooked to a machine by thick wires reminiscent of umbilical cords, which establish his intimate association with technology. Resembling a large bug or octopus, Chew is hysterical and servile, in sharp contrast to Roy, who is physically and verbally poised. Their class disparity is racialized, made apparent in the different forms and styles of speech they use. Chew speaks in incomprehensible gibberish with Cantonese tonal patterns, while Roy misquotes William Blake in controlled, clipped English.

Chew occupies the lowest rung in the process for manufacturing the replicants. A subcontractor whose work recalls that of present-day Asian American workers in the garment and microchip industries, he "only does eyes." In awe of Roy's superior capabilities as an advanced Nexus 6 model, he

James Hong in *Blade Runner.* Chew examines artificial eyes through a microscope before his fatal encounter with Roy Batty and Leon.

whispers, "I gave you your eyes." And Roy acknowledges their connection when he responds, "If only you could see what I've seen with your eyes." If the eye is the final physical site for the determination of one's identity as human or not human, what does it mean that a lowly Asian American worker has created the replicant leader's eyes? Perhaps one of the reasons that Roy and the other replicants can never become wholly human has something to do with the fact that they have eyes, which in the film are intimately related to one's identity, that were made by someone who is not quite human himself.

Like Lee and Chew, the Cambodian Woman (Kimiko Hiroshige), the last secondary Asian American character to appear in the film, functions as a guide, and like Chew, she is closely associated with sight and technology. Before she is introduced, Deckard uses the Esper machine, a criminal investigation device that zooms in and magnifies images, to analyze a photo that he has retrieved earlier in Leon's apartment along with a scale from an artificial animal. He becomes convinced that the two clues are related and promptly leaves for Animoid Row, a section of town that looks like a mélange of East Asia, South Asia, and the Middle East, to get information about the scale. Deckard approaches the stand of the elderly Cambodian Woman, who, upon examining the scale under her microscope, tells him that it belongs to an artificial snake—knowledge that helps Deckard locate the female replicant Zhora (Joanna Cassidy).

Unlike the other Asian American characters, the Cambodian Woman speaks English fluently with a slight British accent. Also, although her help remains unacknowledged by the narrative, it differs noticeably from the kind of aid associated with Lee and Chew. Before giving Deckard important information about the scale, she repeats the same scientific procedure that he has used in the previous scene to examine the photograph. Her microscope, like the Esper machine and the Voigt-Kampf device, reveals crucial traits of the objects under observation that can be seen only with the help of machines. In other words, the Cambodian Woman, who remains unnamed even in the credits, is the only secondary character represented as potentially equal, linguistically and technologically, to the principal character she aids.

Why is this? And what might her gender have to do with the difference in her representation from those of the other male Asian American characters? One clue lies in the landscape.

The Orient as Consumable Style

The second kind of East Asian presence, as noted earlier, appears in the spectral form of foreign economic and cultural capital: visually in Asian-inflected images, architecture, and props; textually in the neon signs that splice the darkness; aurally in cityspeak, which privileges East Asian languages, and in the music and sound design, which features the electronic strains of Vangelis punctuated by Asian instruments and singing. Embodying and performing these exotic representations of the Orient are two eroticized "oriental" women: the billboard image of what Bruno has called the "'Japanese simulacrum,' the huge advertisement, which alternates a seductive Japanese face and a Coca Cola sign,"[40] and the female replicant Zhora, the first of the fugitive replicants to be "retired" by Deckard.

The depiction of a young East Asian woman dressed as a geisha, popping what has been variously described as a digestive, a birth control pill, or a piece of gum, recurs throughout the film. The image is usually accompanied by the ominous sound of *taiko* drums, eerie electronic strains of the samisen, and quick shots of bicyclists in Asian straw hats and loose tunics streaming diagonally into the foreground. The camera cuts to the image, projected on an enormous screen above the city, after significant scenes of violence.

For instance, it first appears immediately after the opening scene in which Holden administers the Voigt-Kampf test to Leon, one of the four fugitive replicants at large in the city. Holden asks Leon to describe his mother and is killed in response. The next image we see is that of the virtual geisha. She appears again after Deckard and Rachael first kiss and later presumably have sex. Their verbal foreplay is tinged with hints of sadomasochism as Deckard grows more aggressive physically and as Rachael repeats his declarations of desire. Finally, the image is visible through the staircases of Sebastian's apartment building in the violent chase scene between Roy and Deckard. Nonreproductive sexuality is showcased in all three instances: like all the replicants, Leon has no biological mother; Deckard and Rachael engage in interspecial (human–replicant) sex; and, as Scott Bukatman has noted, the chase scene between Roy and Deckard is replete with homoerotic overtones.[41]

The advertisement falls somewhere between those of the Asian American workers and the nonanthropomorphic oriental tropes of the city. It is clearly an object; however, it projects the facsimile of a human face—that of

Alexis Rhee in *Blade Runner.* The image of the virtual geisha pulsates in the cityscape, punctuating moments of spectacular violence.

a young, pretty, presumably Japanese woman. This electronically pulsing face transforms the foreign female East Asian body into palatable consumer iconography. It suggests that racial difference can be transcended in two ways: through (hetero)sexual and commodity consumption—both forms of consumption linked to the exoticized eroticization of Asian women in various service roles. Perhaps this is why the Cambodian Lady was given a slightly more dignified representation than her male peers—because the idea of East Asia in the orientalist consciousness has been, and to a large extent continues to be, gendered female, as the virtual geisha demonstrates so spectacularly.

The two categories of Orient as worker and as iconography are also collapsed in Zhora's death scene in Chinatown. This Chinatown is multiracial, a conglomeration of Middle Eastern, East Asian, white, and racially ambiguous faces and bodies—all exuding an air of bustling decadence. Once again Deckard looks distinctly out of place as he tracks Zhora to Taffy's Bar, where she works as an exotic dancer. When Deckard catches her after the show, she nonchalantly rebuffs his advances, wearing nothing but an artificial pet snake, a nude-colored body glove, and some body glitter. Zhora plays the role of the unruly woman who uses her sexuality to return and subvert the male gaze. In that sense, she is the only real femme fatale in the film. The other female replicants are defined through their relationships with men. Pris (Darryl Hannah), despite her athletic struggle with Deckard before dying orgasmically, remains a beautiful sex toy, baiting Sebastian and partnered with Roy, who is obviously her superior. Rachael also takes a submissive position to men throughout the film, first to her father/creator, Tyrell, then to Deckard, who assumes the paternal role as her lover.

In contrast, Zhora is never partnered with anyone, male or female. Her power and appeal stem from her fallen state. Zhora's disguise as a white exotic dancer in Chinatown conflates oriental otherness with deviant female sexuality—deviant in the sense that it exists purely as and for pleasure, with no reproductive value. The character is part of a long lineage of women who have appropriated oriental tropes to enhance their erotic appeal, including the self-styled Mata Hari (Margaretha Zelle), credited with inventing the strip tease; actress Myrna Loy in a number of yellowface roles, including that of Fu Manchu's daughter in *The Mask of Fu Manchu* (1932); and even, arguably, Chinese American actress Anna May Wong, whose Dragon Lady roles required a kind of self-orientalization to appeal to the Hollywood audience.[42]

Like the virtual geisha, Zhora self-consciously functions as a sex commodity and, in doing so, performs and exposes the spectacle of race and gender as such. However, unlike the virtual geisha, who remains safely contained within the screen of the advertisement, Zhora triply transgresses the boundaries of proper womanhood established in the film: racially (as an orientalized white woman), ontologically (as a human being), and sexually (as a single, empowered female). She is duly punished for her transgressions when Deckard shoots her in the back after chasing her through Chinatown.

This chase scene provides one of the longest sustained depictions of urban mise-en-scène in the film, giving viewers a heightened sense of disorientation through techniques such as the use of a busy camera, long and medium-long shots of Zhora and Deckard at the beginning of the chase as they run against the crowds, and fast cuts to the expressionless faces of people they pass.

Throughout the sequence, the viewer is not quite sure with whom to identify. Deckard is drawn as the protagonist of the story: we have had more exposure to him than to any other character; we see the city through his eyes; and we are with him as he hunts down the replicants. However, Zhora, in her distanced, objectified position, arguably elicits more sympathy. Unlike Deckard, she is associated with the city and its inhabitants. Shots foregrounding her face and figure are presented through a blue filter, as are those of the streets and extras. Conversely, Deckard is shot mostly through a red filter; the contrast becomes most striking in the glance-object cut toward the middle of the chase when Deckard spots Zhora blending into the wall of the subway station entrance. Deckard (illuminated behind by red neon) looks down at Zhora (in blue neon).

Zhora's panic is palpable. Her chest heaves and her eyes dart everywhere, whereas Deckard shows no emotion. Deckard finds her and lunges, at which point Zhora commences running with superhuman speed. Her attempt at

Joanna Cassidy in *Blade Runner.* Zhora lies dead in her plastic raincoat on a street of Chinatown after being shot in the back by Deckard.

escape ends only when Deckard shoots her in the back. The cowardice associated with this particular method of killing is compounded here by the victim's gender. Even after she has been shot, Zhora continues to run, crashing in slow-motion agony through several sheets of department-store glass, referencing Sam Peckinpah's *The Wild Bunch* (1969). Her clear raincoat matches the transparent glass, which reinforces her identity as commodity. She is pure surface, her subjectivity wholly exteriorized. In this sense, Zhora is no different from the mannequins whose plastic parts fall off and bounce around her as she plunges to her death on the street.

Zhora's termination and the consistent presence of the virtual geisha highlight the underlying artificiality of a specific kind of racialized gender identity—that of the orientalized woman. Their brief, secondary roles in the narrative provide a counterpoint to the definitions of normative humanity, in terms of gender and race, supplied by the other principal characters. In other words, Zhora and the virtual geisha force the narrative (and the audience) to push the boundaries between human and thing.

The Orient as Raced Replicant

In the overmediated, oriental space of the city with which Zhora and the billboard geisha are conflated, the replicants attempt to change their virtual, illegitimate identities into concrete, legitimate ones. Their displaced and unwanted presence in the city categorizes them as social contagions that need to be contained, processed, and either expelled from or incorporated into the dominant culture. In this respect, the plight of the replicants resembles those of undocumented immigrant Latino/a workers, as Charles Ramírez Berg has suggested.[43] At the same time, references to their "slave" status recall the experiences of enslaved Africans in the antebellum period and of poor African Americans in contemporary urban ghettoes.

Yet even as they might allude to historical and popular representations of these nonwhite groups, all the renegade replicants are phenotypically white, and the leader of the rebellion and his partner, in particular, are stunningly Aryan, with blond hair, pale skin, and blue eyes. How, then, are we to read the replicants in terms of their racial identity, performance, and representation? Are they black? Asian? Latino/a? White? Can they be read racially at all?

In "Back to the Future," Kaja Silverman posits that the replicants are black to the extent that they assume the symbolic space of slavery, which in the United States has been associated with African Americans. She argues, "By putting Batty in the position classically occupied by those with dark skin, the film obliges the white spectator to understand the relation between that position and those who are slotted into it as absolutely arbitrary and absolutely brutal."[44] Brian Locke rejects this argument, citing Silverman's failure to consider the ways in which the replicants and her own reading appropriate the moral power of the victim position (i.e., the replicants' symbolic blackness) without acknowledging the imperialist origins and ramifications of that position. Instead he argues that her reading of race in the film retains the social, political, and representational power of whiteness much as the replicants do through their excessively white phenotypical features, "incorporat[ing] blackness on the level of metaphor and yet at the same time . . . exclud[ing] blackness on the level of the literal."[45]

Locke suggests that the replicants are racially schizophrenic, both black and white, and thus representative of the best of both cultures and histories.[46] Robert Lee goes further, drawing a parallel between the Asian American model minority and the replicant in that they are "the perfect workers, virtually indistinguishable from humans . . . yet completely inauthentic. Replicants can be expected to perform humanly, yet need not be treated humanely."[47] While Locke and Lee provide insightful readings of the replicants, they leave little room for movement between or outside the racial poles of black and white. Locke reproduces the black/white binary by displacing the Orient onto the landscape, while Lee's interpretation does not take into account the racial, economic, and symbolic *elasticity* of the model minority position.

Conversely, one might view these artificial humans as non–racially specific model minorities rather than assigning them a specific racial identity. Although the role of the model minority most often has been associated with Asian Americans, it can be extended to apply to all marginal subjects who desire the legal, economic, and cultural privilege of whiteness. The emphasis here is on *class* as a crucial element of how one is read racially. The resulting variation on the model minority is based on the idea of race as social performance, namely, that the spaces one occupies, the people with whom one associates, and the behaviors and attitudes one displays determine how one is racially defined. One important way in which people of color have been able to perform whiteness is through their possession of class and cultural capital. In the plight of the replicants one sees the costs and benefits of wanting to become human—a humanity that, in the logic of the film and of dominant culture, easily conflates with whiteness.

The replicants have come to earth to "meet their maker" in hopes of extending their termination dates, which would allow them to pass completely as human subjects. Like immigrants and refugees, they have come to the United States for certain social and economic opportunities. Although none of the fugitive replicants successfully assimilates into U.S. society, both Roy and Rachael manage to transcend its boundaries through their relationships with Deckard, the prototypical middle-class white male, whose own ontological status becomes more ambiguous as the film progresses: the former through homoerotic doubling and the latter through heterosexual coupling. According to Bukatman, Roy is Deckard's cyborgian, homoerotic double, who must be eliminated for the protagonist to claim and assert his heterosexual masculinity.[48]

Yet this abject, transgressive figure rescues Deckard in an unfathomable Christlike gesture before he dies in the climax, which begins with a monologue by Roy and ends with a dove mysteriously manifesting itself in his arms before it flies up into the morning sky. The religious reference here is hard to miss. Deckard is a changed (perhaps saved?) man after his encounter with Roy, who in this melodramatic death scene is represented without overt irony in the position of Jesus Christ. Similar to the way in which Christ's deific status is revealed through his death and subsequent resurrection, Roy's gesture of grace toward Deckard before his death implies that he is "more human than human."

Meanwhile, Rachael achieves the same ends by rejecting her newly discovered replicant identity to couple with a human being. Her romance with Deckard structurally bears a strong resemblance to the interracial romance narratives that Gina Marchetti describes, in which "the nonwhite lover completely relinquishes his or her own culture in order to be accepted into the American bourgeois mainstream, usually represented by the creation of a 'typical nuclear family.'"[49] Rachael becomes human in much the same way that East Asian women in films such as *Teahouse of the August Moon* (1956), *Sayonara* (1957), and *The World of Suzie Wong* (1960) become or try to become white through their hyperfeminized performance of sexual difference vis-à-vis an Anglo-American male.

More specifically, Rachael's initial femme fatale demeanor and behavior link her character with the figure of the Dragon Lady persona established in early Hollywood cinema through the vampish, orientalized roles of actresses such as Myrna Loy, Theda Bara, and Anna May Wong. However, her performance later in the love scene with Deckard recalls the Lotus Blossom stereotype most famously associated with the docile characters played by Miyoshi Umeki in *Sayonara* and *Flower Drum Song* (1961). Rachael utters her lines passively, repeating after Deckard the words he wants to hear from her. Essentially, he teaches her, rather forcefully, how to be a real (i.e., heteronormative) woman in love.

Multiracial Traces

Whether we see Rachael and Deckard actually leaving the city for greener pastures (domestic cut) or are left imagining that they will (director's cut), the film ends with the two as a newly formed couple. Regardless of their ability to reproduce, the closing image of two members of the opposite sex in love is an established Hollywood trope that signifies the reproduction of the nuclear family, which functions as an analogy for the nation. At the end of *Sayonara,* a classic East Asian–white interracial romance film, Captain Gruver (Marlon Brando) asks entertainer Hana-Ogi (Miiko Taka) to marry him and return with him to the United States. She worries about the social fate of their biracial offspring, asking, "What would happen to our children? What would they be?" He answers confidently, "What would they be? They'd be half Japanese and half American. They'd be half yella and half white."

The specter of the unborn biracial child overtly addressed in Gruver's response to his Japanese bride-to-be haunts the ending of *Blade Runner.* If Deckard and Rachael have kids, what will they be—human or replicant? Will they fit into the off-world suburbs where the two may be headed? Or is there an idyllic world that lies beyond the off-worlds where humans and replicants peacefully coexist? In the logic of the film, this kind of utopia is the stuff of dreams, a musing that brings us to the enigmatic last scene of the director's cut.

Edward James Olmos in *Blade Runner.* Gaff is a metonym of the multicultural orientalized city he inhabits.

Before Deckard and Rachael prepare to depart from Los Angeles in the 1992 version of the film, Gaff leaves an origami unicorn in Deckard's apartment, alluding to an earlier scene in which Deckard has dreamed of a unicorn, then awakened at a piano surrounded by random photographs much like those that the replicants carry as externalizations of their false, implanted memories. The origami figure hints that Gaff has access to Deckard's memories and dreams as he does to those of the replicants. It is significant here that the key to our hero's suddenly ambiguous identity lies in a mythological symbol from the West expressed in an Eastern aesthetic. It is just as significant that the one who delivers this message, like the city he lives in, looks multiracial and speaks a multitude of languages with a deliberately strong Asian accent.

According to Olmos, who not only played the character but heavily contributed to its development, Gaff's backstory was that he "was primarily

Mexican-Japanese, and . . . his lineage stretched back at least five generations."[50] Olmos later mentioned that he saw the character as multiracial but
predominantly Asian: "I began to feel that, despite his mixed blood, Gaff
was more Asian than anything else. So I asked Marvin Westmore to make up
my skin in yellowish tones before every shot. Yet I also felt Gaff had some
other nationalities in him, too. So we gave him a French-Spanish mustache,
an Italian punk haircut, and China-blue eyes."[51]

Gaff's multiracial, multicultural look was complemented by his use of
multilingual cityspeak. Fancher, who is part Chicano himself, first came up
with the idea of cityspeak based on the speech patterns of Latino youth in
East Los Angeles; he also gave the character its name, Gaff, based on the word
gaffe, meaning a mistake. Cityspeak was fleshed out some more by Peoples,
who followed Scott's instructions to make the character speak Japanese then
added Tagalog when Scott and coproducer Powell later suggested "maybe
Gaff should speak in some sort of weird, futuristic gutter language." Finally,
Olmos added the crucial finishing touches when he translated bits of Gaff's
dialogue into Spanish, French, Chinese, German, and Hungarian with the
help of instructors at the Los Angeles Berlitz School.[52]

Fancher's decision to name the character "mistake" recalls the history
of antimiscegenation law and sentiment in the United States, which is embodied in Gaff's visibly multiracial roots. However, there is another possible
interpretation of the name based on phonetic similarities: Gaff as short for
gaffer, the person responsible for lighting the film set. In *Blade Runner* particularly, lighting is extremely important because it determines what the
audience can and cannot see. Besides, it can change not only the ambience
surrounding an object, body, or space but also our perception of its very
dimensions, textures, and function. An opaque, ambiguous character, Gaff
lies between these two interpretations of his name—gaffe (an object of fun
and ridicule) and gaffer (a subject with the power to transform space)—
in much the same way that the city lies between future and present, East
and West.

In the years following the release of *Blade Runner,* popular media representations began to depict East Asians and Asian Americans in similarly
ambivalent ways. During this period the Japanese, in particular, gained
more visibility through their association with economic capital, which imbued them with forms of privilege associated with whiteness even as their

inassimilable "oriental" traits continued to be highlighted. The next chapter explores how depictions of relationships between Japanese, Japanese American, and Anglo-American characters in Hollywood films from the 1980s negotiated national anxieties around the emergence of this new yellow peril cloaked as model minority—anxieties that reached a fever pitch at the end of the decade.

4

Oriental Buddies and the Disruption of Whiteness

Everyone around me is a total stranger
Everyone avoids me like a cyclone ranger
Everyone
That's why I'm turning Japanese I think I'm turning Japanese I really
think so

—The Vapors, "Turning Japanese"

The specter of the unborn child of *Blade Runner*'s Deckard and Rachael, a mixture of human and machine, recalls the largely forgotten figure of the "television child" introduced by Marshall McLuhan a little over forty years ago at a television studies conference in Austin, Texas. In his paper McLuhan associated the nonlinear mode of watching TV with the East (Asia) and the linear mode of reading books with the West (United States and Europe).[1] He concluded that North American youth, assumed to be of European descent, were becoming more Asiatic through their exposure to television. According to McLuhan,

> The television form of experience is profoundly and subliminally introverting, an inward depth, meditative, oriental. The television child is a profoundly orientalized being. And he will not accept goals as objects in the world to pursue. He will accept a role, but he will not accept a goal. He goes inward. No greater revolution has ever occurred to western man or any other society in so short a time.[2]

The troubling cultural reductions in McLuhan's theorizing aside, his image of youth orientalized by the new medium of the time bears some resemblance to current news coverage bemoaning the rising number of U.S. adolescents, mostly male, who are "addicted" to video games and the Internet.[3] Descriptions of this demographic resemble those of technologized Japanese youth known as *otaku,* a derogatory term loosely translated as "geek." Karl Taro Greenfeld provides the following description of the *otaku,* which reads like a darker, post-Internet version of McLuhan's "television child": "The *otaku* may be the final stage in the symbiosis of man and machine. Their points of reference are all derivative of computers, mass communication, and media. And their technology-generated world is unfamiliar terrain, a new frontier where the morality and ethics of the old world no longer apply."[4]

In a fascinating twist of cultural appropriation, the *otaku* label became a badge of honor among hard-core U.S. anime fans, a phenomenon I discuss in the next chapter, where I trace the development of oriental style as a response to the popularity of certain East Asian media forms and genres such as anime, video games, and martial arts movies.[5] In this chapter I lay the groundwork for that discussion by looking at changes in dominant perceptions of East Asians and Asian Americans in the 1980s, which facilitated the incorporation of these Asian media imports in the following decade.

As should be apparent by now, Asiaphilia and Asiaphobia form two sides of the same ideological coin, orientalist misrepresentations of East Asia used to secure the tenuous centrality of whiteness as the racial and cultural norm. The Vapors' one-hit wonder pop song "Turning Japanese" (1980) provides a good example of this racist dialectic from that period. Its lyrics encapsulate the ambivalent forms of exoticization and identification that Japan's growing visibility generated among U.S. youth. Rumored to be slang for masturbation (playing on the idea that Western eyes squinted in orgasm resemble "slanted" Asiatic eyes), the expression "turning Japanese" constitutes the song's manically repetitive refrain. Outside this refrain and the oriental flourishes that punctuate its synthesizer-heavy musical backdrop, however, "Turning Japanese" appears to have little to do with Japan, fixated as it is on an alienated, presumably white male's obsession with a photograph of a presumably white girl. Like other popular songs of the period, such as The Cure's "Japanese Whispers," Styx's "Mr. Roboto," and David Bowie's "China Girl," "Turning Japanese" activates an updated fantasy of technologized East Asia to showcase alternative, orientalized white male identities.

More specifically, the song foregrounds a sexually perverse and socially challenged male who fantasizes about his crush object as he consumes her image. The mechanistic, marginalized masculinity displayed here resembles historical stereotypes of East Asian men in the United States. Although the narrator is not a sympathetic character (especially for women and Asian Americans), the song is sung from his point of view, so it is reasonable to assume that listeners are supposed to identify with him. Why, then, does "Turning Japanese" highlight an abject oriental masculinity through its default white male narrator? And how does the emergence of this subsequently orientalized subject—the white man who has "turned Japanese"—correlate with the rising visibility of East Asian and Asian American images in the 1980s?

In the following pages I approach these questions by analyzing the relationships between white male characters and their Asiatic friends and nemeses in a number of Japanese American buddy films from this period, focusing on *The Karate Kid, Gung Ho,* and *Black Rain.* All of these movies reinforce the U.S.-centric ideology that drives the Hollywood narrative, namely, that personal relationships between individuals can transcend cultural, racial, and national differences. Robert Lee, Dorinne Kondo, Gina Marchetti, and others have provided useful critiques of this ideology in readings of such films as *Year of the Dragon* (1985) and *Rising Sun* (1993), illuminating the ways in which Asiatic characters and motifs are reduced to simple narrative devices that function chiefly to aid the development of white male protagonists.[6] These critiques center on explicitly racist depictions of East Asians and Asian Americans that play off a relatively uncomplicated neoconservative white male presence.

What has been less closely examined are the ways in which the terms of those and other Asiatic representations were closely intertwined with dramatic changes in depictions of American whiteness and masculinity during this period. The scholars just mentioned discuss how negative orientalist film stereotypes of Asians and Asian Americans are tied intimately to the positive orientalist ideology that implicitly grounds these film narratives, namely, the notion that East Asia—especially Japan—is superior to the United States technologically, economically, culturally, and/or spiritually. As noted earlier, this notion of Asiatic superiority lies at the heart of the model minority thesis, which coincidentally appeared the same year that McLuhan presented his paper on the "television child."

In this chapter I look at how Hollywood films of the 1980s reactivate this thesis in their representations of the relationship between Asian American assimilation and Anglo-American appropriation of particular aspects of Japanese culture. More specifically, I focus on how the presumed superiority of Japan and the Japanese simultaneously appeals to and threatens the protagonists of these films, who are defined by physical and/or moral fallibility and marginalization within their own (white) communities and become fully developed characters only when they absorb Asiatic cultures, economics, and ethics.

In its celebration of Anglo-Americans' benevolent appropriation of Asian "know-how" this narrative strategy is obviously orientalist. My interest here, however, lies not in the fact that such appropriation occurs repeatedly in the movies but rather in how the protagonists' desperate need to imitate and absorb what passes for Japanese culture—especially those traits associated with honor, integrity, and productivity—is crucial to the films' resuscitation of what might be called the (Anglo-) American spirit. Such desperation reveals serious fissures in the paradigms of normative whiteness, heterocentrism, and the nuclear family that epitomized the Reagan era—fissures along and through which current representational models for Asiatic and other nonwhite groups developed.

Exploring the relationships among Anglo-Americans, Japanese, and Japanese Americans and the various spaces they inhabit, cross, and transgress in popular movies of the 1980s can lead to a more nuanced sense of how Asiatic bodies and cultures have come to signify certain styles and sensibilities in contemporary Hollywood. With that goal in mind, I have organized this chapter broadly into two sections. The first section discusses Asiatic stereotypes in 1980s Hollywood and the representation of Asiatic masculinities in the dominant culture. The second section draws on ideas from the first to analyze the dynamics of race, gender, class, and nation in *The Karate Kid, Gung Ho,* and *Black Rain.* Let me start by introducing three key East Asian icons that populate the media landscape of the 1980s: the Oriental Monk, the Asian Pocahontas, and the techno-oriental other.

East Asia as the Past

In "The Oriental Monk in American Popular Culture," Jane Iwamura identifies the "Oriental Monk" as a now familiar icon in U.S. film and television:

a desexualized Asiatic male character with no discernible familial or community ties who "represents the last of his kind."[7] The Monk becomes a surrogate father to a troubled child likewise shunned for his difference, whether the difference is racial (in *Kung Fu* the child is biracial), economic (in *The Karate Kid* he is working-class), or ontological (in *Teenage Mutant Ninja Turtles* the "children" are giant mutant turtles).[8] As an ambivalent "bridge figure," this child proves to be the perfect inheritor of the Oriental Monk's skills and wisdom. Together the interracial father–son/teacher–student duo comes to "embody a new hope of saving the West from capitalist greed, brute force, totalitarian rule, and spiritless technology."[9]

According to Iwamura, "This narrative implicitly argues that Asian religions are impotent within their racial context of origin, and are only made (re)productive if resituated in a Western context and passed on to white practitioners who possess the daring and innovative sensibilities that their Eastern counterparts presumably lack."[10] I want to underscore two points in Iwamura's incisive critique. First, the Oriental Monk exists primarily for and through his Anglo-American protégé. Second, the icon embodies an old, distant, and dying culture—mythic rather than historic—in sharp contrast to that of the modern, industrialized West. Significantly, both traits also characterize the figure of the noble savage in the dime novels and Wild West shows of the nineteenth century as well as in liberal revisionist films about white encounters with Native Americans such as *Soldier Blue* (1970), *Little Big Man* (1970), and *Dances with Wolves* (1990).[11]

In *Romance and the Yellow Peril: Race, Sex, and Discursive Strategies in Hollywood Fiction,* Gina Marchetti notes the link between Hollywood's infatuation with accommodating Native and Asiatic characters in the figure of the "Asian Pocahontas." Exemplified by the Vietnamese female protagonists of such war films as *China Gate* (1957) and *Good Morning, Vietnam* (1987), this figure synthesizes the sacrificial traits of the mythologized Powhatan princess and Puccini's famous operatic geisha, Madama Butterfly.[12] Marchetti notes that both Pocahontas and Butterfly betray their own ethnic communities for the love of an Anglo-American male and pay for their transgression by being forced to leave those communities, either through literal death in the case of the latter or through social death, that is, assimilation into her lover's culture, in that of the former.[13] These icons thus epitomize the subaltern women in Gayatri Spivak's pithy formulation of the gender politics that buttress the imperialist project, namely, "white men seeking to save brown women from brown men."[14]

Like the Oriental Monk, the Asian Pocahontas lives for and through an extraordinary white man, thereby affirming American exceptionalism and imperialism in their most baldly patriarchal forms. As Marchetti puts it, "She [the Asian Pocahontas] is saved either spiritually or morally from her own 'inferior' culture, just as she physically saves her lover from her own people. Ideologically, the narrative can be looked at as either a liberal call for assimilation or as a portent of the annihilation of a conquered people. In either case, these stories legitimize Anglo-American rule over a submissive, feminized Asia."[15] Like Stepin Fetchit, Tonto and Cochise, the Cisco Kid and Poncho, and Charlie Chan, the Oriental Monk and the Asian Pocahontas function as objects of "racist love."[16] The white male protagonist learns the spiritual, kinetic, and erotic secrets of the Far East from these icons, which are associated with traditional oriental spaces, props, costumes, and music harking back to the preindustrial (read pre-Western) past and/or to nature. Through his engagement with the palatable, classical Orient as embodied and performed by these figures, our hero is reeducated, remasculinized, and ultimately reborn.

In other words, the Asian Pocahontas and the Oriental Monk play the roles of figurative mothers or "ideological caregivers" to white protagonists, a pervasive trend in contemporary Hollywood movies, which Cynthia Sau-ling Wong concisely breaks down in "Diverted Mothering: Representations of Caregivers of Color in the Age of 'Multiculturalism.'"[17] Wong points out that nonwhite supporting characters in such films as *Driving Miss Daisy* (1989), *Passion Fish* (1992), and *The Hand That Rocks the Cradle* (1992) "nurtur[e] white patrons, even rescuing them from acute . . . crises," with no expectation of economic, social, or emotional recompense. By suggesting that the non-white caregivers are richer spiritually and culturally than their white care receivers *and* that they are eager to cede their cultural legacy to these "poor" protagonists, such films project the *illusion* of equality between the two parties in each film, thereby reinforcing and justifying the latter's structural privilege.[18] As Wong goes on to note, the figure of the ideological caregiver contains the initially radical concept of multiculturalism by swerving the narrative focus, again, onto the needs and desires of white people, and it endorses their appropriation of nonwhite cultural capital both onscreen and off.[19]

To fulfill these roles of selfless caregivers of color who help birth and rear the new and improved politically correct white male, the Oriental Monk and the Asian Pocahontas cannot be associated with any traits that threaten U.S. hegemony, such as modernity, technology, or assertive forms of sexuality. Not surprisingly, these are precisely the characteristics that define the hero's evil Asiatic counterpart: the techno-oriental other.

East Asia as the Future

I use the descriptor *techno-oriental other* to refer to the male antagonist, usually (though not always) of East Asian ancestry, who has become a fixture in contemporary Hollywood cinema, including, in addition to the films discussed in this chapter, *Year of the Dragon, China Girl* (1987), *Teenage Mutant Ninja Turtles* (1990), *Showdown in Little Tokyo* (1991), *Rising Sun, Lethal Weapon 4* (1998), *Die Another Day* (2002), and many others. If the Oriental Monk and the Asian Pocahontas exemplify the first half of Robert Lee's binary of the "model minority" and the "gook," the techno-oriental other exemplifies the second half. Again, these two seemingly opposite Asiatic stereotypes are implicitly linked, because the popular perception of Asian Americans as inassimilable hinges on white fears of the model minority turning into the "gook."

The latter figure appears in a number of movies about the Vietnam War released in the 1980s, including *Rambo: First Blood Part II* (1985), *Platoon* (1986), and *Full Metal Jacket* (1987), even as it haunts cinematic depictions of East Asians and East Asian Americans in urban action films of the same period. The military peril represented by the Viet Cong in the 1960s and 1970s thus becomes conflated with the economic and social perils represented by Asiatics in the 1980s. Associated with postindustrial transnational capitalism, technological power, and foreign Asiatic masculinity, the symbolic "gooks" in these films—from the *yakuza* (Japanese gangsters) in *Black Rain* to the Chinese American gangsters in *Year of the Dragon*—rework traditional oriental villains such as Fu Manchu and Ming the Merciless.

Similar to these characters, the techno-oriental other is well educated and cosmopolitan, usually bicultural and bilingual, and loaded with economic and cultural capital. Like his predecessors, he is violent, morally bankrupt, and sexually perverse, exhibiting repressed homoerotic, sadistic, and/or masochistic tendencies.[20] Yet unlike cinematic versions of Ming and Fu Manchu, the techno-oriental other is not situated in fantastic alien settings but in contemporary global cities such as Los Angeles, New York, and Tokyo. He also diverges stylistically from the baroque, explicitly orientalized image of traditional Asiatic villains with his nonculturally specific, stylishly minimalist black clothing and his cutting-edge weapons. Finally, the techno-oriental other shows little to no emotional expression. Instead, his power lies in his terrifying control and calmness. All in all, he thinks, acts, and moves much as a sleek and effective *machine*. Put simply, this icon embodies the notion of techno-orientalism.

Significantly, in the analysis of Morley and Robins the figure of the *otaku* mentioned earlier comes to stand for the contradictions and ambivalences in techno-orientalism. As Morley and Robins put it, "The Japanese are unfeeling aliens; they are cyborgs and replicants. *But there is also the sense that these mutants [the otaku] are now better adapted to survive in the future.*"[21] In other words, these socially challenged, mediated Japanese youth are "unfeeling aliens"—not quite human, much like the doomed replicants in *Blade Runner*—yet, precisely due to their automatization, they are seen as the natural inheritors of the inevitably technologized future.

The same ambivalence lies at the heart of the relationship between the techno-oriental other and the white male protagonist in 1980s Hollywood. On the one hand, this figure projects the worst fears of perilist discourse by showing the potential of enterprising East Asians to turn (Anglo-) American, to occidentalize, and thereby destabilize the cultural and economic power of the United States. At the same time, he acts as a necessary foil for the protagonist, exemplified either in his doomed role as worthy adversary or in his domestication as the Asian sidekick, or what I call the oriental buddy.

The Oriental Buddy

Stories about friendships between white protagonists and their nonwhite sidekicks permeate U.S. popular culture. Well-known examples include Huck Finn and Jim, the Lone Ranger and Tonto, the Green Hornet and Cato. In the postwar period, as the United States was trying to project a more liberal and harmonious image of national race relations, a handful of films and television shows, such as *The Defiant Ones* (1958), *The Crimson Kimono* (1959), *I Spy* (1965–68), and *Brian's Song* (1971) featured nonwhite characters in primary roles alongside white protagonists.

Yet, as Ed Guerrero discusses in *Framing Blackness: The African American Image in Film*, it was not until the 1980s that the biracial buddy narrative became an established film subgenre in Hollywood. Drawing on and replacing the previous cycle of (white) buddy films in the 1970s, these movies, usually featuring black and white dual protagonists, became the primary vehicles through which black actors—most prominently Eddie Murphy in *48 Hrs.* (1982) and *Another 48 Hours* (1990) and Danny Glover in the *Lethal Weapon* series (1987, 1989, 1992, 1998)—achieved star status. According to Guerrero, the black biracial buddy film epitomized the reactionary traits of 1980s Hollywood cinema in its attempts to recuperate the myth of a cohesive national identity, which had corroded with the tumultuous political events and social movements of the previous two decades.[22]

Guerrero points out that the unequal power dynamics between the white and black characters serve to contain the latter, placing the black character "in the protective custody . . . of a white lead or co-star and therefore in conformity with white sensibilities and expectations of what blacks . . . should be."[23] According to Yvonne Tasker, elements of the black buddy's sanitized racial difference complement and bolster the fragmented masculinity of the white buddy, whose body, representative of the white nation, was consistently rendered weak, suffering, and physically vulnerable on the big screen in the 1980s.[24] Within the ideological parameters of a genre that "offer[s] . . . a space for the covert exploration of the homoerotic possibilities of male bonding," the black buddy provides a palatable, whitened version of black masculinity to be consumed by his white partner as well as the mainstream audience.[25]

In *Race Men* Hazel Carby provides an excellent close reading of Danny Glover's initial appearance in *Grand Canyon* (1991) that illustrates this particular dynamic. In the scene Carby analyzes, the white protagonist, Mack (Kevin Kline), inadvertently has taken a turn into the mostly poor and black south central section of Los Angeles. Conflated visually and aurally with cinematic representations of war-torn Vietnam, this "urban jungle" is also filled with enemy aliens. The same formal techniques used to dehumanize the Viet Cong in the war film *Bat 21* (1988) are deployed here to depict young inner-city black men.[26] As Carby points out, these secondary characters are othered through their representation in and as the mise-en-scène—specifically through the gangsta rap that blares from their car and the predatory gazes they fix on Mack, painted as the terrified victim, who is rescued in the nick of time by Simon, an older black tow-truck driver (Danny Glover).[27]

Like many of the Hollywood movie characters that Glover has played, Simon is the good black male, the redemptive counterpoint to the specter of the bad black male embodied in the criminalized, rap-listening, gun-toting youth. Whereas the good black male assuages white fear and guilt by reassuring white characters and viewers that racial differences no longer matter, the bad black male, by highlighting those differences in dramatic, often stereotypical ways, serves to remind us of the cultural and economic divide between black and white communities in the United States and the continued existence of white privilege.

Yet toward the end of the 1980s and into the 1990s, it was also precisely the outlaw quality of the bad black male, expressed through the powerful rhythms and lyrics of rap, that enthralled U.S. youth of all colors and led to the global incorporation of hip-hop culture first in music then in other popular media, including film. In *Representing: Hip Hop Culture and the Production of Black Cinema* Craig Watkins provides a social, cultural, and industrial analysis of this progression, tracing the impact of hip-hop style and politics in Spike Lee's early films and ghettocentric pictures of the 1990s, such as *Boyz N the Hood* (1991) and *Menace II Society* (1993). Watkins presents a solid case for the active role played by disenfranchised black youth not only in the artistic development of hip-hop but also in its commercialization and incorporation into mainstream media.[28]

At the same time, as Patricia Hill Collins notes, this empowerment has proven to be a double-edged sword. The success of young hip-hop artists—much like that of black athletes—affirms the postindustrial consumer capitalist system, which shapes the racial ideology that marginalizes young black men socially and politically even as it elevates them culturally to celebrity status, especially in the entertainment arenas of music and sports.[29]

The bifurcation of black masculinity into reductive "good" and "bad" categories speaks to the continued role of black men specifically, and black people generally, in the national imaginary as the "primitive" black other, which frames and helps produce the "civilized" white self.[30] As noted in the introduction, the fantasy of a superior white subject requires that black bodies and cultures be turned into objects for consumption. Along with establishing control over the black other, incorporating certain "black" traits keeps white subjects from losing their humanity to the burdens of maintaining the very sense of modern identity and culture upon which their claims to racial superiority are based.

In *Playing in the Dark: Whiteness in the Literary Imagination*, Toni Morrison connects the popularity of blackface minstrelsy in the nineteenth century with American Africanism, or consistent metaphors of blackness as embodied, sexual, and/or primal, to articulate white subjectivity in U.S. literature: "In minstrelsy, a layer of blackness applied to a white face released it from law. Just as entertainers, through or by association with blackface, could render permissible topics that otherwise would have been taboo, so American writers were able to employ an imagined Africanist persona to articulate and imaginatively act out the forbidden in American culture."[31]

In *Love and Theft: Blackface Minstrelsy and the American Working Class*, Eric Lott examines the historical foundations of American Africanism in blackface performance. Like Morrison, Lott reveals the seemingly contradictory binaries that structure white male fantasies of black masculinity in the United States, such as fascination and fear, homage and appropriation, "love and theft."[32] He describes how in the nineteenth century white ethnic working-class performers, themselves excluded from definitions of citizenship, were able to solidify their claims to white identity and privilege by performing its racial opposite in blackness. Like other historical work on whiteness, Lott's study demonstrates the fluidity and instability of this invisible racial category, which defines itself through less assimilable or inassimilable nonwhite others.[33]

Given these contours of American Africanism, one might ask, To what "taboo" traits of blackness have white authors and performers been drawn? Embedded in dominant representations of African Americans in the United States, these fantasies point to the slippery concept of *authenticity*. I want to make it clear here that the notions of authenticity I discuss with respect to black and other nonwhite masculinities have been constructed by and primarily for white people. Although people of color sometimes perform these racialized traits, both consciously and unconsciously (particularly in popular films), and although some of these traits may be rooted in non-Western cultural, social, and epistemological forms, they are, at base, Anglo-American creations that have been used to keep the cultures of nonwhite groups subordinate to the Eurocentric culture of the United States. In the African American instance, the same primitivist stereotypes that served to justify the enslavement of black people in the antebellum era and to limit their enfranchisement until the Voting Rights Act of 1965 also were and continue to be celebrated as emblematic of a kind of natural, embodied humanness.

Collins's description of the reception of black male bodies in contemporary popular culture carries the same mixture of fear and fascination around black masculinity that once lay behind the appeal of blackface minstrelsy.[34] That mixture of emotions in white audiences toward blackness as spectacle relies on the signification of the black male body as more physically and emotionally authentic—as somehow more *real* in its corporeality—than the white male body. In this context, the idea of authenticity comes to stand for the power and potency of a racialized masculinity, which is desirable only when excised from the bodies and communities of its origin and transformed into a cultural commodity for white consumption.

Within the racial category of blackness, media constructions of the bad and good black male designate different degrees of authenticity, as Collins points out: "Some representations of Blackness become commonsense 'truths.' For example, Black men in perpetual pursuit of booty calls may appear to be more authentically 'Black' than Black men who study, and the experiences of poor and working-class Black men may be established as being more authentically Black than those of middle- and upper-middle-class African American men."[35] The dangerously appealing authentic black other is distinguished from the comfortingly appealing, less authentic black buddy primarily through *class lines*. Authenticity becomes attached to the bodies and experiences of poor and working-class black men due to their proximity to marginalized Afrocentric U.S. culture, whereas middle- and upper-middle-class black men are seen as less black due to their proximity to dominant Eurocentric U.S. culture.

Meanwhile, degrees of authenticity—again, defined in this context as a form of racialized masculinity deemed worthy of white appropriation—are determined mostly along *national lines* in representations of East Asian and Asian American men. In Hollywood cinema East Asian men—especially when they perform martial arts—are considered more authentic than their

Asian American counterparts. A quick glance at contemporary male stars of Asian descent reveals that most are foreign-born, recent immigrants to the United States who regularly travel between Asia and America, literally inhabiting two worlds. Further, the current popularity of such Asiatic male actors as Jet Li, Chow Yun-Fat, and Jackie Chan is a historical anomaly in U.S. cinema. With the exception of Bruce Lee's anti-imperialist roles as a kung fu screen hero in the 1970s, this authentic Asiatic masculinity has been, for the most part, demonized in Hollywood films in the figure of the gook, as noted earlier.

Carby points out that shared hatred of this figure plays an important role in the bonding that occurs between racially diverse groups of U.S. soldiers in war films from *Bataan* (1943) to *Windtalkers* (2002) and describes the interracial friendships that result (mostly between black and white men) as rooted in "a *shared experience as oppressors* . . . outside the continental United States."[36] Not unlike earlier white ethnics, nonwhites must align with the white establishment against another other to be included in the national body. Here, following the logic of racial triangulation, the other is an Asiatic antagonist consistently coded non-American as well as non-Western.

Although marginalized in multiple ways, black characters in Hollywood movies are nonetheless usually presumed to be *African American,* not African. In this sense they are known entities, familiar to U.S. audiences, for better or worse. In sharp contrast, Asiatic characters—whether of East Asian, Southeast Asian, South Asian, or Middle Eastern descent and whether Asian or Asian American—seldom are presumed to be American. Instead they remain unknown and unknowable beings.

Important exceptions to this rule are what might be called the assimilated Asian American woman (hereafter, AAAW), a version of the Asian Pocahontas, and the oriental buddy, a version of the Oriental Monk that began to appear more frequently onscreen in the 1980s. Both character types navigate a predominantly white world and develop close relationships with white male leads. The relationship is almost always sexualized and/or romantic in the case of the AAAW and platonic, though often with homoerotic undertones, in the case of the oriental buddy.

Played by actresses such as Lucy Liu, Tia Carerra, and Kelly Hu, the AAAW demonstrates the acceptance of a certain kind of Asian American presence onscreen: female, sexually desirable, and white-identified. As a love interest for white men, the ideological role of the AAAW resembles that of most Latina and Native American female characters in Hollywood cinema. African American female characters comprise the glaring exception to this trend, for they are almost never paired romantically with white male leads, demonstrating the continued salience of the dominant notion of black female sexuality as taboo.[37] In this context, the black buddy functions as a sublimated surrogate for the absent black female romantic interest even as his sexuality enhances the masculinity of the white buddy.

Meanwhile, heterosexual coupling between Latina characters and white male leads in such films as *Lone Star* (1996) and *Bread and Roses* (2000) seems to obviate the need for Latino buddies to project the illusion of interracial harmony. Since the 1980s, Chicano and Chicano-coded men have played leading roles in such popular films as *La Bamba* (1987) and *Stand and Deliver* (1988) but seldom have been placed in buddy relationships with white men. Native men, on the other hand, play either sidekicks or antagonists to white male leads in contemporary westerns such as *Dances with Wolves* (1990), *Black Robe* (1991), and *The Last of the Mohicans* (1992) and occasionally appear as strong protagonists, but only in less well-known independent films such as *Pow Wow Highway* (1989) and *Smoke Signals* (1998).

Unlike these other men of color, Asiatic men rarely appear at all on the big screen as humanized characters, that is, in dramatic rather than physical (action) and comedic roles. When they do appear in the foreground, the following patterns define their characters. First, Asiatic men play sidekicks (oriental buddies and Oriental Monks) to white male leads even when an Asiatic woman (AAAW or Asian Pocahontas) is romantically available to these leads. Examples of this curious phenomenon can be found in such films as *Heaven's Burning* (1997), *Shanghai Noon* (2000), and *The Transporter* (2002). Second, until the cycle of East Asian (not Asian American) martial arts and action films became popular in the early to mid-1990s, Asiatic men almost never had starring roles in popular Hollywood films. A notable exception to this rule was Japanese American actor Sessue Hayakawa, a silent screen luminary most famous for his charismatic performance in *The Cheat* (1915). Third, and perhaps most pertinent to this discussion, Asiatic men are seldom shown in overtly romantic relationships with *any* women, white or nonwhite, including Asiatic women, with whom, significantly, they are least often paired.

As Palumbo-Liu stresses in his explication of the model minority thesis, the white dominant culture lauds and desires the traits of *foreign* Asian masculinity; hence its perceived authenticity over Asian American masculinity and its subsequent visibility on the big screen, historically in the form of the powerful enemy and, more recently, in that of the skilled martial arts hero. Yet even this more visible form of Asiatic masculinity is rendered less authentic, less masculine than other forms of nonwhite masculinity. For along with their perpetual foreignness (characterized by their thick Asian accents, retention of traditional Confucian ideas and customs, propensity for martial arts, and association with Asiatic tropes such as Chinese and Japanese restaurants, orientalized clothing, stereotypical Asiatic music, etc.), these Asian male characters are erotically and romantically underdeveloped. Unlike other men of color in Hollywood movies, we seldom see them on the path to becoming fathers, husbands, and patriarchs in nuclear families, and the patriarchs we see onscreen are usually much older, emasculated, and pushed to the background.

If the masculinity (and, by extension, authenticity) of East Asian men in U.S. culture is questionable, then what of Asian American masculinity—or, in the case of Japanese American buddy films, the masculinity of the oriental buddy? Do such characters have a masculinity, or are they feminized men, that is, sexually neutral versions of the AAAW and the Asian Pocahontas?

The dominant view of Asian American men in the United States has historically been, and for the most part continues to be, that they are asexual, sexually repressed, and/or gay. Regardless of sexual orientation, Asian American men are considered *sexually passive*. To quote filmmaker Richard Fung, they are defined by a "striking absence down there."[38] Whereas (foreign) Asian men have a symbolic phallus exemplified by their traditional values (e.g., their work ethic, emphasis on family, brotherhood, etc.) and their martial arts abilities, Asian American men, in many ways, are characterized by their lack of a phallus. As discussed in chapter 1, exclusionary policies on Asian immigration kept Chinese American communities in a state of gender imbalance for most of the nineteenth century and the early twentieth, perpetuating the "bachelor societies" on the West Coast, whose members performed mostly domestic labor due to discriminatory employment practices. This socioeconomic situation created and solidified dominant stereotypes of Asiatic men as emasculated and effeminate.

Indeed, for most of U.S. history, Asian American men were considered neither men nor women but rather something in between and neither: *machines* that provided cheap, expendable labor at precisely the moment when industrial capitalism began to take on steam, so to speak. In this sense, the popular perception of Asian American masculinity has always been "queer" in the broad sense of the term, that is, following David Eng, not simply as a sexual orientation but as an erotic sensibility that is multiple, shifting, and undefinable.[39] Asian American masculinity is thus sexually and ontologically *inauthentic* by the standards of white U.S. patriarchy, which finds its *authentic* counterpoint in African American masculinity. This binary plays out in representations of Asiatic men, which conflate their power with those of machines and technology, and those of black men, which emphasize their superhuman sexuality and physicality.

In the 1970s a few Asian American male writers voiced their resistance to being stereotyped in this way. In "Fifty Years of Our Own Voice," the introductory essay in *Aiiieeeee! An Anthology of Asian American Writers*, editors Frank Chin, Jeffery Paul Chan, Lawson Fusao Inada, and Shawn Wong present a stinging indictment of the model minority myth in the form of a kind of manifesto for the then-burgeoning Asian American movement. At the core of the essay, Chin et al. argue that in order to gain political power in the dominant culture Asian Americans must create their own language instead of mimicking that of white America. In this respect they echo activist intellectuals and writers such as Audre Lorde and Gloria Anzaldúa, who present a similar argument in their writings, which intimately link the personal with the political.[40] Like Lorde and Anzaldúa, the *Aiiieeeee!* editors also associate the profoundly political act of creating a new language with the activation and expression of a hitherto submerged non-Western sexuality.

However, unlike these lesbian feminists of color, Chin et al. promulgate a (hetero)sexuality that finds expression in a form of Asian American masculinity that is primarily *reactive* with respect to white masculinity and *reactionary* with respect to heterosexual Asian American women and certain Asian American men (gay men and lesbians are not mentioned). The *Aiiieeeee!* editors define the explicitly "authentic" and implicitly "masculine" literary works of the mostly male Asian American authors in the anthology against the popular "feminine" works of Asian American women and feminized men, which are condemned as "fake" expressions of colonized subjects.[41] Not surprisingly,

Asian American feminists were quick to attack this essay for its sexist and homophobic overtones, and it came to occupy a marginal position in Asian American Studies.[42]

As James Kyung-Jin Lee points out, although critiques of the essay remain valid, reducing its initial attempt to interrogate stereotypes of Asian American men to a simple form of cultural nationalism leaves a glaring gap in the history of the Asian American movement as well as in the intellectual and political terrain of Asian American studies.[43] Since the publication of "Fifty Years of Our Own Voice," several studies on Asian American masculinity have appeared that wrestle with issues of Asiatic manhood in the United States in multiple, often overlapping ways. The approach that has been favored in the field, responding in part to the heterocentrism and sexism of Chin et al. and in part to the dominant trend in masculinity studies generally, has been informed by feminist and queer theories and has focused on representations of gay men.

In "Looking for My Penis" Richard Fung performs brilliant close readings of gay porn films that reveal the ways in which gay male subculture replicates dominant stereotypes of Asiatic men as passive and feminized. Fung notes that in North America Asiatic men are assumed to be asexual or homosexual (the two are often conflated in the postindustrial West) and that within this framework they are further emasculated as sexual and social "bottoms."[44] Although various manifestations of the feminist movement have led to more legal rights and social freedoms for women, the political, social, and cultural institutions of the West remain patriarchal. Within this phallocentric system, feminized "bottoms," or objects of sexual penetration—whether passive queer male partners or passive straight or queer women—are considered subordinate to the masculinized "tops," the ones doing the penetrating. In *Racial Castration: Managing Masculinity in Asian America,* David Eng further explores these issues in literary studies through nuanced readings of symbolically queer representations of Asian and Asian American men in canonical Asian American literary texts. In the process Eng weaves together various strands of psychoanalytic theory, queer theory, and Asian American studies to examine the complex role of Asiatic masculinities in literary and filmic texts with Asian American themes and tropes.

Drawing on the theoretical framework established by Fung, Eng, and others working at the intersections of Asian American studies and queer studies, emerging scholarship reexamines the issues introduced by Chin et al., addressing the ways in which straight Asian American men negotiate the emasculating stereotypes conferred on them by the dominant culture.[45] On a related note, studies that use a comparative approach to look at the historical experiences and representations of African Americans, Latinos/as, and Asian Americans have begun laying the theoretical foundations for future studies that might examine the masculinities of various nonwhite groups—not simply through the filter of Eurocentric culture but also through the overlapping histories and stories of our own indigenous, if displaced, roots.[46]

All of these studies in some way or another grapple with the racial ordering of American masculinities in which Asiatic men occupy the position of social and cultural "bottom," which places them directly opposite black men, who are seen as hypermasculine and as hypersexual "tops."[47] Moving between the two poles of the hypermasculine (black) and the nonmasculine (Asiatic) are Latino, American Indian, and mixed-race men, while the specter of the white male hovers outside and around this racialized hierarchy of masculinity as the invisible (though not invincible) standard. This racial ordering is a political sexual fantasy in which all men of color are relegated to the social and cultural bottom of the dominant culture insofar as they are rendered racially exoticized subordinate objects of the white gaze. Within this hierarchy, the status of the Asian American male onscreen is tenuous, if visible at all, because in Hollywood cinema Asian American masculinity continues to be defined through the tropes of its foreign Asian counterpart.

As a result, Asian and Asian American actors working in Hollywood have been forced to stay within the boundaries of these orientalized representations in order to be recognizable to and recognized by Western audiences. Put another way, these actors have had to negotiate between embodying character type and racial stereotype—the two often conflated in self-orientalizing roles that require the actor to perform a kind of double consciousness onscreen and sometimes off, which vacillates between their (projected) oriental Asian identities and their (lived and/or suppressed) Asian or Asian American identities.[48] Such racial performances shape the roles of the Oriental Monk and the oriental buddy, which are played by Asian American actors Pat Morita in *The Karate Kid* and Gedde Watanabe in *Gung Ho,* respectively, as well as by Japanese actor Ken Takakura in *Black Rain.* It is to these actors and movies that I now turn.

A Beautiful Friendship

In a DVD special-feature documentary film on the making of *The Karate Kid*, director John Avildsen, writer Robert Mark Kamen, and principal cast members Ralph Macchio, Pat Morita, William Zabka, and Martin Kove recount their experiences on the set and pay homage to this classic coming-of-age movie. Morita ends the string of nostalgic reminiscences with the following words: "It [his involvement in *The Karate Kid*] brought me . . . a family [deep pause]. A family [Morita's eyes tear] of wonderfully diverse people and backgrounds. And I'm not simply referring to the cast and the powers that be . . . but a beingness, a belonging to this family of earth . . . people."⁴⁹

Morita's reflection on the role of the film in his life is incredibly moving, yet its emotionally charged delivery is also a bit unsettling, especially compared with the more restrained comments of the other actors. We could interpret this moment of mediated disclosure as one in which Morita self-reflexively performs the figure of the Oriental Monk, serving up Asiatic New Age "wisdom" à la the spirit of Mr. Miyagi—winking at Asian American audiences while engaging in subversive mimicry of the powers that be. Or, conversely, we could point to this moment as evidence of his successful interpellation in the Hollywood system as an "abject" Asian American actor for whom the part of the Oriental Monk in this film represented the pinnacle of a lifelong career in the entertainment industry. Ultimately I hope to show that neither critical position adequately captures the complexities of Morita's performance in *The Karate Kid* or, for that matter, the many onscreen performances that distinguish the prolific actor's dramatic life and career.

The role of the karate sensei in the film, which was supposed to go to legendary Japanese actor Toshiro Mfume, went instead to Morita, a diminutive Japanese American stand-up comedian well known for his many comic roles in television and movies.⁵⁰ The first Asian American to be nominated for an Oscar and one of the few actors of Asian descent to be honored with a star on the Hollywood Walk of Fame, Noriyuki Morita was born in 1933 to migrant fruit pickers in Isleton, California.⁵¹ At the age of two Morita contracted spinal tuberculosis and spent most of his childhood bedridden in a Catholic sanatorium where the nuns and priests gave him his Anglicized name. He was released nine years later after undergoing spinal surgery and learning to walk—only to be sent, after the Japanese attack on Pearl Harbor, to a relocation camp at Gila River, Arizona, where he joined his family before they were taken to the internment camp in Tule Lake, California.[52]

When the war ended, Morita's family opened a Chinese restaurant in Sacramento due to continued anti-Japanese sentiment.[53] Soon thereafter his father was killed in a hit-and-run accident. Morita took data processing jobs at the Department of Motor Vehicles and the Aerojet-General Corporation to support his wife and child. At the age of thirty, he decided to pursue his dream of becoming a stand-up comic. Calling himself the "Hip Nip," he performed in clubs in San Francisco, Los Angeles, and Las Vegas, opening for performances by Ella Fitzgerald, Johnny Mathis, the Supremes, and others. He once had a particularly harrowing experience filling in for Don Ho in Hawaii in which he learned just before going onstage that the audience was composed mostly of disabled Pearl Harbor survivors. Morita recounts the moment thus: "I turned on all the angelic, cherubic charm I could find and I went out and I said, 'Before I begin, I just want to say I'm sorry about messing up your harbor.' There was a second of silence, and then a big wave of laughter started at the back and rolled forward. That was all it took."[54]

The ingenious comic skills and timing Morita demonstrated in this charged situation became the comedian's signature mark onscreen as well. He broke into the movies in 1967 playing the utterly silent Oriental Number 2 in the musical movie *Thoroughly Modern Millie* (1967) alongside Jack Soo (Oriental Number 1), best known for his role in the television sitcom *Barney Miller* (1975–82). However, with the exception of the *Karate Kid* series, Morita was not as successful in cinema as he was on television, where he played such familiar and memorable roles as diner owner Arnold in *Happy Days* (1974–84) and Lamont's friend Ah Chew in *Sanford and Son* (1972–77). Furthermore, he made TV history by starring in two short-lived shows: *Mr. T and Tina* (1976), the first sitcom with an Asian American in the lead role, and the detective series *Ohara* (1987), which he created.

A member of the Los Angeles–based national Asian American theater organization East West Players, Morita was also active in the Asian American drama and independent film scene. In 1976 he appeared in the TV movie *Farewell to Manzanar* (1976), which recounts the World War II internment experience through the rare perspective of a Japanese American female lead, and four years later in *Hito Hata: Raise the Banner* (1980), the first feature film about Japanese Americans produced and distributed entirely by Asian Americans. More recently, in *Only the Brave* (2005), a film about the highly decorated Japanese American 442nd Regimental Combat Team that was written, directed, and produced by Lane Nishikawa, Morita played a Buddhist monk imprisoned in Hawaii during World War II.

Yet despite all these accomplishments, the image that most of the world associates with Pat Morita is that of the Asian sidekick. In a thoughtful *New York Times* editorial, Lawrence Downes provides a snapshot of the screen caricature that the actor, who died in 2005 of chronic alcoholism, was consistently chosen to play:

> Whenever a script called for a little Asian guy to drive a taxi, serve drinks or utter wise aphorisms in amusingly broken English, you could count on Mr. Morita to be there. Those who knew Mr. Morita say he was a man of uncommon decency and good humor. He fulfilled the actor's prime directive, to keep busy. But it's distressing to think that the life's work of one of the best-known, hardest-working Asian American actors is mostly a loose collection of servile supporting roles.[55]

Of these roles, certainly the best known and the one for which Morita was most highly acclaimed was that of Kesuke Miyagi in *The Karate Kid*. It took Morita two auditions to convince producer Jerry Weintraub to choose him for the part. Weintraub initially rejected the actor because he felt the audience would associate him too closely with his role in *Happy Days*. Undaunted, Morita grew a beard and affected his uncle's Japanese accent for a second screen test. According to Weintraub's wife, Evelyn, the producer failed to recognize the self-orientalized Morita and declared, "'That's what I want—a goddamn actor,' not realizing it was Pat."[56] For Morita, getting into this character was an almost mystical experience, which he described in the following way: "I don't know how, I don't know where it came from . . . *Miyagi voice. Miyagi presence. Miyagi spirit* . . . emerged."[57]

Whatever spirit the actor was able to channel through Miyagi clearly resonated with many viewers—especially young boys in need of strong male role models. Avildsen's rhetorical question "Who wouldn't want to have a

Mr. Miyagi as a surrogate father?" sums this up.[58] After all, *The Karate Kid* is about a bullied teenage boy coming into manhood, a passage usually facilitated by a father or father figure. The film emphasizes the importance of karate as a family tradition handed down from father to son in Okinawa (Miyagi's hometown), a theme further developed in *The Karate Kid II* (1986). Yet in *The Karate Kid* Miyagi has no son or wife or any family to speak of, at least in the United States, to whom to bequeath his familial and cultural legacy. As much as Miyagi functions as a surrogate father for Daniel Laruso (Ralph Macchio), Daniel also functions as a surrogate son for Miyagi. More than any other Hollywood film character in the 1980s, the teen hero of this movie series typifies the geeky orientalized white male protagonist, who has since become a staple in popular media.

Bowing at cineplexes in the summer of 1984, *The Karate Kid* was the fifth-highest-grossing domestic film that year. It garnered an Academy Award nomination for Morita—who lost to Haing Ngor, who won for his supporting role in *The Killing Fields* (1984)—and led to a resurgence of interest in martial arts among U.S. youth (the first wave of interest, in the 1970s, had been sparked by the "kung fu craze," which is mentioned in the next chapter). The film centers on the unlikely friendship between two outsiders: an unpopular, working-class Italian American teenager and a solitary Japanese American janitor. Miyagi teaches Daniel how to defend himself against the Cobra Kai, a gang of wealthy white youth from the San Fernando Valley who victimize him for his ethnically coded class difference and for his romantic interest in Ali (Elisabeth Shue), the gang leader's former girlfriend.

It opens with a sulky Daniel leaving New Jersey with his mother (Randee Heller) for California, where she has accepted a job as the manager of a new computer firm. Their journey reworks the Manifest Destiny narrative of "going West," in which California represents the dream of the frontier. However, this new frontier is characterized less by the values and iconography of the Old West than by those of the Orient: along with the obvious foregrounding of karate, a Japanese martial art, and allusions to Japanese culture (bonsai, sake, etc.), one important scene is prominently set in a Chinese restaurant. Interestingly, this scene shows the last heart-to-heart conversation in the film between Daniel and his mother before Mr. Miyagi enters Daniel's life.

Miyagi is the literal embodiment of the Asiatic mise-en-scène: through him the initially foreign and menacing Oriental other, which structures the new rules that Daniel must learn to survive in Los Angeles, becomes a friendly and familiar presence. Daniel first encounters Mr. Miyagi when he and his mother move into their new apartment. Searching for the maintenance man, Daniel finds him in a cluttered office trying to catch a fly with chopsticks. The first shot shows Miyagi from behind in shadow, framed by chimes and bonsai trees. The following close-up reveals that he is wearing a Japanese headband and an almost fanatic expression of concentration. He replies to Daniel's questions only with "hai" ("yes" in Japanese), gibberish, and exasperated grunts.

As the relationship between the two characters deepens, however, the janitor turned karate instructor is both Americanized and humanized, as is signaled by a shift in the extradiegetic music used to signal Miyagi's presence—from low, menacing string chords to the clear, peaceful strains of Zamfir's pan pipe. We eventually learn that Miyagi is just as adept at repairing vintage American cars as he is at trimming bonsai trees and that, despite his heavily accented English, he is an American citizen and has lived in the United States for a long time.

In the vein of Wong's "caregiver of color," Miyagi assumes the parenting roles of Daniel's absent father and his single working mother, who can neither protect her son from the bullies nor provide him with the skills he needs to keep from being assaulted. As a substitute father, Miyagi teaches Daniel how to defend himself through karate. He is also linked with the transportation vehicles that represent Daniel's adolescent male freedom: he repairs Daniel's bike when the Cobra Kai run him into a ravine with their more powerful motorbikes and later, on his sixteenth birthday, presents him with his first car, a 1947 Ford coupe, significantly yellow, that Daniel chooses from a line of vintage cars that Miyagi has restored. Meanwhile, as a substitute mother Miyagi takes care of Daniel when he is beaten up by the Cobra Kai and performs domestic duties, such as making him a Halloween costume and baking him a birthday cake.

The film privileges the familial relationship that evolves between Miyagi and Daniel over those of other, whiter families, namely, the violent, homosocial male family of the Cobra Kai and, to a lesser but related extent, Ali's uptight, upper-class nuclear family. In contrast to Daniel's family, defined by the close-knit relationship with Miyagi and his mother, both of these white, Anglo-Saxon Protestant families are defined by their cultural and emotional lack, which the film links to excessive capitalist consumption.

Unlike Miyagi, who teaches Daniel the philosophy of karate and its in-separability from one's mode of being in the world, John Kreese (Marin Kove), the psychopathic sensei of the Cobra Kai, teaches his students the techniques but not the spirit of karate. His highly regimented lessons are given in the enclosed, artificial, and commodifed space of an expensive dojo, unlike Miyagi's lessons, which unfold organically in the outdoors and con-nect martial arts training with daily acts of labor that Daniel obediently per-forms for his teacher (e.g., "paint the fence," "sand the floor," "wax on, wax off"). Providing an ironic twist on the stereotype of the Japanese as imita-tors of the West, the Anglo-American sensei appropriates karate, emptying it of its history, spirituality, and philosophy in order to turn the martial art form into a commodified weapon for bored and angry rich American youth.

Although Ali's parents are not psychopathic, they, too have a flat and mechanistic affect, which likewise belies a moral and emotional bankruptcy. This becomes apparent in a scene toward the end of the second act. Ali has promised to meet Daniel outside her parents' country club but is trapped into dancing with her ex-boyfriend, Johnny (William Zabka), the Cobra Kai leader and Daniel's chief rival. After waiting a while, Daniel enters the build-ing through the kitchen and spies Ali and Johnny dancing from the window

Pat Morita and Ralph Macchio in *The Karate Kid* (1984). Mr. Miyagi teaches Daniel how to "paint the fence."

Ralph Macchio in *The Karate Kid*. A humiliated Daniel at the country club had spied Johnny stealing a kiss from Ali.

of the kitchen door. He and Johnny exchange a shot-reverse-shot glance; Johnny grins and attempts to kiss Ali. We hear a crash, quickly followed by a zoom-in to an embarrassed Daniel, sprawled on the floor and covered with spaghetti sauce, a sight that immediately elicits cruel, amused laughter from the wealthy Anglo-Americans at the club.

The audience is clearly supposed to sympathize with Daniel in this moment of abjection, which is linked to and amplified by his racially liminal position: he is defined *against* the white privilege of the country club and *alongside* the marginalized experiences of nonwhite and working-class groups. Daniel is othered with regard to ethnicity and class as a poor Italian American youth from Reseda, a less affluent part of Los Angeles. He enters the club from the back and is mistaken for a servant, a position that has historically been relegated to African Americans and other people of color. In addition, his difference as an ethnic American is encoded in oriental style: he wears an ill-fitting outfit (white shirt and pants, red jacket) that sports the colors of the Japanese flag.

Furthermore, this scene is preceded and followed by scenes that emphasize the bond between Daniel and Mr. Miyagi by highlighting the latter's ethnic and cultural difference. In the first scene, two lower-class white men yell racial slurs at Miyagi as he and Daniel leave the beach, calling him a "pet Nip" and "Mr. Moto." When Miyagi politely asks them to remove their beer bottles from his truck and leave, they refuse until he karate-chops the bottles. In the second scene, Daniel arrives at Miyagi's home after being humiliated at the country club. He discovers his teacher dressed in a military uniform, singing a Japanese song, and drunkenly toasting a photograph of his wife.

Through a poignant monologue delivered by Miyagi, we learn that his wife and newborn son died due to complications of birth in the Manzanar internment camp while he served in Germany during World War II. As Daniel tucks his teacher, who has passed out, into bed, he finds Miyagi's Congressional Medal of Honor on the night stand. The scene ends with Daniel gazing back at Miyagi's house in the darkness and respectfully bowing in the direction of his sleeping master before going home.

According to Avildsen, this scene earned Morita the Academy Award nomination, yet it was also one that studio executives originally wanted to cut, a decision Morita opposed for the following reason: "I get a call from Jerry and John [the producers] who wanted to cut the scene out. I'm like, wait a minute. It's the only real moment of Miyagi's fallibility and being

Pat Morita and Ralph Macchio in *The Karate Kid*. Mr. Miyagi offers Daniel a drink on the anniversary of his wife's death in the Manzanar internment camp.

human. And we get a sense of the surge of Daniel's emergence into his own manhood. Recognition of life ain't all about me. Look at this man."⁵⁹ Tellingly, Miyagi's fallibility and humanity, which in Morita's opinion is a major catalyst for Daniel's "emergence into ... manhood," are intimately connected to Miyagi's identity and experience as a *Japanese American man*. The unspoken subtext of this scene is that the deplorable living conditions in the Manzanar camp most likely led to the death of his wife and child. Furthermore, these conditions were created by the government that Miyagi was serving to prove his loyalty—that is, to show that he was American, or not Japanese, at a time when those identities were seen as mutually exclusive.

In the same way that Miyagi serves as Daniel's father figure, Creese serves as the father figure for Johnny and the other Cobra Kai members. Like Miyagi, he is associated with a U.S. war in Asia and embodies a particular kind of East–West hybridity. However, whereas Miyagi is Americanized through his patriotic service in World War II (a war the United States played a key role in winning), Kreese is orientalized through his dishonorable service in the Vietnam War (a war the United States lost). The film thus posits as more authentic a hybridized Orientalism expressed through an Asiatic character rather than a non-Asiatic one, drawing on the popular conflation of Asian Americans with Asians.

At the same time, the film ultimately privileges the appropriation and performance of this "authentic" oriental identity by certain white men. After all, it is titled *The Karate Kid*, not "The Karate Sensei." When Daniel wins the tournament at the end of the film, he does so as the ethnic and working-class underdog, much like the title character in *Rocky*, which John Avildsen had directed a few years before this movie. However, unlike Rocky, the youthful Daniel finally emerges as a new liberal subject curiously dependent on oriental otherness for self-expression.

Japanese Invasion

The theme of U.S. dependence on Japan moved from the arena of sports to that of the workplace two years later in *Gung Ho*, a comedy about the culture clash that ensues when Tokyo-based company Assan Motors reopens an auto plant in Hadleyville, an economically depressed small town in Pennsylvania. Based on a *60 Minutes* news segment about the opening of a Nissan plant in rural Tennessee, the Ron Howard–directed film received mixed reviews but performed well at the box office and even led to a short-lived television sitcom of the same name.[60]

Most of *Gung Ho* predictably contrasts Japan and the United States with regard to notions of identity, work, family, and community, depicting the Japanese as communal, unemotional, and work-focused and the Americans as individualistic, expressive, and leisure-focused. These differences are epitomized in the personalities of the two protagonists: Hunt Stevenson (Michael Keaton), a wise-cracking, washed-up former local basketball star, and Kazihiro Oishi (Gedde Watanabe), an overworked manager and family man who is transferred to the United States for failing to meet the production quota at the home office. Their friendship transcends the cultural and national differences between their communities, saving the town morally as well as financially.

Watanabe, a Japanese American native of Ogden, Utah, and graduate of the American Conservatory Theater in San Francisco, got his big break in 1984 playing the caricature of a Japanese foreign exchange student in the teen film *Sixteen Candles*. Like Morita, Watanabe gave an orientalized performance in his audition, complete with a thick faux-Chinese accent. During the audition Watanabe became aware that neither the director, John Hughes, nor the casting person realized he was actually playing a part. He recalls approaching the latter afterward to tell her it had been an act: "So I went back to her and said, 'Look, I'm really sorry but you have to know that I don't have an accent, and I'm from Utah and everything like that.' She said, 'Well, don't tell the director.'"[61] Watanabe subsequently stayed in character during the entire shooting of the movie.

Perhaps due to his extensive experience playing such roles, Watanabe is outspoken with regard to the stereotypes Asiatic men are forced to perform in the industry: "I think the Asian male [in movies] is pretty . . . shit. And I mean that. You don't see them as lovers or that they've got full lives. . . . It's always made me feel, like, who writes this shit?!"[62] Yet like Morita and many other Asian American actors, he has managed to work within these limitations, emerging as a notable presence on Broadway and in voice-overs as well as in film and on television.

Although critics praised Watanabe's performance of his stereotypical role in *Gung Ho*, they were less generous toward Keaton, as is apparent in the following comment from a review in the *Washington Post:* "Watanabe . . . is turning into a charming comic actor, which is something that Keaton is not. Keaton . . . does so much mugging, so much Mr. Wise Guy, that you can't really see the character for the schtick."[63] One of the most popular comedic actors of the 1980s, Keaton was coming off of several successful films, including *Night Shift, Mr. Mom* (1982), and *Johnny Dangerously* (1984), when he was cast as the star in *Gung Ho.* Like all buddy movies, the film has a dual protagonist but focuses heavily on the development of Keaton's character.

We are introduced to Hunt in the expository section of the film when he flies to Tokyo to meet with the executives at Assan Motors. After making several off-color sexist jokes and cultural faux pas, he is somehow able to convince them to reopen the Pennsylvania auto plant. Kazihiro and the other executives soon arrive with their families and are given a warm reception by the optimistic townspeople. The reception grows chilly, however, when the Japanese attempt to impose their corporate structure on the Hadleyville plant: they institute longer work hours, stress the importance of the company's productivity over the workers' relationships with their families, and try to instill a stronger sense of teamwork in the workers through such Japanese corporate practices as morning calisthenics. Depicted throughout the film as fat, lazy, loud, whiny, and undisciplined, the workers make fun of their new Japanese bosses, loudly resisting when the latter try to get them to exercise. Eventually the Americans realize they are inferior to the Japanese in the workplace—especially when the Japanese effortlessly beat them at the all-American sport of baseball—and by the end of the film they have adopted the Japanese work ethic with a few American tweaks.

In contrast to its rather pedantic and sometimes heavy-handed depiction of Americans incorporating Japanese culture, the film renders the effects of American culture on the Japanese in light, absurd tones. For example, one of the important turning points in the romantic B plot is a scene in which Audrey (Mimi Rogers), Hunt's girlfriend, remains at the dinner table to join a business discussion among the men instead of politely leaving like the Japanese wives. When she tries to support Hunt, he rudely reprimands her in front of his coworkers, and, in response, she breaks up with him on the drive home. The film thus warns of the dangerous influence of Japanese patriarchal values on American men even as it critiques the feminist attitudes of U.S. women in the 1980s.

Meanwhile, Kazuhiro's wife and children also undergo a change as they consume American products, including Jimmy Dean sausages, Hawaiian punch, Cabbage Patch Kids dolls, and MTV. However, their Americanization is played to high comic effect in a peripheral scene in which the company president pays Kazuhiro an unexpected visit. The household is shown to be in complete chaos: the wife is cooking a frozen dinner, the daughter is making a mess in the kitchen, and the son, dressed in army fatigues, greets the important guest by shooting him with his toy machine gun and yelling, "GI Joe!"

As the primary "buddy" of the film and the mediator between the white-collar Japanese management and the blue-collar American workers, Hunt tries to play the smart orientalist with such lines as "We're lucky to have the Japanese over here right now. We just gotta know how to play them." However, his strategy backfires when the Japanese bosses continuously reject the workers' requests for more pay and fewer hours. Hunt finally strikes a deal for those benefits on the condition that the Hadleyville plant meet the same monthly quota of cars required in Japan. Too cowardly to tell the workers that this is an all-or-nothing deal, he lies to them, saying that they need to meet only half the quota to receive half the benefits. This leads to several predictable complications, which are resolved when Kazihiro and Hunt, who have become fast friends after a drunken night at the local bowling alley, are able to convince their men to work together to manufacture the rest of the cars.

When the deadline arrives, the workers have met the quota except for one defective car, which Hunt desperately claims is a symbol of the new, collaborative spirit between Japan and the United States. The car disastrously falls apart in front of the company president, who has come to inspect the plant. Rather than closing the plant as expected, however, the president, inexplicably charmed by Hunt's wacky sense of humor, congratulates the two leaders on their teamwork and gives everyone a raise.

The movie ends by repeating the initial scene of morning calisthenics with Kazuhiro and Hunt wearing business suits onstage leading the workers, wearing blue jumpsuits, below. The camera moves from a wide aerial shot of the workers as an undistinguished moving mass to medium and close-up shots of individual workers smiling and exercising cheerfully. Somewhat incongruously, the rock song "Working Class Man" by Jonathan Cain plays both diegetically and extradiegetically in this final scene as the credits roll. In a *Cineaste* review Jim Naureckas notes, "The final scenes almost demand to be taken ironically, as smiling, uniformed workers do their prescribed jumping jacks in perfect synchronization."[64] And this disconcerting image certainly does make one wonder to what extent Hunt or any of the Americans in the film have learned to "play" the Japanese.

Emphatically antiunion, *Gung Ho* conflates Japan with white-collar economic prosperity and hints that the U.S. working class needs to be morally resuscitated by its Japanese competitors. In so doing it elides the domestic problems in the United States brought on by the conservative policies of Reagonomics. Furthermore, it presents the U.S. working class as economically and morally dependent on the Japanese, from whom, ironically, they relearn the joys of the postwar American work ethic. East and West meet through this hybridized work ethic, which is channeled to meet the goals of global industrial capitalism. The somewhat jarring happy ending feels false not only within the logic of the film but also in the period in which it was released, when fears of Japan taking over were percolating as Japanese corporations invested in important symbols of American culture, including Hollywood.

In *Gung Ho* (1986), auto factory workers happily perform morning calisthenics under the leadership of their new Japanese bosses.

The Ugly American

In November 1989 the Japanese electronics giant Sony bought Columbia Pictures Entertainment Inc. for the highest amount paid by a Japanese company for a U.S. corporation to that time, a record that Matsushita broke just a few months later the following year when it bought MCA/Universal.[65] With these buyouts, Sony and Matsushita acquired a library of U.S. cultural software for their Japanese hardware—the audiovisual electronics products that had established both as international corporate giants. This synergistic move signaled a shift to what Joseph Nye calls the "soft power" of Japanese cultural commodities, which became more pronounced in the 1990s as Japan's technological prowess morphed into a "hip" new style in global popular culture.[66] In the late 1980s, however, these purchases fueled a panic in Hollywood and the nation at large that foreign industries would take over U.S. businesses and culture. As Janet Wasko observes, no such panic had ensued when Australian mogul Rupert Murdoch's News Corporation bought Twentieth Century Fox in 1985, demonstrating that in this instance "foreign" was coded not just nationally but culturally and racially.[67]

Drawing on this anxiety, in 1992 Congressman Leon E. Panetta (later White House chief of staff under the Clinton administration) proposed a bill to limit foreign ownership of entertainment companies and national landmarks to 50 percent.[68] Although the bill did not pass, it was against this politically charged backdrop that Ridley Scott's *Black Rain* was released in late September of 1989 amid much controversy and some confusion, for Shohei Imamura's film with the same title would premiere just a few days later at the New York Film Festival.[69] In both movies, "black rain" refers to the toxic chemical residue from the atomic bombs that the U.S. planes dropped on Hiroshima and Nagasaki in World War II. However, this reference is all they have in common: Imamura's quiet art house film focuses on the effects of the bomb on a Japanese family, while Scott's unabashedly commercial action movie centers on a New York cop who discovers his moral core while pursuing a *yakuza* killer.

A slick thriller, travelogue, and buddy film, the latter met with considerable success at the box office and received Academy Award nominations for sound and special effects. Whereas Japan remains safely contained on U.S. soil in *The Karate Kid* and *Gung Ho*, Scott's *Black Rain* takes us directly to the oriental other in Osaka, which, as many critics noted, eerily invokes the orientalized city in his earlier film, *Blade Runner*.[70] This was no coincidence. According to Michael Douglas, who plays the protagonist, he and producer Sherry Lansing asked Ridley Scott to direct the film after being struck by the resemblance between Tokyo's Ginza Strip and the *Blade Runner* set.[71]

Scott's rendering of urban, modern-day Japan in *Black Rain* both recalls and realizes his earlier fantasy of a techno-orientalized future in *Blade Runner* and provides a way for us to look at the multiple levels on which the film deals with the issues of cultural authenticity, appropriation, and commodification that have been introduced in this chapter. At the most basic level of plot, the story capitalized on the fears of the time of a destabilized U.S. economy: New York police officer Nick Conklin (Douglas), his partner Charlie Vincent (Andy Garcia), and Osaka police officer Masahiro Matsumoto (Ken Takakura) work to expose a Japanese counterfeiting ring that has the technological ability to make perfect replicas of U.S. currency. Meanwhile, Scott's decision to shoot on location for a more realistic portrait of contemporary Japan illuminated these issues offscreen. After scouting out Tokyo and Kyoto, the director decided to film in Osaka for its densely packed streets and polluted skies, which he felt would provide the desired image of a high-tech, distinctly Asiatic industrial center. Once in Osaka, casting sessions and location shooting proved awkward and difficult because, according to associate producer and "resident Japanologist" Alan Poul, respectable Japanese actors did not audition, and most Japanese films were shot in studios.[72]

Yet in interviews Scott and the U.S. actors were quick to celebrate the "international language in filmmaking" that emerged in interactions between the U.S. and Japanese film crews. Scott described the Japanese crew and actors as "an army . . . [that] would die—absolutely die—for you." Furthermore, he and Michael Douglas both expressed surprise at the skill of the Japanese actors. Scott found them "brilliant": "I thought I was going to get Kabuki Theater and I didn't get that at all."[73] Douglas concurred: "We tend to have preconceived ideas that the Japanese are very stylized, almost ritualistic, but to see how natural and honest their actors really are was a big surprise to me."[74] One of these actors, costar Ken Takakura, recalled the shooting process in slightly less effusive terms: "I've done a lot of physically demanding films. I've been dragged to the South Pole and the North Pole. I've had to climb glaciers and stand naked in sub-zero weather in Hokkaido, and I would say that making this film was just as tough, maybe even tougher, than any of them."[75] Interestingly, the film did well in Japan, where it was nominated for Best Foreign Language film and performed better at the box office than all of the domestic films in 1989.[76]

Japanese critics and audiences lauded the film for its "accurate" depictions of Japanese culture and for using prominent Japanese actors who spoke in Japanese with English subtitles. In fact, according to Douglas, audiences at the Tokyo Film Festival saw Masahiro (Takakura) "as the hero who shows [Nick] the way."[77] In stark contrast, the film received mixed reviews and scathing responses in the United States from liberal intellectuals who critiqued what they saw as its racist stereotypes of Japan.[78]

The contradictions in these multiple responses to *Black Rain* can be traced to the film's ambivalent treatment of cultural, national, and racial differences between the United States and Japan. As in *The Karate Kid* and *Gung Ho,* these differences are projected onto and contained by the relationships that develop among the male characters. In *Black Rain* notions of cultural authenticity among Japanese men are determined along generational lines, while among Japanese and American men they are shaped by class divisions. The *yakuza* are split between Sugai (Tomisaburo Wakayama), the honorable old boss, and Sato (Yusaku Matsuda), his dishonorable young protégé. Sato steals one of Sugai's counterfeiting plates during a lunch between his boss's representatives and Italian American mob bosses in New York. Nick and Charlie chase him out of the restaurant and, after a struggle, capture and take him to police headquarters. Much to Nick's frustration, the Japanese embassy grants Sato diplomatic immunity, and the two U.S. cops are ordered to escort him back to Osaka. Before they deplane, they stupidly make the mistake of handing him over to his *yakuza* friends, who are disguised as the local police.

Sato continues to elude the Osaka police while Nick and Charlie pursue him on their own, chaperoned by a thoroughly unimpressed Masahiro. After Sato kills Charlie in a brutal scene on which I will elaborate shortly, Nick offers Sugai his services for capturing the traitor. Sugai agrees, dismissing Sato as morally and culturally lost: "He might as well be American. His kind respects just one thing: money." At this point Nick asks Sugai what impelled him to join the *yakuza* and receives the following response: "I was ten when the B-29s came. My family lived under the ground for three days. When we came up, the city was gone. Then the heat brought rain, black rain. You made the rain black. You shoved your barrels down our throat. We forgot who we were. You created Sato and thousands like him. I am paying you back."

Sugai justifies his turn to crime in a postcolonial critique of the role of the United States in Japan during and after World War II. The United States dropped atomic bombs on Japan, effectively ending the war and securing itself as an economic and military superpower while castrating Japan, which was stripped of its military power and given a new constitution by its former enemy. According to Sugai, the American values that have dominated Japan since World War II have corrupted members of the postwar generation, who are epitomized by Sato and his underlings: a future of increasingly Americanized young Japanese who have lost their sense of cultural identity, history, and ethics.

Whereas the techno-oriental other is performed in symbolic yellowface by Creese and the Cobra Kai in *The Karate Kid* and displaced onto the specter of globalized Japanese corporate culture in *Gung Ho,* in *Black Rain* it sports the cool young face of Japan's technologized present and future. The ultimate techno-oriental other, Sato displays a ruthless and mechanistic approach to life defined purely by acquisition and style. As one critic adroitly put it, he is a "viciously hip villain . . . a renegade mobster cleverly portrayed as a smirking adolescent by Yusaku Matsuda."[79] Dressed in black and wearing sunglasses, Sato easily blends in with the industrial materials—steel, glass, and neon—that define the Osaka cityscape as interpreted through Scott's design-heavy lens even though his weapons of choice are not guns but anachronistic traditional knives and swords.

Much like the face of the billboard geisha and the replicants in *Blade Runner,* Sato functions as a metonym of the city itself. Shot through a deep red filter, his subterranean steel plant resembles a kind of technological hell in which his adolescent underlings roar about on their motorcycles like urban, Japanized versions of the suburban Cobra Kai. According to Greenfeld, these youth are known as members of the *bosozoku,* or "speed tribes," the "proving grounds for the Yakuza," with an estimated 40 percent eventually entering the ranks of the Japanese underworld.[80] The dehumanized images of the *bosozoku* are linked with the speed and power of the motorcycles they ride. Indeed, motorcycles, a recurring motif in the film, come to represent potentially dangerous transnational technology, masculinity, and youth—all important components of the techno-oriental other.

Yusaku Matsuda in *Black Rain* (1989). Stylish techno-oriental other Sato rides his motorcycle through the urban street tunnels of Osaka.

Black Rain opens to a screen drenched in red, which gradually condenses into a circle. The title appears vertically against this backdrop to the sound of metallic oriental chimes, associating the circle with the sun of the Japanese flag. As the filter shifts from red to blue, this flat symbolic sun fades into a wire sculpture of a dark metallic globe toward which we see the silhouette of Nick riding on his motorcycle. The next shots track Nick on the Brooklyn Bridge as dawn breaks, riding toward a group of motorcycle racers who congregate under the bridge. Nick challenges one of them to a race and wins, establishing his masculinity in this shady, working-class subculture.

Nick's illusory sense of power is quickly undercut in the following scenes when we learn that he is divorced, struggling to put his children through private school, and being accused of stealing confiscated money by Internal Affairs. En route to an interview with the "suits," he gives his partner Charlie a ride to work. Charlie is introduced dressed impeccably in a fashionable suit. He playfully greets Nick (on his motorcycle) by taunting him with his coat the way a matador taunts a bull with the red cape.

This scene foreshadows Charlie's death scene in Japan, where Sato (also on his motorcycle) snatches his coat in a subway mall, leading Charlie down to an underground parking lot where the *bosozoku* surround him on their motorcycles and ritualistically slice him with their knives. Wielding a *katana* (samurai sword), Sato decapitates Charlie as Nick watches helplessly from behind a wall of wire. Later, in the film's climax, Nick avenges Charlie's death and reestablishes his own masculinity and honor when he finally captures Sato in the countryside. As Pat Dowell insightfully points out in a *Cineaste* review, Nick can defeat the villain only outside the urban context and then, significantly, by pushing him off his motorcycle.[81]

Through the shared trope of the motorcycle, the film reinforces the doubling between Nick and Sato and paints the former as a flawed antihero. An angry version of *Gung Ho*'s Hunt Stevenson and very much in line with the white male victim types Douglas played throughout the 1980s and 1990s, Nick is lost in a shiny, labyrinthine Japan that functions as a foreign metonym for the white-collared establishment that he blames for his impotence. The film keeps us wondering about his guilt with regard to the accusation by Internal Affairs until Charlie's death, when he confesses to Masahiro that he committed the crime to support his children financially. Much like the protagonist in *The Last Samurai*, Nick is spiritually rejuvenated and reborn in Japan. In both cases, the "caregiver of color" is a variation of the Oriental Monk who functions initially as antagonist, then as both sidekick and mentor.

In *Black Rain* this oriental buddy role is performed by Ken Takakura, well known in Japan for playing honorable old-school *yakuza* in a number of Toei Film Company gangster films during the 1960s and in the United States for playing opposite Robert Mitchum in the Hollywood film *The Yakuza* (1974). The antithesis of Sato and Sugai, Masahiro is a working-class *sarariman* (salary man), dutiful father, and citizen. He represents the honorable side of Nick just as Sato represents the dishonorable one. The two bond through their jobs as working-class police officers trapped in state bureaucracy. As Mr. Miyagi did for Daniel, Masahiro provides Nick with (Japanese/Eastern) moral guidance. And as Hunt did for Kazuhiro, Nick provides Masuhiro with the (American/Western) will to "just go for it"—to assert his individual desires in ultraconformist Japan.

The film concludes happily with Masahiro rather improbably presenting Nick with the counterfeit plates as a gift for his kids. By showing that Masahiro has taken Nick's advice to heart, the gesture humorously hybridizes Hollywood's rendition of the Japanese sense of honor and ethnics. At the end of the film, Masahiro is supposed to have provided a human face for Japan and Nick is supposed to have recuperated U.S. masculinity—or at least given us some faith in its continued potency.

U.S. critical response seems to indicate that Takakura was effective in this regard, while Douglas fell flat. Indeed several reviewers noted that although Nick is supposed to be our tour guide and cultural representative, his sexism, racism, and general boorishness keep viewers from liking or identifying with him much. Dowell points out the deep insecurity underlying his hypermasculine bravado:

> In another decade Lee Marvin or Clint Eastwood might have played this role, but in the Eighties, America's champion is Michael Douglas—weak-chinned, unable to muster an assured tough guy manner, given to impotent screaming tantrums [and] *Black Rain*'s furious contradictions reveal more insecurity about America than about Japan. . . . At the heart of Nick Conklin's hysterically threatening brush with Japan is the nightmare, not of being bested, but of being transformed: that "we" will become "them."[82]

Given the general critical dissatisfaction with the primary protagonist, the reviewers' consistent praise of Takakura and then–rising Cuban American star Andy Garcia stands out.[83]

An examination of the relationship between these two characters vis-à-vis Nick reveals the complicated state of Anglo-American masculinity at the end of the 1980s. This relationship is particularly illuminated in one scene in which the three soon-to-be buddies are drinking in a sleek, upscale Osaka bar. Charlie invites Masahiro to join him and Nick. Nick and Masahiro already have been set up as antagonists, the former as the rebel cop and the latter as the cop that plays by the rules. These roles are generalized onto their national and cultural identities: Masahiro tells Nick he should try to act "more Japanese," declaring that the United States has lost its economic edge and is good only for "music and movies," while the Japanese "make the machines [and] build the future." Nick responds, rather unoriginally, that the Japanese are unoriginal and "tight," adding a nonsensical chain of expletives. Charlie tries to mediate, asking them to "smoke a little peace pipe" and toasting the two with *kampai* ("cheers" in Japanese). Nick leaves the frame to talk with Joyce (Kate Capshaw), a blond American ex-pat hostess who functions throughout the film as a combination of orientalized femme fatale, cultural translator, and informant for Nick.

Like Daniel in *The Karate Kid,* Charlie represents an orientalized, multicultural U.S. male subject—defined against Nick's WASP persona and alongside that of Masahiro, the Japanese male who, like Miyagi, is Americanized and humanized as the film progresses. Like Daniel, Charlie functions as a kind of ethnic cipher that references and combines the histories of marginal nonwhite groups in the United States. Although his ethnicity is never made apparent, early in the film he is associated with Latin culture through his play bullfighting, and in the bar scene he alludes superficially to both Native

Ken Takakura and Andy Garcia in *Black Rain.* Masahiro and Charlie perform a karaoke duet of Ray Charles's "What'd I Say" to a delighted Japanese audience.

American culture (through the peace pipe reference) and African American culture. After Nick leaves the table, he persuades Masahiro to perform a karaoke duet with him, paying homage to jazz and black style in his charismatic performance of Ray Charles's "What'd I Say." Masahiro, crookedly wearing Charlie's sunglasses, joins in toward the end, mechanically and rather incongruously singing backup for Charlie.

Significantly, the two bond here over and through the structuring absence of an alternative, African American masculinity that does not include Nick. The doubling between the two characters is further reinforced by the cross-cultural references in their names: Charlie latinizes Masahiro by calling him "Mas" (Spanish for "more"), and of course the U.S. military used the term *Charlie* to refer to the Viet Cong during the Vietnam War. The doubling becomes glaringly obvious when Charlie's death by the swords of the motorcycle gang leads to Nick and Mas's partnership. Charlie is the ethnic other who is sacrificed for the needs of transnational collaboration—this time in the realm of law enforcement—between the United States (Nick) and Japan (Masahiro). Ultimately, then, the film ends, like *The Karate Kid* and *Gung Ho,* with the message that the oriental other, in the figure of the oriental buddy, is an important and necessary complement to the survival of white American masculine identity in an increasingly transnational world.

Conclusion

The movies discussed in this chapter have been largely dismissed or mentioned only in passing in Asian American studies and film studies. Although in film studies this elision may be due primarily to the films' commercial success and conventional themes and narratives, in Asian American studies it is more likely due to the complex and often ambiguous ways in which they render visible Asiatic characters, tropes, and spaces. Put another way, these films, unlike such movies as *Year of the Dragon* or *Rising Sun,* are neither explicitly nor consistently racist in their representations of the oriental other. Even though Asiatic characters remain in the background as sidekicks and nemeses, their development in the scripts—as well as the virtuoso performances by Asiatic actors that give them texture, dimensionality, and humanity—gesture toward a growing sense in Hollywood, and in the nation at large, of the need to better understand East Asia, especially Japan.

The oriental nightmare that structured the dystopic future of *Blade Runner* in the early 1980s had been transformed into palatable celluloid visions of collaboration with East Asia by the end of the decade. In all of these movies, the absence and/or dysfunction of Anglo-American masculinity and the nuclear family leads to the increased importance of surrogate, non-Anglo-American homosocial male families in the public spaces of sport, industry, and law enforcement. Intercultural and interracial friendships between Japanese, Japanese American, and Anglo-American males in these spaces are depicted as not only plausible but necessary for the global survival of "American" ideologies—albeit hybridized with Japanese ones.

In the 1990s the East–West connections celebrated in these movies were paradoxically naturalized through the transnational tastes of the culturally hybrid youth that are demonized in all three movies. Asian, American, and Asian American, these youth are defined by their consumption of popular media culture. Examples include the motorcycle gangs in *The Karate Kid* and *Black Rain*, Kazihiro's undisciplined children in *Gung Ho*, and, to a large extent, the impossibly cool young antagonist of *Black Rain*. In the 1980s such youth were seen as corrupted by a cultural hybridity coded in terms of Japanese technology and Asiatic difference.

However, these same youth became celebrated and almost quotidian in the early to mid-1990s for two reasons. First, a major economic recession hit Japan and the newly industrialized countries, bursting the bubble economies of these countries and rendering them less economically threatening to the United States. Second, young filmmakers who grew up on these images of orientalized heroes and their oriental buddies came of age to inaugurate a new multicultural and transnational oriental style. As I show in the next chapter, this style draws as much from the West as from the East, dehistoricizing and destabilizing both, though in different ways and to different ends.

5

Martial Arts as Oriental Style

Silly Caucasian girl likes to play with samurai swords.

—O-Ren Ishii, *Kill Bill: Vol. 1*

A year after Sony acquired Columbia Studios, Japanese auteur Akira Kurosawa won an Academy Award for Lifetime Achievement and the fifth–highest-grossing movie in the United States was *Teenage Mutant Ninja Turtles*.[1] This live-action film was based on a comic by Peter Laird and Kevin Eastman that featured a quartet of pizza-eating, genetically altered street turtles trained in the martial arts by their sensei, a wise first-generation Japanese American rat. According to Marsha Kinder, the film helped solidify an already existing "supersystem" of media and consumer products around the *Teenage Mutant Ninja Turtles* concept, including an animated television show, a Nintendo video game, books, toys, and clothing lines.[2]

To explain the huge popularity of *Teenage Mutant Ninja Turtles*, Kinder cites the "amazing powers of assimilation and accommodation" that characterize both its media-savvy youth audience and its narrative fluidity. In other words, the concept was successful because the film's characters and stories were able to appeal to various demographics while moving seamlessly across different forms of media—"powers" that Kinder significantly traces to Japanese sources.[3] More precisely, she links the use of cultural pastiche in *Teenage Mutant Ninja Turtles* with that in the samurai and *Gojira* movies of Akira Kurosawa and Eiji Tsuburaya, respectively. According to Kinder, *Teenage Mutant Ninja Turtles* producers referenced Japanese popular culture to create universally appealing American characters in the same way that Kurosawa and Tsuburaya drew on Western popular culture to fashion Japanese films that likewise appealed to audiences outside their national production context.[4] Kinder argues that this imitation of Japanese narrative and marketing strategies on the part of mostly U.S. media producers challenges Said's model of Orientalism. As she puts it, "The *Teenage Mutant Ninja Turtles* movie breaks with the traditional conception of orientalism, where one is defined strictly in opposition to the alien Other, and instead adopts a postmodernist form of intertextuality and accommodation, fluidly consuming and becoming the Other."[5]

Kinder's gestures toward a kind of postmodern Orientalism as it pertains to youth and media are evocative and problematic in ways similar to McLuhan's description of the orientalized "television child," which I referenced in the previous chapter—evocative in pointing out that popular media can familiarize as much as it can exoticize the Asiatic for Western audiences, problematic in failing to acknowledge the continued cultural and economic dominance of the West over the East and the rest of the world, a dominance apparent in the global reach of the U.S. military and entertainment industries.[6] Cinematic allusions to East Asia and Asian America, especially since the 1990s, have been defined by the ambivalence that results from the interplay of these two dynamics, which to some degree derives from the media consumption practices of youth in the period between McLuhan's talk and the publication of Kinder's book.

According to demographers, McLuhan's "television child" grew up to become a member of Generation X, the thirteenth generation of Americans, born roughly between 1961 and 1981.[7] In the same year that *Teenage Mutant Ninja Turtles* debuted on the big screen, the stereotype of then twenty- and thirty-something youth as cynical, underachieving "Gen X slackers" was popularized in Douglas Coupland's novel *Generation X* and Richard Linklater's independent film *Slacker*. The characters in these novels, like the orientalized "television child," "accept a role, but . . . not . . . a goal."[8] McLuhan's prescient description of Generation X recalls the poststructuralist notion of identity as performance, which regards the self not so much as a stable and coherent entity but instead as a constellation of various roles played out within constantly shifting social, cultural, and political contexts. Ironically, this initially radical idea proved to be an immensely successful marketing strategy that continues to be used to target multiple niche audiences in the United States and, increasingly, around the globe.[9]

In a small act of defiance against these seemingly relentless forces of commodification, Coupland announced the death of Generation X in *Details* magazine a few years after his book was published.[10] But it was too late. Generation X as a stereotype and market group had become entrenched in popular culture. As much as Xers like Coupland railed against their pigeonholing by media, the rapid incorporation of this subculture made perfect sense given its members' tight relationship with the very same media. According to television critic Rob Owen, "Xers are the first group for whom TV served as a regularly scheduled baby-sitter . . . the first to experience MTV and the Fox network and . . . are an audience many advertisers are eager to reach. Xers are the most media-savvy generation ever."[11]

It should come as no surprise, then, that at the time of this writing, members of Generation X (and their children who experienced *Teenage Mutant Ninja Turtles* as a retro event) play a leading role in media culture as producers, consumers, and critics. Directors such as Quentin Tarantino, Brett Ratner, Antoine Fuqua, Justin Lin, Robert Rodriguez, Alexander Payne, McG, and others fall under the Gen X umbrella and exhibit its so-called postmodern traits in their films, including irony, nostalgia, clever self-reflexivity, a penchant for pastiche, and an emphasis on style.[12] Most of these filmmakers grew up watching *Speed Racer* (1967), *Kung Fu* (1972), and *Battle of the Planets* (1978) on television and playing Japanese-produced video games on consoles "made in Japan." In other words, representations of Asia in films by these younger auteurs are based primarily on the East Asia–produced media that they avidly consumed as youth. Two of the most popular of these media imports have been and remain Hong Kong martial arts and action movies and Japanese animation.

In this chapter I consider how the visibility and popularity of these East Asian media, rising since the 1990s, have helped to influence concurrent shifts in cinematic representations of the Asiatic. I begin with a brief overview of the reception of Hong Kong films and anime in the United States, then go on to examine the ways in which four U.S. filmmakers have referenced their narrative and stylistic characteristics, bearing in mind the following questions. In what ways do non–Asian Americans who claim to identify with and/or celebrate Asiatic cultures critique traditional orientalist attitudes? In what ways do they reiterate those attitudes? And how, if at all, are their cultural (mis)translations opening up an alternative, transnational space within the formal and ideological constrictions of Hollywood?

Kung Fu, Hong Kong, and Hollywood

In his article "Fists of Legend and Fury," Glenn Omatsu points out similarities in the reception of Hong Kong martial arts–trained actors Jet Li and Bruce Lee. Like Lee almost three decades earlier, Li has been able to cross over to various audiences, including the same immigrant, working-class, nonwhite viewers that constituted Lee's substantial fan base in the 1970s.[13] In performances that range from playing an anti-colonialist national hero in *Once Upon a Time in China* (1991) and its numerous sequels to costarring with black music icons the late Aaliyah and DMX in *Romeo Must Die* (2000) and *Cradle 2 the Grave* (2003), respectively, Li courts what constitute urban (read black) and other marginal audiences in the United States within the parameters of Hollywood cinema. Meanwhile, affable Jackie Chan has successfully franchised himself around the world. Trained in the Peking Opera, Chan entertains children as an animated character in the *Jackie Chan Adventures* (2000–present) on the WB television network; owns several businesses, including fitness chains, restaurants, a clothing label, and a skin care line; and continues to churn out blockbuster action films.[14]

The two martial arts superstars Li and Chan recently costarred for the first time in *The Forbidden Kingdom,* a martial arts action film loosely based on the Chinese legend of the Monkey King directed by Rob Minkoff, coproduced by Casey Silver and the Huayi brothers, and distributed by Lionsgate and the Weinstein Company. A commercial success, the film was shot mostly in China, with action sequences choreographed by Yuen Wo Ping.[15] This kind of international coproduction follows in the wake of the popularity of films such as *The Matrix* and *Crouching Tiger, Hidden Dragon,* which sparked the current interest in the martial arts genre and the near ubiquity of martial arts action sequences in U.S. film and television.

Although it is only recently that such sequences have become a fixture in American popular media, scattered references to martial arts were present in Hollywood before the 1970s. A famous example is the scene in which Frank Sinatra shows off his karate skills while fighting Henry Silva in North Korean yellowface in *The Manchurian Candidate.* Nonetheless, the origins of the martial arts film proper in the United States can be traced to the stunning materialization on the silver screen of martial arts teacher, philosopher, and Hong Kong cha cha champion Bruce Lee in the early 1970s. According to David Desser, Lee's popularity was due in large part to his positioning within a "veritable wave of Hong Kong action movies" during the period. That wave climaxed in the United States in the spring of 1973 when three martial arts films—*Fists of Fury* (1971), *Deep Thrust—the Hand of Death* (1972), and *Five Fingers of Death* (1973)—dominated the Hollywood box office. With Lee's mysterious death in 1973, the kung fu "craze" migrated underground and to the small screen.[16]

Throughout the 1970s and 1980s, martial arts films continued to be screened in inner-city second-run theaters and small-town drive-in theaters, where they provided emotional catharsis for mostly working-class audiences. These films were linked commercially, stylistically, and politically with blaxploitation films, which, along with the films of the Hollywood Renaissance, helped rescue the studios from financial ruin in the 1970s.[17] Cultural blending between representations of Asian martial arts and black political empowerment underlie the themes and style of movies such as *Super Fly* (1972), *Black Belt Jones* (1974), *Three the Hard Way* (1974), and *Cleopatra Jones and the Casino of Gold* (1975). Although this blending had a strong cultural and political impact on the popular imaginary, its origins were economic in nature. As Desser notes, the blaxploitation–kung fu hybrid film was the result of specific marketing and distribution strategies used by Warner Bros., which produced *Super Fly* and *Five Fingers of Death:* "Warner Brothers [sic] placed its films in downtown theatres, double-billed many of its martial arts offerings after 1973 with blaxploitation films . . . and advertised its product along familiar generic and exploitation lines. Other distributors followed suit."[18]

When the cycle of blaxploitation and kung fu movies reached an end, martial arts as theme and trope continued to appear in television programs such as the drama *Kung Fu* (1972–75), the animated *Hong Kong Phooey* (1974–75), and the comedy *Sidekicks* (1986–87), as well as in the home video market.[19] In these domesticated forms the stylized, orientalized moves of Chinese, Japanese, and Korean martial arts were actively consumed by American youth. Throughout the 1980s, the spectacle of martial arts also spiced up Hollywood action films targeted toward male viewers. Prominent among these were action and war movies starring white male actors with martial arts training, including Chuck Norris, Steven Seagal, and Jean-Claude Van Damme, as well as films targeted toward youth, such as the *Karate Kid* and *Teenage Mutant Ninja Turtles* movies.

In the early 1990s Hong Kong cinema experienced a revival in the United States with the popularity of action films directed and produced by Stanley Tong, Corey Yuen, Ronnie Yu, John Woo, Tsui Hark, and others that showcased stars such as Chow Yun-Fat, Michelle Yeoh, Tony Leung, and Jackie Chan. These films combined elements of 1970s martial arts movies with those of 1980s New Hollywood action films—a formula that enabled the sleek new Hong Kong cinema to cross over into the U.S. mainstream.

As David Bordwell notes, this occurred through its transformation into a "subcultural cinema"—both in the highbrow arena of film festivals and in the lowbrow arena of youth fan culture. Although film scholars, critics, and festival programmers celebrated the elegantly choreographed expressions of physicality in these movies, often comparing them to Hollywood silent movies, Hong Kong cinema became a staple in U.S. culture due mostly to the enthusiasm of young film fans who wrote and disseminated commentary about these movies in fanzines. With the introduction of the Internet, these zines evolved into electronic texts—web sites, chat rooms, listservs, and blogs that connected ever more members of the growing international fan community.[20]

This subcultural cinema entered the mainstream in the mid-1990s, when Hong Kong and Chinese directors, producers, distributors, and actors such as Jet Li and Jackie Chan, John Woo, Michelle Yeoh, Chow Yun-Fat, and others immigrated to the United States in response to the impending handover of Hong Kong to the People's Republic of China in 1997. The notion of Hong Kong cinema as a Hollywood success story intensified steadily during the decade with these players functioning as model minorities of a sort in the U.S. film community. Their presence in Hollywood seemed to affirm the idea that Asia had arrived, so to speak, at the threshold of American and, by implication, global popular culture.

Film scholars have attributed the international popularity and economic success of Hong Kong cinema as the largest film exporter in the world after the United States to its unique reworking of the Hollywood style, an uncanny, hyperbolic mimicry of films. Esther Yau describes this process of translation in the following way: "If commercial Hong Kong movies are shamelessly derivative and creatively irreverent at the same time, their culturally androgynous features are not just local, nor are they a cause for celebration; rather, they register the industry's pursuit of the global market, a pursuit that mirrors Hollywood's, whose 'inauthentic' productions consolidate its screen hegemony."[21] Along the same vein, Bordwell suggests that the choreographed violence and celebration of chivalric themes in these stories rings culturally specific and universal at the same time. He ascribes the cross-cultural quality of these films to their formal and cultural hybridity, which satisfies the primary criterion of the successful genre film, namely, the ability to depict familiar narrative and visual patterns with an unfamiliar twist.[22]

Bordwell goes on to note that Hong Kong filmmakers "scavenge" equally from foreign and local cinematic sources—from Hollywood genre films, French *Nouvelle Vague* cinema, and Japanese *jidai-geki* (Edo-period drama) films to Chinese and Hong Kong kung fu (martial arts) and *wuxia-pian* (swordplay) films.[23] Furthermore, as Vijay Prashad points out, Chinese cinematic traditions themselves have multiple, heterogeneous roots. For example, the kung fu film has elements derived from Peking Opera, Shaolin temple, and U.S. boxing traditions.[24] Like Hollywood, Hong Kong cinema has been able to cater to different markets by cobbling together and blasting on the screen at dizzying speeds numerous generic and cultural histories whose original integrity is necessarily lost in the process of such mixing. The attraction of both Hong Kong and Hollywood blockbusters, then, does not lie simply in their many, seemingly incongruous, parts but rather in their ability to suture those parts together into a style at once new and familiar.

As discussed in previous chapters, Hollywood projects a predominantly white, liberal image of the United States through films that promulgate the idea of the melting pot, incorporating racial, gender, sexual, class, national, and regional differences into grand narratives that reiterate the promise of the American dream. In turn, Hong Kong cinema and other contemporary Asian cinemas borrow and rework the metaphors of both the melting pot and the American dream, extending them in films that perform a consciously exaggerated homage to the Hollywood paradigm. At the same time, these films display the visual and visceral tropes associated with East Asia, which allude subtly and sometimes not so subtly to the layered cultural nuances of their local contexts. In other words, internationally marketed Hong Kong movies place *national* metaphors in an ostensibly borderless *transnational* space, a process Kwai-cheung Lo describes thus:

The local site [Hong Kong], rather than being an enclosed place for delineating a well-established homogeneous identity, is relatively fluid and porous to the infiltration of alien elements. . . . The meaning of the Hong Kong local is always already overdetermined by the framework of the transnational that structures our perception of its reality. *In the case of Hong Kong, the local is the transnational itself in its becoming.*[25]

As Lo goes on to point out, this process is driven by a diasporic desire not for national, ethnic, or cultural unity but rather for capital growth, and as such it can be seen primarily as a "strategy of overseas marketing undertaken to serve commercial purposes."[26]

To get a sense of how these transnational narratives resonate in the United States, I now turn to examine two different but complementary modes of representing the East Asian Orient in Hollywood.

Whiteface/Yellowface: Performing Race in Hollywood

In *Recentering Globalization: Popular Culture and Japanese Transnationalism*, Koichi Iwabuchi introduces the idea of "cultural deodorization" to explain the current appeal of Japanese style and popular culture around the world. He uses the term *mukokuseki* (someone or something lacking nationality, implying the erasure of racial and ethnic characteristics) to describe Japanese export products, from electronic hardware such as game consoles, Walkmans, televisions, and other consumer technologies to software such as cartoons, toys, and computer and video games. According to Iwabuchi, Japan's economic success in the international marketplace stems largely from the marketing decisions of large electronics and auto corporations in the 1970s and 1980s, which aimed to erase signs of Japanese national difference specifically and Asiatic cultural difference generally in the products they marketed to the West.[27]

The notion of cultural deodorization can be applied to the films and career trajectories of John Woo and Ang Lee, two of the most successful Asian directors who have worked in Hollywood. Much like the Japanese exports that Iwabuchi describes, their work has been deliberately crafted for an international audience. Kenneth Chan notes that Lee's *Crouching Tiger,*

Hidden Dragon "had to be accessible to a Euro-American audience, but it also had to have cultural appeal to Asian audiences, who are generally more familiar with and nostalgic about the conventions and styles of sword-fighting movies."[28] Likewise, Kenneth Hall insists on the cultural syncretism of Woo's films, refuting the idea of the director as "merely a Western epigone," asserting instead that he "brings a Western-hued sensibility to his deep interest in, and romanticization of, his own heritage."[29] What Woo and Lee exhibit in and through their films, then, is a creative hybridity necessitated by the economic and ideological constraints of a form of cultural globalization that continues to be defined in Western terms. The content, production, and reception of their work reveal the complex ways in which formal and cultural elements defined as Asian and Euro-American are rooted in specific places and histories yet always in conversation with forces outside those contexts.

Many of the stylistic techniques of Woo's beautifully choreographed films, which stress the importance of honor, loyalty, and friendship in a corrupt dog-eat-dog world, have become standards in action cinema. The son of poor immigrants from Guangdong province in mainland China, Woo received his film education while working in the Hong Kong studio system. He began his career in the 1970s at Cathay and Shaw Brothers, where he learned how to shoot action scenes under Zhang Che, renowned director of the swordplay drama. In the 1980s he then moved on to Cinema City and Golden Harvest, where he continued to direct kung fu films and honed his skills at comedy with Michael Hui, a master of that genre.

With the release of *Hard Target* in 1993, Woo became the first Asian filmmaker to direct a Hollywood movie, a feat made possible in large part due to his growing U.S. fan base for *A Better Tomorrow* (1986), *The Killer* (1989), and *Hardboiled* (1992). After the disappointing box office sales of his second U.S. film, *Broken Arrow* (1996), Woo emerged as a major Hollywood player with the blockbusters *Face/Off* (1997) and *Mission Impossible 2* (2000). These were followed by the less stellar but still bankable *Windtalkers* (2002), about Navajo code-breakers stationed in Europe in World War II, and *Paycheck* (2003), a science-fiction movie based on a short story by Philip K. Dick. Since *Paycheck* Woo has worked on several nonfeature projects, including *The Robinsons: Lost in Space* (2004), a pilot for a science-fiction TV series, a segment for the French- and Italian-produced film *All the Invisible Children*

(2005), and *Stranglehold* (2007), a video game closely based on *Hardboiled*. Although Woo has professed a desire to expand his generic scope, the less impressive financial and critical draw of his last two feature films suggests that the action genre remains his calling card in Hollywood and the entertainment media industry. Perhaps as a response, he has turned to focus on audiences in China and the Asian region—a move that seems to be paying off. His two-part film *Battle of Red Cliff*, a historical martial arts epic, recently became the most successful Chinese blockbuster film to date when it beat previous bestseller *Curse of the Golden Flower* (2006) at the Chinese box office just a little more than a month after its release in July 2008.[30]

Unlike Woo, Taiwanese native Lee was trained in filmmaking in the United States. He received his graduate degrees in theater and theater direction from the University of Illinois at Urbana–Champaign and in film production from the Tisch School of Arts at New York University. In contrast to Woo, who is known for his synergistic approach to one genre in various media, including television, video games, and commercials, Lee is known for his wide generic range in one medium: film. His first feature films explored the conflict between Confucian group values and Western-style individualism in a trilogy that focused on generational relationships in Chinese families: *The Wedding Banquet* (1993), *Eat Drink Man Woman* (1994), and *Pushing Hands* (1995).[31] *The Wedding Banquet*, his first major hit in the United States, respins the East-meets-West narrative in fresh ways through a love triangle involving a wealthy gay Taiwanese American man, his bohemian Anglo-American lover, and a struggling female artist from mainland China, all masquerading in compulsory heterosexuality to please the protagonist's parents, who are desperate for their only son to get married.

Lee's next projects, adaptations of Jane Austen's Victorian novel *Sense and Sensibility* (1995); Rick Moody's nostalgic novel of New England in the 1970s, *The Ice Storm* (1997); and Daniel Woodrell's novel of the Civil War, *Ride with the Devil* (1999), diverged sharply from the Chinese themes, settings, and characters of his previous films. They also heralded his acceptance by the U.S. film industry as an Asian director who could make universal (i.e., white-centered) films as well as art house vehicles that could cross over into mainstream theaters. *Crouching Tiger, Hidden Dragon* combined Lee's previous approaches to filmmaking in that it placed Asian themes and motifs within the fantastic past of another adaptation—this time of an early twentieth-century Chinese novel set in the Quing Dynasty. The film did spectacularly well both on the festival circuit and in mainstream theaters, receiving ten Academy Award nominations, including one for Best Picture, to become "the most commercially successful foreign-language film in U.S. history and the first Chinese-language film to find a mass American audience."[32]

Since *Crouching Tiger, Hidden Dragon* Lee has directed a wide variety of movies that move between Western and Eastern themes and settings, including *Chosen* (2001), *Hulk* (2003), and *Brokeback Mountain* (2005). Of these, Lee's adaptation of Annie Proulx's poignant short story about gay white cowboys in rural 1960s Wyoming, nominated for an Academy Award, struck an unexpected chord in both mainstream and art audiences, much as had *Crouching Tiger, Hidden Dragon*. Lee's most recent film, *Lust, Caution* (2008), a World War II espionage thriller set in Shanghai adapted from a short story by Eileen Chang, which received mixed reviews in the United States, marked his cinematic return to Asian themes.

The success of these two director-producers puts in bold relief the rewards and challenges for nonwhite filmmakers of negotiating the burden of cultural representation in the United States, both commercially and politically. Until more people of color have financial and creative control in the media, high-profile filmmakers such as Lee and Woo will be held responsible for representing the difference written on their bodies not only by Asian American media activists and viewers who demand so-called authentic representations but also by media producers and financiers who demand authenticity of the kind that appeals to as many demographics as possible. Woo and Lee's responses to these pressures have been read in two contrasting ways.

On the one hand, the filmmakers have been seen as playing down to Hollywood style, selling out, so to speak, to the dominant U.S. culture. On the other hand, their ability to learn and execute another cinematic language has been celebrated as an example of resistant mimicry and a smart way to extend the range of their career choices to boot. Yet the kind of strategic essentialism that Lee, Woo, and other transnational Asiatic filmmakers such as Wayne Wang, Mira Nair, Justin Lin, Gurinder Chadha, and M. Night Shyamalan are practicing as artists and businesspeople in the media is much more complex, lying somewhere between and sometimes outside these two representational strategies.

Further complicating the pattern of cinematic cultural exchange between East and West is the fact that Hollywood is not the only entertainment industry that has appropriated and incorporated elements of Asian cultures. Although cross-over Asian filmmakers cater to a Westernized audience, interest in East Asian martial arts, fashion, and philosophies has also became pronounced in the now ubiquitous culture of hip-hop, which originated in the 1970s among poor and working-class black and Latino youth in the Bronx.[33] The songs and videos of De La Soul, R. Kelly, Wu Tang Clan, and many others, as well as films such as *Blade* (1998), *Ghost Dog* (1999), and *Romeo Must Die*, incorporate elements of martial arts moves and philosophies much as their blaxploitation predecessors had done. The Afro Asian connections in hip-hop hark back to those that existed in the black reception of kung fu films and the short-lived subgenre of kung fu blaxploitation films in the 1970s.

Several scholars have discussed the ways in which the celebrated reception of Bruce Lee's kung fu movies in the 1970s among African Americans, diasporic Chinese, and other formerly colonized peoples illuminated the cultural and political links among these groups.[34] Bill Mullen uses the term "Afro Orientalism" to describe the interest in Asia and the Middle East since the early twentieth century among black radicals and artists who sought non-Western forms of knowledge, religion, and spirituality as part of a rejection of—and alternative to—Western bourgeois norms and values. According to Mullen, Afro Orientalism opens a third, potentially transgressive, space even as it reiterates some of the exoticizing elements of European and Anglo-American Orientalisms.[35]

Although this critical potential remains somewhat operative in more independent forms of artistic expression, contemporary Afro Orientalism differs from its predecessor in its explicit emphasis on both black and Asiatic cultural signifiers as consumable commodities. Within this context, the embrace of the martial arts and action style of Hong Kong cinema by the dominant culture of Hollywood and the no longer marginal subculture of hip-hop demonstrates the complex, contradictory, and increasingly blurred relationship in the United States between dominant culture and subculture, between white and black, with yellow often posed as a disembodied mediator between the two color poles.

To sum up, two forms of stylized racial presentation appear in the broadly defined Hollywood martial arts and action movie. The first is a kind of *Asian whiteface* in which Asian and Asian American filmmakers appropriate and perform the Hollywood paradigm, making films for an international audience, sometimes with stylistic nods to Asian cinema and culture and sometimes with no reference at all to the Asiatic. Along with the films of John Woo and Ang Lee, prominent examples of Asian whiteface include the coproductions of Asian and Asian American directors such as Stephen Chow, Corey Yuen, Wayne Wang, and Mira Nair. Complementing whiteface is a kind of *celebratory yellowface*—a process in which white, black, and Latino/a filmmakers appropriate and perform their renditions of East Asian cultures and stereotypes. Examples include *Ghost Dog, Cradle 2 the Grave*, and the *Kill Bill* dyad (2003, 2004), which will be examined later in this chapter. Whiteface and yellowface constitute a complex loop: the two merge in the enactment of an ostensibly recognizable oriental style, which, at the same time, is extremely malleable, fluid, and hybrid.

For instance, John Woo's camerawork, while devoid of overt East Asian signifiers (Asian whiteface), is seen as representative of Hong Kong cinema and categorized as East Asian cinema more generally. As a result, when Quentin Tarantino or Robert Rodriguez borrows his trademark camera style, the homage is read as a reference to East Asian cinema (celebratory yellowface). These two forms of oriental style make it clear that categorizing whether something or someone is nationally, culturally, or racially authentic per se is no longer relevant or useful. Instead it is more productive to ask how such authenticities are being invoked, *and being made to matter,* by and for whom, in specific historical and cultural contexts.

The Art of Action: Martial Arts in the Movies, a documentary that aired on the Encore cable television network in the spring of 2003, provides an example of one such context. African American actor Samuel Jackson hosts and narrates the film. His figure merges the dichotomies of Asian whiteface and celebratory yellowface, dominant culture and subculture, white and nonwhite. In his role as the viewers' guide to the world of the exotic martial arts film, Jackson dons the symbolic whiteness of Hollywood against the foreign yellowness of the marital arts film. His fashionably fly figure is set against a spare backdrop with the term *wu xia* (Chinese martial-chivalric fiction) painted in calligraphy in large red Chinese characters. Jackson opens and ends the film by defining the term, accompanied by his use of stereotypical martial arts hand gestures and sound effects. In this way he literally and symbolically performs a kind of colorblind yellowface that links white and black America through their fascination with the foreign martial arts film.

The fact that Jackson was chosen to host a program on martial arts movies illustrates the continued invisibility of Asians and Asian Americans in dominant U.S. media as well as the ease with which non–Asian Americans are able to appropriate East Asian cultural forms. This becomes clearer when one tries to imagine, for instance, an Asian American actor hosting a documentary on blaxploitation movies. Such a scenario will probably be quotidian in a few years given the increasing participation of Asian Americans in hip-hop culture, including journalists Jeff Chang and Oliver Wang, MCs Jin and Cool Calm Pete, and DJs Kuttin Kandy and QBert.[36] However, the still limited exposure and success of Asian Americans in black cultural space— of which hip-hop has become one of the most commercially visible—attest to the fact that at this juncture such forms of Afro Asian collaboration remain inaccessible and therefore unfamiliar to mainstream audiences.

After walking viewers through a celebratory history of the martial arts film genre, complete with clips of interviews with key Hong Kong players, *The Art of Action Movies* ends rather predictably by touting the success of *Crouching Tiger, Hidden Dragon*. The film is upheld as the ultimate example of the culturally and nationally mixed future of the martial arts movie in Hollywood. What the documentary does not address is the film's significantly less enthusiastic reception in East Asia, which hints at another aspect of that future. *Crouching Tiger, Hidden Dragon* performed poorly at East Asian box offices with the exception of those in Taiwan and Singapore—both markets dominated by Hollywood products.[37] No doubt piracy was linked to the low number of ticket sales in the region. However, the disappointing theatrical turnout also might have resulted from the fact that *Crouching Tiger, Hidden Dragon* targeted a Western audience unfamiliar with the martial arts genre more aggressively than it did the East Asian audience, which had a different set of standards and expectations for the film.

The appeal of *Crouching Tiger, Hidden Dragon* specifically and Asian genre films generally in the United States suggests that in order to find a space in dominant culture, non-Western popular forms must continue to cater to and promote a universal sensibility. In the process, however, these forms also are redefining the hitherto Western cultural, formal, and economic terms of this universality. A similar kind of cultural mixing can be discerned in the growing visibility and popularity of anime in the United States.

Mecha Anime

In the fall of 2003 a *Village Voice* article titled "Extreme Makeovers" listed several personae for New York college students to "try on for size," offering the tongue-in-cheek aside "After all, authenticity is just another commodity." Amid identities such as "Original 1970s Punk Rocker," "Wannabe," and "The Artiste" was the nationally specific category of the "Japanophile." According to the article, "the basics" for this identity included "strange creatures with noodles. Techy gadgets. *Anime*."[38]

After years of being associated with geeky white adolescent boys, anime had broken into the ranks of coolness as defined by the New York weekly. Originally a Japanese appropriation of the French word for animated films, the term *anime* has come to refer to animation specific to Japan.[39] The medium is easy to recognize: it features striking characters with huge eyes and vividly colored hair, less fluid temporal rhythms than Disney animation, and panels that integrate negative space, opening the action to the extradiegetic world.[40] Visually, ideologically, and narratively, anime differs, sometimes quite radically, from U.S. animation and films. According to Susan Napier, "Much of the best of anime resists any attempt at 'ideological containment' and, given the dark tone of many of its most memorable texts, could well be considered a cinema of 'de-assurance' rather than one of 're-assurance,' which . . . is the dominant tone of most Hollywood films."[41]

How does this cinema of de-assurance work? The narrative characteristics of anime provides one inroad into understanding why the medium is so popular among youth in the United States and Europe as well as in Japan and other East Asian countries. To begin with, anime plotlines tend to be more complex and multiple than those of Disney animation; problems are not easily resolved, if at all. Also, character development is emphasized, complementing the serial nature of the medium. As a result, characters' attitudes and actions exhibit a higher degree of moral ambiguity than those of their American counterparts. Over time, good characters can become bad, and vice versa, based on changing narrative situations. Finally, anime posits a different relationship among characters, action, and mise-en-scène than is found in U.S. animation. With roots in traditional Japanese art such as the Edo-period woodblock prints known as ukiyo-e, as well as noh, kabuki, and bunraku theater, mise-en-scène plays a crucial role not just in setting the tone of anime but also in shaping its narratives. Rather than functioning as mere backdrop, the mise-en-scène prompts the viewer to participate actively in interpreting the story.

Exhibiting these traits, anime, like the martial arts film, has become accessible to foreign audiences while retaining its national identity. Douglas McGray locates Japan's "secret to thriving amidst globalization" in its double positioning: "There exists a Japan for Japanese and a Japan for the rest of the world."[42] Interviews conducted by Napier with undergraduate anime fans at University of Texas at Austin seem to confirm his observation. Many of the students said they liked the medium because of what they perceived to be its radical difference from American animation and Hollywood narratives.[43] That anime functions as Hollywood's aesthetic and narrative other in the minds of these U.S. fans confirms Japan's ability to cross-market itself to audiences both within and outside of East Asia. This section offers some preliminary thoughts on how such positionality (which bears some resemblance to the concept of whiteface introduced earlier) may function in the case of anime reception in the United States.

During the same period that Hong Kong film celebrities moved to the West Coast, a wave of bohemian Japanese youth immigrated to New York in response to dismal employment prospects at home thanks to the continuing recession. In much the same way that the bodies of John Woo and Chow Yun-Fat gave belated evidence of Hong Kong cinema's entrance into Hollywood, these hip, young bodies from Japan announced the acceptance of techy *Japonoiserie* as a new style commodity in American youth culture. Along with cute *(kawaii)* toys and accessories, Japanese food, art, and popular music, anime was a distinctive style marker among members of this set and their American friends and admirers. Of course anime was nothing new to hard-core U.S. fans, most of whom have tended to be young, Anglo-American males studying or working in the fields of science, technology, and graphic design.[44] As noted earlier, many of these fans were introduced to anime in its Americanized form through television cartoons or *terebi manga* (television comics) such as *Astro Boy* (1963), *Speed Racer* (1967), *Battle of the Planets* (1978), *Voltron* (1984), and *Transformers* (1985).[45]

However, anime first appeared in the United States in the early 1980s as an explicitly Japanese product through the videotapes of American students who had studied abroad in Japan. Viewed as an international economic success story, Japan was a popular foreign exchange destination during this period. The increased affordability of VCRs made possible the dissemination of anime among fans who met in burgeoning anime clubs on U.S. college campuses. Over time, these fan communities and their conventions grew, as did the number of anime distributors that emerged to meet their demand. Streamline Pictures, AnimEigo, and the Right Stuff opened up shop in the late 1980s; since then they have been joined by U.S. Manga Corps, AD Vision, Pioneer, Central Park Media, Manga Entertainment, Viz Video, and now Buena Vista Pictures (owned by Disney), the official distributor for Studio Ghibli, Hayao Miyazaki's production facilities.[46]

In the past ten years, anime as a medium and a style has spread to the dominant culture, appearing on web sites as well as in fashion and in American-based comics and cartoons such as *The Power Puff Girls* (1998–present), *Samurai Jack* (2001–present), *Xiaolin Showdown* (2003–present), *The Life and Times of Juniper Lee* (2005–present), *American Dragon: Jake Long* (2005–7), and special episodes of *The Simpsons* (1989–present) and *South Park* (1997–present). Similar to the way that critical recognition for *Crouching Tiger, Hidden Dragon* repopularized and legitimated martial arts cinema, the conferral of the 2003 Academy Award for Animation on Miyazaki's *Spirited Away* (2002) appeared to signal the arrival of anime. In 1998 the *Pokemon* phenomenon had achieved this sort of legitimization in a more overtly commercial way, targeting primarily younger children with a successful television program, movie, videos, video game, and toys. The rising visibility of Miyazaki's gorgeous animated fairy tales indicates a shift toward a wider audience range, which seems to be leading to a wider variety of anime imports. Nonetheless, the form of anime still most familiar to Americans remains the genre known as "*mecha* anime" (*mecha* is short for "mechanical").

In Japan *mecha* belongs to myriad different genres in the related media of anime and *manga* (Japanese comics), including high school, horror, historical, instructional, romance, porn, and children genres. These genres target multiple audiences: businessmen, housewives, career women, adolescents, and children. Initially, *manga* and anime were categorized according to their gendered content and audience (*shojo* for girls; *shonen* for boys). However, these divisions began to erode in the 1980s as *shojo* anime assumed characteristics of *shonen* anime, and vice versa, and as viewers' gender and sexual orientation became less significant in determining what kind of anime is consumed.[47]

Although anime in Japan is multiple and varied, *mecha* narratives in the United States have come to represent anime as a whole, in part because *mecha* has been the preferred genre of the primary American anime audience. Marketed historically to young boys and adolescent males, *mecha* anime centers around technological and science-fiction themes and motifs, featuring giant robots, high-tech vehicles, cyborg characters, outer space, cyberspace, and apocalyptic urban settings.[48]

Like martial arts films, *mecha* anime showcases the violent, repressed, usually male (though increasingly female), and usually young body. In both genres bodies resemble machines. However, the martial arts body and the *mecha* body have different narrative functions. In the martial arts film, disciplined, mechanical moves transcend the limits of the physical body to assume a spiritual quality. When weapons are used, they are limited to simple, nontechnological instruments such as nunchakus, wooden sticks, and kendo swords. The primary weapon is the spiritually and physically disciplined body flowing in elegantly choreographed motion.

Conversely, in *mecha* anime the body is technologized through prosthetics and/or body- and mind-altering drugs so that the body's owner is rendered a cyborg. This transformation occurs through the consistent use of highly technological weapons such as handguns, machine guns, and lasers and through the replacement or enhancement of body parts with weapons.[49] Finally, while most martial arts films are characterized by an optimistic, sometimes anticolonialist tone, the majority of *mecha* anime works along a nihilistic and decidedly antiheroic register that parallels the tone of U.S. cyberpunk narratives.

The stylishly violent films of filmmakers and animators such as John Woo, Takeshi Kitano, Mamoru Oshii, and Katsuhiro Ôtomo blend elements of martial arts cinema and *mecha* anime, resulting in striking contrasts between the controlled and uncontrolled body, the vulnerable and the armed body, the hero and the antihero. Such work provides "authentic" examples of the techno-orientalism that continues to reign in popular (especially youth) culture and that appears in the work of the Gen X American filmmakers mentioned at the opening of the chapter and to whom I now return.

"Hip-Hop Kung Fu"

On the set of *Romeo Must Die* in 2000, legendary action movie producer Joel Silver coined the phrase "hip-hop kung fu." He used this phrase to describe a then-emerging trend in U.S. cinema, which he and Larry and Andy Wachowski had introduced to mass audiences a year earlier in the sleeper cyberpunk hit *The Matrix*. Since then, the fusion of gritty hip-hop music and graceful martial arts sequences has become a standard stylistic formula in Hollywood. Films that use this formula, including *The Replacement Killers* (1998), *The Corruptor* (1999), *Charlie's Angels* (2000), *The Transporter* (2002), *Bulletproof Monk* (2003), and *Volcano High* (2003), are characterized by multicultural casts, martial arts action sequences, and hip-hop and industrial soundtracks.[50] Critics often compare such films to video games and music videos, usually disparaging their tendency to privilege style over substance.

In this final section of the chapter I offer some comments on the racial and gender dynamics of three very different hip-hop kung fu movies: the Hollywood action films *Rush Hour* and *Rush Hour 2* (1998 and 2001), directed by Brett Ratner, and *Cradle 2 the Grave,* directed by Andrzej Bartkowiak, and the independent films *Ghost Dog,* directed by Jim Jarmusch, and *Kill Bill: Vol. 1* and *Kill Bill: Vol. 2,* directed by Quentin Tarantino. The readings examine how these films pay homage to East Asian cultural and aesthetic forms, particularly martial arts, and consider some of the larger social and political implications of these forms of homage.

The *Rush Hour* Movies

Let us begin with *Rush Hour*. How are Asiatic and black masculinities represented in this series, which stars two nonwhite characters? More specifically, what happens to the ideological dynamics of the interracial buddy formula when an African American male and an Asian male work together to "fight the (white) man?" In *Rush Hour* and *Rush Hour 2* Jackie Chan assumes the historically subordinate position of the foreign Asian male type but renders it central in ways that complement Chris Tucker's performance of the funny angry black male type made famous by Eddie Murphy in the 1980s.

In *Rush Hour* Detective Inspector Lee (Chan) arrives in Los Angeles to help his former boss, Consul Han (Tzi Ma), find his daughter Soo Young (Julia Hsu) and her kidnappers. The FBI try to keep him out of the investigation by placing him under the supervision of Los Angeles police officer James Carter (Tucker). But the two eventually team up to rescue Soo Young from Juntao, the mysterious Hong Kong crime lord who has abducted her and who turns out to be none other than her father's friend Thomas Griffin (Tom Wilkinson), the British commander of the Royal Hong Kong Police. After Griffin and his snarling young sidekick Sang (Ken Leung) are killed and the case is solved, Lee invites Carter to vacation in Hong Kong.

The arrival of Griffin and Sang in Hong Kong opens *Rush Hour 2,* where Carter now plays the fish out of water, unwittingly accompanying Lee as he pursues Ricky Tan (John Lone), a Triad leader suspected in the deaths of two U.S. Secret Service agents who have been investigating a counterfeiting operation. As he pleads with Lee to take him out of the country, Tan is shot by his assistant Hu Ling (Zhang Ziyi) and presumed dead. The Secret Service orders Lee off the case and Carter back to the United States for losing the prime lead. When Carter learns that Tan was responsible for the death of Lee's father and that solving the case is a personal matter for his friend, he invites Lee to accompany him to Los Angeles. There they help Secret Service agent Isabella Molina (Roselyn Sanchez) expose the ringleaders behind the counterfeit scheme: hotel billionaire Steven Reign (Alan King) and Tan, who faked his death. Like *Rush Hour, Rush Hour 2* ends with the villains dead and the protagonists boarding a plane.

Asian American groups widely protested against the release of *Rush Hour* as they had that of *Lethal Weapon 4* earlier in 1998 for its invocation of orientalist stereotypes, including the use of the gong to herald Lee's arrival in Los Angeles, Carter's jokes making fun of Lee's ethnicity and poor command of English, and the emphasis on martial arts to represent the Asiatic male protagonist. Meanwhile, the film and its sequel went on to do very well at the box office for New Line Cinema, known for targeting niche markets, especially youth and urban audiences. *Rush Hour* catapulted stand-up comedian Chris Tucker to the actors' A-list, established Jewish American director Brett Ratner as a key industry player, and, perhaps most significantly, became the

Hollywood vehicle through which Jackie Chan finally successfully crossed over to U.S. audiences.

Focusing on different aspects of the film, Mita Banerjee and LeiLani Nishime argue that *Rush Hour* offers moments of resistance against racial stereotypes but ultimately reproduces them. Banerjee writes, "Chan's and his black sidekick's registering on the American scene . . . must be seen in terms of the filmic narrative's indebtedness to a . . . fundamentally racist . . . theatrical form: the performance of minstrelsy," while Nishime writes, "The film offers a vision of cross-racial identification and bonding, and . . . also undercuts the possibility of hybridity by reinforcing national, geographic, and sexual boundaries."[51] Banerjee upholds the notion that the film does not provide an authentic black/Asian political message as in the Bruce Lee films, whereas Nishime suggests that the film gestures toward but never quite achieves a representation of Afro Asian cultural hybridity.

Nishime lists two characteristics of the film that offer libratory readings of racial difference. First, the protagonists share command of the camera. Neither buddy chaperones the other: Tucker dominates the dialogue, while Chan dominates the action sequences. Second, the two characters bond over their marginalization by the white establishment, specifically the FBI, which ignores Han's request to use Hong Kong police. Nishime goes on to argue, however, that the film ultimately decontextualizes and dehistoricizes the African American and Asian cultures by promoting the liberal idea that exchange between these two cultures is easy and pleasurable. This is exemplified in performative scenes showcasing Lee and Carter's racialized bodies bonding over music and food, which actively disrupt the narrative. While agreeing with Nishime that this notion of exchange is based on essentialized notions of cultural ownership (i.e., Asians are earnest and do kung fu; African Americans are funny and dance), I would like to extend her terrific reading of the relationship between the protagonists with a few larger structural points.

First, rather than interpreting the performative aspects of the film (e.g., the montage sequences, the ways in which Tucker and Chan interpret the script) solely as narrative ruptures, I would argue—as I have been doing throughout this book—that these aspects are a fundamental part of the narrative, especially with respect to character development, establishment of tone, and deployment of space. Both actors supplement the plot-oriented buddy formula with non-Western modes of performance: Chan brings the martial arts tradition (as rendered onscreen in Hong Kong action movies, where action sequences dominate and the plot is fairly inconsequential), while Tucker brings the African American comedy tradition (based on verbal improvisation, active audience participation, and cultural critique embedded in black trickster discourse). Foregrounding these traditions thus, the film hybridizes the Hollywood narrative, assimilating it as much as being assimilated into it.

Like many young directors currently working in the action genre, Brett Ratner got his start in the movies by shooting rap videos, which emphasize style, performance, and image over more conventional modes of linear narrative—all elements of the high-concept style that have become even more pronounced in Hollywood cinema since the 1980s. Second, although *Rush Hour* was targeted toward the niche urban audience, it was commercially successful precisely because its appeal extended beyond that particular group, which begs the following question: what universal tropes and themes did this film draw upon and/or promote that made it appealing to a wide audience base?

At the level of narrative, the superficial ways in which the film shows the development and consolidation of Lee and Carter's friendship obscure a deeper impulse behind their bonding. For along with being excluded from the investigation by the FBI, both also share a desire to find the rapidly Americanizing Soo Ling and restore her to her father, thereby restoring Consul Han's wholly patriarchal nuclear family. This two-person family conspicuously lacks a mother; we learn early in the film that Soo Ling's mother is dead, though her image is constantly before us in a family oil painting on a consulate wall. Also, Soo Ling is a tomboy who is doubled with the protagonists: she aggressively resists capture using the marital arts skills Lee has taught her, and at the end of the film she comically imitates Carter as he challenges Juntao to "push the button" that activates the bomb attached to her vest.

Furthermore, Lee and Carter's investment in restoring this father–daughter relationship is indirectly linked to their relationships with their own fathers, both of them police officers who died in the line of duty while serving their respective nations. It is significant that the crucial turning points in both movies, when the buddies threaten to separate but remain together, occur at the airport and invoke the memory of these fathers. In

Rush Hour Lee has been ordered back to Hong Kong after Carter's actions lead the FBI to lose their trace on Soo Ling. He accuses Carter of "dishonoring" his father's name, at which point Carter tells Lee his father was killed in a routine traffic arrest. Carter then asks Lee to stay in Los Angeles and help him solve the case so that his father will not have died in vain.

In *Rush Hour 2* the roles are reversed: Carter is mad at Lee for depriving him of the promised holiday in Hong Kong, instead dragging him along in his pursuit of Tan. As he is about to board the plane, he learns from Lee that Tan betrayed and killed his father. When Carter realizes that, for Lee, the case is about vindicating the death of his father, his anger vanishes. He invites Lee to join him on the flight back to Los Angeles to pursue the "rich white man" who, according to his "theory of criminal investigation," holds the key to solving the case. To sum up, the protagonists bond over father figures and the paradigm of the patriarchal family, a symbolic microcosm of the nation.

As is typical in buddy films, women play a peripheral role in these movies, functioning primarily to alleviate the homoeroticism between the two buddies, which is played for laughs throughout *Rush Hour* and *Rush Hour 2*. In both films the romantic potential resides in the figure of an unattainable Latina woman. In the first she is Tucker's partner at work: Americanized Latina LAPD officer Tania Johnson, played by Cuban American actress Elizabeth Peña, at whom Carter constantly directs inappropriate sexual innuendos. In the second she is the foreign-accented Puerto Rican Secret Service agent Isabella Molina, played by Puerto Rican actress Roselyn Sanchez, who is partnered romantically with Lee, albeit ambiguously. During a clichéd voyeuristic scene in *Rush Hour 2,* Carter and Lee bond through their sexual desire for Molina (which she plays to her advantage), and in both movies the women represent the promise of family, the birth of sons, and the continuation of the father–son relationship that the protagonists so clearly miss. Through the miscegenation implicit in this promise, the presence of these women also offers a vision of the larger cultural and racial hybridity that the film itself cannot permit. That is, the Latina women fulfill the function of a kind of hybrid mestiza racial and cultural identity that lies in between the black and Asian identities of the protagonists and characterizes the multiracial and multicultural landscape of Los Angeles itself.

That the protagonists never achieve relationships with these or any other women is important for two reasons. First, their erotic energies, which in the normative model of heteromasculinity would be channeled into procreation and the establishment of nuclear families, are channeled instead into scenes of cultural bonding that occur through the body (e.g., martial arts and dance choreography, the consumption of food and music) and through language. More specifically, the mistranslations and gaps that characterize their verbal communication point to the fissures and limitations in the "free cultural exchange" the film seems to promote superficially through the fluid, syncretic nature of their physical performances. In a similar way, the irony and self-reflexivity with which Carter and Lee perform racialized stereotypes of black and Asiatic men, respectively—and the ways in which the script itself complicates and undoes some of these stereotypes—posit alternative modes of masculinity that gesture beyond representations of nonwhite manhood as defined through white heterocentric norms.

Rather than reading Lee as emasculated and Carter as hypermasculine in accord with dominant cultural stereotypes, I would suggest that both characters present more humanized forms of masculinity that emphasize soft over hard depictions of manliness. Not only are both characters hopeless at getting dates; they are also infantilized, Lee due to his foreignness and Carter due to his constant "playing"—or dissembling—to get the information he needs. Yet the vulnerability displayed in the childlike masculinity of these characters "playing" together contributes to the wide appeal of the *Rush Hour* films, especially because the actors are able to showcase non-Western forms of masculinity in less stereotypically feminized and emasculated ways than they would with white partners. Although the films never break completely from the conventionally racist and sexist elements of the buddy formula (which are sadly reinforced in the third film), they do point to new ways in which the presence of nonwhite primary characters reworks these elements. This is exemplified in the two scenes described next.

In the first scene, from *Rush Hour*, Carter has picked up Lee from the airport and taken him to Grauman's Chinese Theatre, which he assumes Lee recognizes, conflating this orientalist simulacrum of China with the images of postindustrial Hong Kong that open the film. On the surface, Carter appears to hold the position of power here: Los Angeles is his home turf, he speaks the language, and he is "babysitting" Lee for the FBI. However, the way the scene unfolds makes it clear that we are supposed to identify with Lee rather than Carter and inserts a moment of confusion in which we wonder if this is a Hollywood film appropriating elements of the Hong Kong action film or a Hong Kong action film merely set in Hollywood.

At the level of mise-en-scène, the simulacral nature of the theater is reinforced by the swarm of primarily East Asian tourists who crowd the frame. That they find this orientalized space so exotic points to their awareness of its fakeness, its inauthenticity. It also illuminates the agency of the economically privileged class of Asian tourists who can indulge in this orientalist fantasy as its subjects rather than its objects. While Carter is interrogating a street contact, Lee escapes, banking on Carter's stereotypical inability to find him among the sea of Asian faces.

From this point on, Lee has command of the camera. In a nod toward *Police Story* (1987), he hops a double-decker tour bus full of East Asian tourists busily snapping pictures of the Los Angeles landscape. Carter spots him, gets on the bus, and confronts Lee, waving his gun around and yelling, "Think I'm playin' with you?"—a spectacle that elicits a collective gasp of fear from the tourists. Carter turns around to reassure them he is FBI, pausing to pose for their cameras. Lee takes this moment to swing outside the back of the bus onto a Hollywood street sign (an overt symbol of Chan's return to Hollywood), where he swings briefly before dropping gracefully

Jackie Chan in *Rush Hour* (1998). Lee dangles on the Hollywood street sign during an action-packed attempt to escape his new partner from the Los Angeles Police Department.

into a family recreational vehicle, followed by a taxicab with Carter in close pursuit. The scene ends with Carter discovering to his surprise that Lee can speak English. His soon-to-be partner from Hong Kong informs him, "Not being able to speak is not the same as not speaking," underscoring the shift of power in this scene from Carter to Lee, the United States to East Asia.

As both Nishime and Banerjee point out, the representation of the United States by a black actor in these films seems to imply that Hollywood and U.S. society at large have moved beyond race. At the same time, it projects anti-Asian racism onto African Americans, providing white and other nonblack viewers an outlet for these racist attitudes while expiating them from the negative consequences of expressing them publicly. For Banerjee, who sees Lee as the protagonist and Carter as his sidekick, the film reinforces black-face stereotypes of African Americans as "both depthless beyond repair and idiotic."[52]

I would argue, instead, that Carter is constantly "signifyin'," the term Henry Louis Gates uses for the allusive, parodic, and ironic verbal play that characterizes black vernacular cultures in the African diaspora, which he traces to trickster tropes in Yoruban mythology.[53] This view is reinforced by the multiple times that Lee uses the verb "playing" (as in "I was just playing" or "He's just playing") to refer to the questionable veracity of an attitude, a potential action, or an event in the narrative. In the process he self-reflexively places distance between himself and the attitude, action, or event being observed and/or "played." Carter thus embodies the central idea of signifying, that words have multiple, often seemingly contradictory, meanings based on how they are uttered and interpreted by different audiences. Although he tricks the other characters and the audience by playing the clown, Carter is quite resourceful in both movies: in *Rush Hour* it is his underground sources that guide the protagonists to Juntao, and in *Rush Hour 2* it is his hunch that leads him and Lee to follow hotel mogul Steven Reign to the Red Dragon Casino, where they uncover the counterfeiting operation led by Reign and his considerably more powerful partner, the not-really-dead Tan, played deliciously high camp by John Lone.

A scene in the buildup to the climax of *Rush Hour 2* highlights the way Carter uses humor both to further the plot (in this case, to act as a distraction while Lee discreetly tries to enter the room where the counterfeit bills are being produced) and to make transparent usually concealed racial and class dynamics. Appropriately enough, the most explicitly political critique of racism in the film occurs at a craps table. Decked out in a rich, butter-colored crocodile suit, Carter asks to join the game and is dealt five hundred dollar chips. After exchanging a quick shot–reverse shot glance with Lee, Carter assumes the "angry black man" pose, accusing the dealer of being a racist and asking, "How come everyone at the table have thousand dollar chips, and the black man have a nickel?" The tight-lipped dealer denies he is a racist, and Carter continues his passionate rant, asking those around him, "How come there ain't no black people performing here?" A manager steps up to proudly announce that in fact Lionel Richie is performing that night, to which an unimpressed Carter retorts, "Lionel Richie hasn't been black since the Commodores." To divert attention from Lee, Carter becomes even more hysterical, jumping up and down on the table and drawing the security guards, who pull him back to the floor.

At this point Carter segues into a short spoof of Martin Luther King Jr.'s "I Have a Dream" speech, enthusiastically cheered on by his fellow players. When Carter intones, "I have a dream that black people and white people . . . and even Chinese people can gamble together without getting different chips," he sums up the economic bottom line behind the tropes of global multiculturalism and Afro Asian solidarity in the *Rush Hour* films. To put it simply, the relationship between the black and Asiatic protagonists in these films suggests that aligning against "the man" no longer has so much to do with bonding over an anti-colonial sense of political solidarity as with learning how to play the field of identity politics strategically in order to gain the power to represent oneself as a subject—a power that increasingly must be *bought,* with real or fake money. Rather than simply condemning this commodity-driven mode of representation, we need to look closely at how such forms of expressing identity and difference present a new kind of racial and cultural politics based more on style and performance than on direct calls for coalition-building among the formerly colonized.

Cradle 2 the Grave, Kill Bill, and *Ghost Dog*

Like the *Rush Hour* movies, *Cradle 2 the Grave* is the product of a multi-racial, multicultural, and multinational collaboration headed by white men. As in earlier Bartkowiak and Silver action vehicles *Romeo Must Die* and *Exit*

Chris Tucker in *Rush Hour 2* (2001). Carter enthralls gamblers at the Red Dragon Casino with his variation of Martin Luther King Jr.'s "I Have a Dream" speech.

Wounds (2001), the action sequences in *Cradle 2 the Grave* were choreographed by Hong Kong filmmaker Corey Yuen and its soundtrack compiled by numerous black hip-hop artists. The action film stars *wushu* champion turned actor Jet Li as Su, a stoic Taiwanese cop, and gangsta rapper DMX as Tony Fait, a thief who dotes on his young daughter. The two nonwhite protagonists join forces to rescue Fait's daughter and to recover a bag of black diamonds (nuclear weapons in disguise!) from Ling, Su's corrupt former partner (Mark Dacascos). Jet Li and DMX perform bankable nonwhite masculine stereotypes of the asexual martial arts machine and the black stud, respectively, while Dacascos and Kelly Hu, both of mixed Asian and European descent, play updated versions of the evil Fu Manchu and his female counterpart, the Dragon Lady.

Cradle 2 the Grave functions as a showcase for Li's fantastic action sequences and for the street glamour of hip-hop culture, expressed visually in Fait and his crew and aurally in the soundtrack by DMX, Eminem, Jay-Z, 50 Cent, and other hip-hop artists. The plot serves only to move us from one action scene to another. In this sense, the film's narrative structure resembles the format of video games, music videos, and amusement park rides, as several reviewers have noted, including Roger Ebert, who quipped, "The film . . . is on autopilot and overdrive at the same time: It does nothing original, but does it very rapidly."[54] The most generous reviews focused on *Cradle 2 the Grave*'s campy elements, usually culminating in descriptions of over-the-top action sequences.[55]

The flat, cartoon elements of the film extend to its representation of women, namely, Ling's partner, the bad Eurasian woman Sona (Hu), and Fait's partner, the good black woman Daria (Gabrielle Union). Daria functions as distracting bait during Fait's heists, and both she and Sona provide eye candy for the target young male audience. Aside from a gratuitous strip scene performed by Union, both women get the most screen time in their martial arts (cat) fight scene, which recalls similar sexually charged scenes between women in blaxploitation films such as *Cleopatra Jones* (1973) and *Foxy Brown* (1974). This mode of representing strong, violent, and often vicious women became exponentially popular in the mid-1990s and early 2000s with the emergence of female characters who used martial arts techniques to kick ass in television shows such as *Xena: Warrior Princess* (1995–2001), *Buffy the Vampire Slayer* (1997 2003), and *Alias* (2001–6) and in movies such as *The Matrix, Charlie's Angels*, and *Lara Croft: Tomb Raider* (2001). From a business angle, these representations of violent femininity are seen as lucrative because, by ostensibly empowering women and titillating men, they appeal to two traditionally separate target audiences.

In the *Kill Bill* dyad Quentin Tarantino attempted to explode these contradictions with his representations of the orientalized martial arts heroine as performed by Uma Thurman and Lucy Liu. Tarantino's most recent epic follows The Bride (Thurman) on a rampage of revenge against the fellow assassins who tried to kill her when she renounced her violent career to assume a life of motherhood in the Bible Belt. *Kill Bill: Vol. 1* focuses on The Bride's standoffs with the two nonwhite villainesses on her hit list: African American Vernita Green (Vivica Fox) and Asian American O-Ren Ishii (Liu). The film swiftly dispatches Green in the setup, then splits the remaining screen time on The Bride's period of training in Osaka and Ishii's backstory as an orphaned transnational Asian American. In her unlikely role as abject, vengeful action hero, The Bride performs a kind of gender-inverted yellowface, displaying an orientalized masculinity cobbled from previous martial arts films and actors that are referenced through her body and her association with other male characters.

Uma Thurman in *Kill Bill: Vol. 1* (2003). The Bride pays sartorial homage to Bruce Lee in her fight with the Crazy 88s at O-ren Ishii's headquarters.

For instance, in the final fight scene against Ishii's *yakuza* army, The Bride wears a yellow jumpsuit with a broad black stripe, a clear allusion to the jumpsuit that Bruce Lee wore in his final film, *Game of Death* (1978). Further reinforcing the association with Lee are the black masks of the Crazy 88s masks, which recall the mask that Cato wore in *The Green Hornet* (1966). In Tarantino's homage to Bruce Lee via Thurman's blond, female, but decidedly uncurvy body, he simultaneously masculinizes the angry, abject white woman and feminizes the ultimate angry Asian American martial arts master. The Bride also assumes an apprentice role with regard to two East Asian martial arts "masters": the Japanese Hattori Hanzo (Sonny Chiba) and the Chinese Pai Mei (Gordon Liu), whose training sequences appear as flashbacks in *Kill Bill: Vol. 2*. Here she follows in the footsteps of her father figure, lover, boss, and narrative foil, Bill (David Carradine), well known for his yellowface role as the biracial Chinese American protagonist Caine in *Kung Fu* (1972).

In contrast to the masculinization of The Bride, Oshii, the primary antagonist in *Kill Bill: Vol. 1,* is hyperfeminized. Japanese Chinese American with a strong American accent, she is a metaphor for the film itself, which derives most of its entertainment value from its clever and cartoonish collage of references to East Asian popular culture. In a clear racial and cultural reference to anime, Oshii is the only character in the film with her own animated segment—the most violent sequence in an already violent film. Like the protagonists played by Jackie Chan and Jet Li, she has no familial or romantic ties.

Furthermore, Oshii's femininity is indistinguishable from that of the hyperracialized and sexualized Dragon Lady persona she inhabits, which contrasts sharply with the humanizing maternal qualities of the other women in the film. The Bride's strong maternal instincts propel the story, and Vernita Green, in her fatal encounter with The Bride, is concerned first and foremost for her young daughter. Conversely, Oshii's maternalism is evil and perverse in that it is linked with the Crazy 88s, a "yellow horde" of *yakuza* henchmen led by Gordon Liu and, in not so subtle lesbian undertones, with her female subordinates, Eurasian Sophie Fatale (Julie Dreyfus) and Japanese schoolgirl assassin–disciple Gogo Yubari (Chiaki Kuriyama). This perverse oriental feminine must ultimately be destroyed—and it is by a "silly Caucasian girl" in the film's homoerotic climax.

What East Asia gives The Bride is the dangerous technology with which to fulfill her vigilante white feminist fantasy against (and through?) the

Kill Bill: Vol. 1. An animated version of young, blood-soaked O-ren after she has achieved revenge for the death of her parents.

Chiyaki Kuriyami and Julia Dreyfus in *Kill Bill: Vol. 1.* Gogo Yubari and Sophie Fatale, O-ren's lead henchwomen, enter headquarters with members of the Crazy 88s.

white patriarchy that has wronged her. In *Kill Bill: Vol. 1* that technology is in the form of the Hattori sword, which allows her to engage in elaborate and effective Japanese swordplay; in *Kill Bill: Vol. 2* it is in the form of the brutal martial arts training she receives from Pai Mei, which gives her the skills to engage in hand-to-hand combat. In these ways, orientalized images and narratives of Japan and China occupy the backdrop and backstory of both films and are closely connected to the development of the heroine's strength and final recuperation of her honor—both as a violent professional killer (an identity coded black and brown; her previous epithet, "Black Mamba," references a Latin dance, and with one consonant dropped becomes "Black Mama") and a devoted mother-to-be (an identity coded white: the not-so-virginal, born-again blond white Bride).

Although director Quentin Tarantino's films are more independent with regard to content, narrative style, and artistic approach than straight-forwardly blockbuster-modeled movies like *Rush Hour* and *Cradle 2 the Grave,* they register as somewhat less independent than the films of such directors as Terrence Malick, John Sayles, and Jim Jarmusch, who do not have—and who have professed not to want—the financial backing of studios in favor of more creative control over their work. As Biskind discusses in *Down and Dirty Pictures,* Tarantino belongs to the new crop of independent filmmakers who emerged in the mid-1990s through the support of the Sundance Institute and Film Festival and Miramax studios.[56] In contrast, Jarmusch, often touted as the quintessential American independent filmmaker and embraced by hipsters the world over, belongs to the previous generation of independents, awkwardly situated between the end of the first phase of the New Hollywood and the beginning of the current hybrid independent-studio system.

About a month before *The Matrix* caught the attention of the nation, Jarmusch's quirky character study of an orientalized black assassin bowed to mixed reviews in New York and Los Angeles. Unlike the other films discussed in this chapter, *Ghost Dog* has no East Asian characters, nor does it have people of Asian descent working behind the camera. Described by Jarmusch as a "gangster samurai hip-hop eastern western," the film stars Forest Whitaker as a likeable sociopath who strictly follows the code of behavior prescribed in the *Hagakure: The Way of the Samurai* by Yamamoto Tsunetomo, and, as in *Romeo Must Die* and *Cradle 2 the Grave,* a gritty hip-hop soundtrack permeates the movie.[57]

A young, working-class black man in a generic urban space with no discernible familial or social ties, Ghost Dog has pledged to serve Louie, a small-time mobster who once saved his life from a gang of black youth. When the daughter of the Mafia leader witnesses one of his jobs for Louie in which he murders her lover (also her father's friend), the mob puts a death warrant out on Ghost Dog. Using sleek high-tech gadgets and weapons, he embarks on a darkly comic killing spree that ends in a doomed Leonesque duel between himself and his "master." Like most of Jarmusch's films, *Ghost Dog* focuses not so much on plot as on character development and setting: most of the film consists of long, nocturnal street sequences in which Ghost Dog listens to Wu Tang Clan member RZA's hypnotic riffs while driving another stolen Mercedes to his next job.

One of the few old-school independent filmmakers left in the United States, Jarmusch has an oeuvre that consistently reflects a progressive liberal perspective. *Dead Man* (1996), his feature film before *Ghost Dog,* was widely admired outside the United States and had a mixed reception within it for its dark and violent vision of the American frontier. When Nobody, the Native American character played by Gary Farmer, mutters "stupid fucking white man" in the film, he critiques not only the history of U.S. imperialism against American Indians and people of color but also the naiveté of his traveling companion, William Blake, the dying white protagonist played by Johnny Depp. By articulating Nobody's perspective and highlighting Blake's ignorance, Jarmusch defamiliarizes whiteness and, in so doing, provides a trenchant critique of the dominant racial order.

When Nobody appears again in *Ghost Dog*, repeating the same phrase to the mobsters who have killed the protagonist's beloved pet pigeons, Jarmusch attempts to reiterate this critique. However, his position on whiteness is less clear here for two reasons. First, the film lacks nonethnic white characters like Blake who might represent the director and his white liberal audience. Second, the ethnic characters that do populate the film constantly appropriate and perform the trappings of other races and cultures for this unmarked audience.

This form of racial drag is seen on several levels. At the most obvious level, the black male protagonist fetishizes Japanese history and culture in several ways: through his consumption of texts such as *Hagakure* and *Rashomon*, through the decorative display of oriental signifiers such as the Asian characters on his clothing and the weapons mentioned earlier, and through his performance of "Japanese" attitudes and actions such as his adherence to a stoic samurai masculinity and his fascination with Japanese swords. At another level, the females in the film are subtly orientalized. Pearline, the precocious young black girl who befriends Ghost Dog, and Trish, the adolescent mob princess mentioned earlier, an anime Betty Boop with large eyes, a Lolita sexuality, and a Louise Brooks bob, are linked to Ghost Dog and to each other through a copy of the Japanese novel *Rashomon*. Finally, at yet another level of racial performance, the film's antagonists—old Italian American gangsters—embrace the black hypermasculinity commonly associated with hip-hop culture. It is telling that Jarmusch depicts Ghost Dog's dedication to the samurai code in a straight, serious, and mostly uncritical mode, whereas he plays the mobsters' fascination with black popular culture for laughs.

As in *Dead Man*, the director critiques whiteness through caricature. However, the critique is less powerful here because it pokes fun at a specific kind of whiteness from which the director and his hipster audience can distance themselves, namely, that of a working-class white ethnic group whose own romanticized stereotypes as mobsters is appropriated by and elevated in gangsta rap. Ultimately, then, Jarmusch diffuses the liberal white male gaze through its exoticization of different racial and ethnic groups exoticizing each other. And the ambiguous nature of the relationship between this gaze and its objects is epitomized in the figure of a black protagonist who assumes narrative power through his performance of an orientalized and decontextualized East Asian masculinity.

Conclusion

As I hope these analyses show, hip-hop kung fu style is racially, culturally, and sexually elastic, based as it is on the construction of an oriental masculinity that can be performed not only by black men *(Ghost Dog)* and East Asian men (*Rush Hour, Rush Hour 2,* and *Cradle 2 the Grave*) but also by white women (*Kill Bill: Vol. 1* and *Kill Bill: Vol. 2*). At first glance, this insertion of mostly non–East Asian bodies in distinctly East Asian styles and settings carries on the Hollywood tradition of marginalizing East Asian and Asian American talent. The majority of Asian and Asian American actors are limited to the background and secondary roles while Asian signifiers are appropriated and performed by white or non-Asian actors. Even when Asian actors appear and Asian choreographers are employed, the superficial level of diversity they provide reproduces old stereotypes in new ways and fails to challenge the existing paradigms of power that created those stereotypes in the first place.

One could argue that these films exemplify the ways in which stereotypes of black and East Asian people from hip-hop and martial arts cultures have become commodified types, able to be taken off and worn by everyone and anyone. Although this form of homage increases the visibility of nonwhite bodies and cultures, it does so in a way that flattens them into cool commodities with no social, political, or historical roots. Paradoxically, then, in this line of thought the rise of multicultural chic seems to have done little to alleviate the burden of representation shouldered by people of color in the popular media.

Yet the power of visibility, even of so-called negative stereotypes, cannot be discounted completely. The translations of cultural forms and styles occurring at present among filmmakers, actors, and fans in martial arts

cinema, anime, and Hollywood films hint at the workings of a phenomenon much more complex than an appreciative form of cultural exchange
or an oppressive mode of cultural appropriation. These films disseminate
images of difference (as problematic as they may seem at times) and, just as
important, provide employment opportunities for nonwhite people in the
entertainment industry. East Asian and Asian American media producers
are using these opportunities to complicate the terms of cultural appropriation in the popular visual culture.

Meanwhile, Asian films continue to be hot both on the festival circuit
and in Hollywood.[58] In the past several years, East Asia has become a source
not only of cinematic inspiration but also of transnational collaboration,
as demonstrated by U.S. and European interest in Hong Kong, Japanese,
and Korean genre films, Chinese Fifth Generation and Sixth Generation art
house epics, and anime. In addition, East Asia is providing narrative ideas
for Hollywood, as highlighted, for instance, in the current interest in remaking Korean films.[59]

Underlying all of this attention, of course, is the desire on the part of
the United States to exploit existing markets and open up new ones in
Asia. According to Toby Miller and his coauthors, "Japan provides 10–20 per
cent of worldwide grosses on blockbuster releases. . . . India and China
account for over two-thirds of film screens around the world. . . . By 2015,
Asia could be responsible for 60 per cent of Hollywood box-office revenue."[60] For Hollywood, whose commodities comprise the second-largest
form of U.S. export after those of the aerospace industry, one of the pressing
questions in the early twenty-first century is this: what images and stories
will these Asian viewers pay to watch? While Hollywood executives work to
transform newly industrialized Asians (particularly those in mainland China
and Southeast Asia) into eager media consumers, Asian American communities continue to grow in the United States. The bicultural Americans who
hail from these communities function both as physical reminders of the
historical oriental other in one's midst and as potential cultural bridges for
understanding what appears, to some, to be an inevitably Asian future.

Whether a fleeting millennial trend or the beginning of a new cultural
wave, the staying power of East Asia in Hollywood seems to be related not
only to the traditional oriental signifiers with which it has always been
linked but also to its relatively recent associations with the technologized

future—a future celebrated and represented by youth audiences, who comprise the fan base for martial arts films, Asian action films, and *mecha* anime. To these youth, growing up in the era of "posts" (postmodernism, postcapitalism, postcolonialism, postfeminism, and post-9/11, to name just a few), what was considered foreign has become familiar as the ubiquity of media has made the familiar feel increasingly surreal, and vice versa.

Even to older Gen Xers and Baby Boomers, Asian cultural forms such as martial arts, anime, yoga, and feng shui may not seem as alien as they did a few years ago for reasons that are linked in the paradigm of techno-orientalism. Namely, the number of Asians in the United States continues to grow, and we are learning to experience space differently thanks to the mediation of advanced telecommunication technologies. The world appears to be shrinking into sound bytes and snapshots mediated through global popular culture. East Asian spaces, cultures, and peoples represent the cutting edge of information technologies. The ensuing logic is that as we in the West grow more entrenched in the visual economy of the so-called information society, we grow to resemble our counterparts in the East.

Here I do not want to imply that by wanting to "turn Japanese" Asiaphilic Gen X filmmakers in the United States have somehow gotten beyond the historical, political, and institutional apparatuses of Orientalism. What I am posing, rather, is the possibility that, as Americans who possess a great deal of knowledge about and appreciation of East Asian popular culture, these media producers may be reflecting and constructing new modes of relating to East Asia. The cross-pollination of oriental and occidental styles in contemporary Hollywood posits an alternate model for exploring the ambivalences in identity and community construction that have always been present in Orientalism.

This model would look at the relationship between the self and the other, the West and the so-called rest, less as a binary and more as a dialectical process focusing on undertheorized elements in Orientalism such as fascination, complicity, and multilateral circuits of exchange. It could critically engage with the "Asiaphilia" that characterizes the appeal of many recent films, including those outside the action genre, such as *Lost in Translation* and *The Last Samurai* (2003) and *Memoirs of a Geisha* (2005). What kinds of stories and attitudes about Asia and its relationship to the West are these movies telling and selling? And how do these images and narratives influence the way non-Asians see Asians and the way people of Asian descent, especially in the United States, see themselves?

The next and final chapter will come back to this question in its examination of *The Matrix*, the already iconic film that displayed a new kind of grim, multicultural, and techno-oriental America for the twenty-first century and that helped introduce the forms of East Asian popular media, which were discussed in this chapter.

6

The Virtual Orient

We wrote the story for ourselves and hoped others would pick up on it. Every studio we showed it to thought no one would understand it. We told them it would be complex and dense, but we were also going to shoot the best action scenes and coolest computer graphics ever. Even if audiences didn't get all of the references, we knew they'd at least have a good time with the visuals.

—Larry Wachowski, quoted in *Time*

Seventeen years after *E.T.* demolished *Blade Runner* at the box office, an eerily similar scenario appeared in Hollywood. George Lucas's heavily publicized first prequel to his space opera *Star Wars* bowed at theaters in May 1999, two months after the debut of an intriguing cyberpunk film by two geeky young brothers from Chicago. Once again, a feel-good, cross-marketed science-fiction blockbuster squared off with a dark, noirish film about human beings and technology. The outcome in 1999, however, was decidedly different than that in 1982. Although *Star Wars I: The Phantom Menace* more than recouped its production costs, it was the sleeper hit *The Matrix,* directed by brothers Andy and Larry Wachowski, that captured and seemed to reflect the public imagination at the cusp of the new millennium.

At the time of this writing, *The Matrix* has grossed $460 million in total box office: $171 million domestically and $288 million internationally.[1] It has generated a synergistic mass of *Matrix*-related paraphernalia, including an award-winning DVD documentary, *The Matrix Revisited* (2001); two sequels, *The Matrix: Reloaded* (2003) and *The Matrix: Revolutions* (2003); a series of animated shorts, *The Animatrix* (2003); a comic book series, *The Matrix Comics,* Volumes 1 and 2 (2003, 2004); two video games, *Enter The Matrix* (2003) and *The One* (2005); and a multiplayer online computer game, *The Matrix Online* (2005). These media products, in turn, have sparked a flurry of journalistic criticism, a formidable international fan base linked though the Internet, and an ever-growing number of academic books and articles.[2]

The Matrix is a futuristic bildungsroman about a somnolent corporate drone by day and hacker by night named Thomas Anderson with the computer alias Neo (Keanu Reeves). Neo learns that what he has accepted as reality is actually a fake world called the Matrix. The Matrix is Plato's cave, cyberspace, and Antonio Gramsci's notion of hegemony all rolled up into one "consensual hallucination"—a simulation of reality fed to human beings in order to keep them blind to the reality that they are energy sources for the alien machines, which have invaded the planet. Neo's mentor on this journey of (self-) discovery is a well-dressed terrorist named Morpheus (Laurence Fishburne), who turns out to be the leader of a resistance movement against the machines. He and his crew, which includes Trinity (Carrie-Anne Moss), Neo's strong and sexy love interest, fly around the ruins of the real world in their ship, the Nebuchadnezzar, evading the metallic surveillance octopi called Sentinels and "jacking in" to the Matrix to fight the evil, blank-faced Agents led by Smith (Hugo Weaving).

Morpheus believes that Neo might be the One (note the anagram)—the savior that the grandmotherly trickster known as the Oracle (Gloria Foster) has prophesied will free humankind from the machines. Once Neo learns and accepts the awful truth that his life has been a lie, the focus of the film shifts to whether he may or may not be the One. Found wanting in several ways, he eschews the issue to rescue Morpheus, who has been captured by the agents while trying to save Neo's life. Neo's willingness to sacrifice himself for his friend and teacher—as well as Morpheus's continued faith in his protégé—leads the audience to suspect that he might indeed be the One, a suspicion confirmed and realized through Trinity's expression of her love for Neo. For it is her kiss that resurrects our hero from the dead and gives him the power to defeat Agent Smith before shooting up to the sky with the promise of more pop-philosophizing and ass-kicking in the inevitable sequels.

Immediately hailed as a classic of postmodern filmmaking, *The Matrix* is both heir and successor to the cinematic legacy of *Blade Runner*—a legacy that stresses mise-en-scène and, more specifically related to this study, depictions of racial, sexual, and ontological difference in and as mise-en-scène. Given the films' shared emphasis on visual and visceral formal elements, especially as they culminate in a kind of cinematic, multicultural Oriental-ism, it is telling that *Blade Runner* was dismissed while *The Matrix* was feted upon the films' initial releases in 1982 and 1999, respectively.

In this final chapter I attempt to account for the striking contrast in crit-ical reception by looking at how *The Matrix* addresses issues of race through the tropes of technology and the Orient. I do so by focusing on the role of Neo as an ambivalent antihero and on Keanu Reeves's embodiment and performance of that role as a mixed-race actor of East Asian and European descent. Therefore, the chapter consists of a brief historical overview of mixed-race representation in Hollywood, a summary of the critical response to the film, and close readings of Neo's body in a few key scenes.

My analysis of *The Matrix* is concerned with the ways in which the film deploys oriental style to activate and disavow the anxieties that undergird the central question in *Blade Runner* and in cyberpunk narratives more broadly: what makes something or someone human? In both films this question is asked along racial lines and answered through contrasting itera-tions of black and Asiatic tropes set against the larger backdrop of a de facto mixed-race future. More specifically, whereas blackness appears only as a metaphor in *Blade Runner,* it is literally embodied by the primary black characters in *The Matrix.* Meanwhile, oriental imagery is more literal in *Blade Runner*—opaque and static, exemplified in its props, costumes, and production design—whereas in *The Matrix* it is more metaphoric—trans-parent and mobile, exemplified in the film's stylistic incorporation of mar-tial arts, anime, and video games.

These differences in how blackness and Asianness become visible in the films can be traced to certain shifts in attitudes toward racial difference since the 1980s. As I have tried to show in my readings of oriental style in Holly-wood films, over the past twenty years representations of nonwhite peoples and cultures have become more fluid, disembodied, and metaphoric and, at the same time, they have been increasingly commodified as exotic objects for mass consumption. Reduced thus to metaphors, different nonwhite groups have come to assume specific aesthetic and ideological functions in popular culture, not only in relation to an increasingly destabilized whiteness but also to each other.

These changes in how we perceive racial difference have occurred as part of a number of socioeconomic and industrial developments discussed in previous chapters, including the social justice movements of the 1960s and 1970s; the post-1965 immigration to the United States from Latin America and Asia; the economic rise of Japan and the newly industrialized countries in the 1980s; the emergence of popular multicultural discourse in the 1980s and 1990s; and the entrenchment of a neoliberal economic system and neo-conservative social policies in the 1990s and 2000s.

At the same time, these changes in popular depictions of race have also been part of larger social, epistemological, and ontological shifts that have accompanied the advent of the Internet and the increased presence of media in our lives, a phenomenon Todd Gitlin calls the "media torrent."[3] Along with other media scholars, Gitlin argues that the quotidian incorporation of digital media (the Internet, video games, cell phones, i-pods, etc.) has rendered our perceptions of reality less stable and concrete, more unstable and "virtual."[4] Journalist Benjamin Woolley gives one of the most concise definitions of this nebulous term in *Virtual Worlds*, a cultural history of simulation. He provides a genealogy of *virtual*, tracing it back to the "origins of modern science" in the early eighteenth century, when it referred to "the refracted or reflected image of an object"; to the nineteenth century, when it was used by physicists to describe "a particle's 'virtual velocity'"; and finally to the twentieth century, when it was adopted by cyberneticists to describe the reproducible memory of the first computer conceptualized by British mathematician Alan Turing in 1936.[5] As Woolley puts it, "A computer is a 'virtual' machine. . . . It is an abstract entity or process that has found physical expression, that has been 'realized.' It is a simulation, only not necessarily a simulation of anything actual."[6]

This definition of *virtual* as simulation, or the concrete manifestation of a fantasy with no point of origin, can also be applied to the myth of race as a marker of difference. As I noted in the introduction, this myth is sustained through the persistence in the dominant culture of attaching certain cultural assumptions to certain phenotypical traits. The racial confusion engendered by the presence of mixed-race people whose racial ambiguity allows them to pass as white and/or nonwhite simultaneously exposes the culturally constructed nature of race and ethnicity and demonstrates the permeability of racial borders. In the next section I give a brief overview of mixed-race reception in U.S. popular culture to frame the analysis of multicultural and multiracial politics in *The Matrix* that follows.

You've Come a Long Way, Baby

The number of multiracial people in the United States has grown substantially since the case of *Loving v. Virginia* struck down antimiscegenation laws nationally in 1967. According to the Population Reference Bureau, children born to parents of different races increased from 1 to 3.4 percent of total births in the nation between 1968 and 1989, and the number of mixed-race couples excluding Hispanics grew from 310,000 to 994,000 between 1970 and 1991.[7] In the 2000 Census, 6.8 million Americans, or 2.4 percent of the population, identified themselves as belonging to more than one racial group when they were given the option to do so for the first time.[8] Such statistics indicate that mixed-race people are becoming more visible in the United States, socially and politically. As I will discuss in more detail shortly, this visibility is currently celebrated in popular media—a reception that runs counter to historical representations of mixed-race people in this country, both onscreen and off.

As Susan Courtney points out, the very origins of U.S. cinema are racially mixed insofar as *Birth of a Nation* (1915), the seminal silent film that established the classical Hollywood style, is driven narratively by the "ostensible fear of black men raping white women." *Birth of a Nation* and other films from that period spectacularized the public's fearful fascination with interracial coupling, particularly between black men and white women during and after Reconstruction. In its institutionalization as a culture industry, Hollywood responded to these popular fears by policing notions of interracial romance from 1930 to 1956 with a specific clause in the Production Code that forbade depictions of miscegenation.[9]

To comply with the code, two practices evolved for the representation of people of color generally and mixed-race people more specifically: the industrial practice of employing white and occasionally racially ambiguous actors and actresses to play nonwhite roles in blackface, yellowface, brownface, and redface and the narrative practice of eliminating characters that embodied racial mixing, killing them off or otherwise expelling them from the story.[10] In this sense, mixed-race types such as the mestizo/a, the half-breed, and the Eurasian all functioned ideologically as variations of the "tragic mulatto" figure, described by Freda Scott Giles as follows: "The mulatto could be identified with and pitied as the victim of the miscegenation taboo while at the same time be feared as the despised other lurking within who had to be punished, either for trying to sneak into the white world as an imposter or for reminding the black world of the mark of the oppressor."[11]

Associated primarily with biracial characters of black and white ancestry, this racial type became the Hollywood standard for depicting mixed-race characters in general. In the tragic mulatto narrative, the children of interracial unions represent the forbidden intersection of white and nonwhite (again, usually coded black). Belonging to neither group, these individuals must renounce a socially subordinate nonwhite identity to retain their tenuous place in the dominant culture. However, in the end, the mixed-race character can survive neither in the dominant white nor in the marginal nonwhite culture.[12] We find examples of the tragic mulatto as the doomed protagonist in such films as *Showboat* (1929, 1936, 1951), *Imitation of Life* (1934, 1959), *Carmen Jones* (1954), and *Love Is a Many Splendored Thing* (1955).

The concept of passing as white that underlay the figure of the tragic mulatto erased, disavowed, or otherwise failed to recognize the social, psychological, and cultural dynamics that shape multiracial identities. As Teresa Kay Williams explains, "Passing in and of itself is problematic for multiracial individuals because it accepts and further reifies the exclusive, oppositionalized, unequal structure of race in which either fluidity across its boundaries or multiple situationality within many boundaries is not permitted."[13] In other words, for someone to pass from one identity or group to another, those identities or groups must be regarded as stable, unified, and distinct. Moreover, the phenomenon of passing presumes a racial binary in which whiteness is associated with empowered subjectivity and blackness with disempowered objectification—a binary based on the idea of hypodescent, also known as the one-drop rule, which dictates that even "one drop" of black blood makes a person wholly black.

Unique to the United States, the black/white binary, as discussed in previous chapters, has shaped national racial discourse regardless of the historical presence of other racial and ethnic groups in the country, namely, American Indians, Latino/as, Pacific Islanders, and Asian Americans, not to mention most African and Anglo-Americans, who have multiracial backgrounds. Most of the new Asian and Latino/a immigrants who entered the United States after 1965, unlike their European predecessors and counterparts, were not able to pass as white phenotypically. Consequently, their arrival led to a browning and yellowing of the hitherto mostly white and black national body. According to demographers, this trend should continue until 2050, when whites will no longer be the racial majority, as is already the case in California, where nonwhites comprise 53 percent of the population.[14]

As a result of these demographic changes as well as the civil rights, Black Power, and subsequent cultural nationalist movements, nonwhite and mixed-race actors who could not pass as white gained more presence in Hollywood during the following decades. Many filmmakers of color, such as Gordon Parks, Wayne Wang, and Gregory Nava, first gained experience in media production by working on documentaries and short films within these movements broadly. Also, thanks to affirmative action initiatives more people of color matriculated into film programs in this period, resulting in the blossoming of the Los Angeles School, Chicano cinema and Asian American cinema as well as the production of documentaries and films about racial minorities on public television in the 1980s. Many of the newly politicized filmmakers, actors and actresses, producers, and writers of color entered the commercial film industry and contributed to the growing visibility of non-Western bodies and cultures behind and in front of the camera. Their presence, along with the commercial popularity of blaxploitation and martial arts films in the 1970s, led in the 1980s to the surfacing on the big screen of more nonwhite imagery, which found expression in multicultural mise-en-scène and racially diverse casting.

The increased visibility of racial difference in Hollywood was followed by the multiracial chic of the 1990s, as epitomized by the magazine cover models of *Time* in November 1993 and *Mirabella* in September 1994. Constructed digitally using photographs of individuals from various racial and ethnic backgrounds, these virtual models looked vaguely ethnic but sported predominantly European features.[15] Similar mixed-race and racially ambiguous characters began to appear soon thereafter and have since become fixtures of U.S. advertisements, commercials, video games, films, and television.[16]

This racially ambiguous media world recalls Gloria Anzaldúa's descriptive framework for multiracial subjectivity. Anzaldúa's idea of a mestiza consciousness draws on her own marginalized experiences as a biracial Chicana lesbian in order to reclaim the liminal status of the mixed-race subject whose phenotypical and cultural ambiguities present a mass of contradictions to the monoracially framed world. In the following passage she defines the mestiza and the spiritual-political consciousness borne out of the attempt to synthesize these contradictions:

> The new *mestiza* copes by developing a tolerance for contradictions, a tolerance for ambiguity. . . . She has a plural personality, she operates in a pluralistic mode. . . . Not only does she sustain contradictions, she turns the ambivalence into something else. . . . In attempting to work out a synthesis, the self has added a third element which is greater than the sum of its severed parts. That third element is a new consciousness—a *mestiza* consciousness— and though it is a source of intense pain, its energy comes from continual creative motion that keeps breaking down the unitary aspect of each new paradigm. . . . The future will belong to the *mestiza*. Because the future depends on the breaking down of paradigms, it depends on the straddling of two or more cultures.[17]

Anzaldúa posed mestiza consciousness as a critical, creative, and spiritual response to a monoracial worldview in which non-Western racial and cultural differences were rendered abject or invisible. Almost twenty years later, a highly commodified form of that consciousness appears to have replaced this worldview: in contemporary popular media, racial difference, *properly contained and sanitized through class and/or cultural capital,* is neither ignored nor reviled but rather actively celebrated and portrayed as desirable.

The current popularity of racially ambiguous characters and the increased superficial visibility of nonwhite peoples and cultures in Hollywood cinema suggest the need to revisit and rework the traditional notion of appropriation as white people stealing and incorporating the cultures of nonwhite peoples. What I call "virtual race," or the technologized performance of racial, ethnic, and cultural traits and styles different from one's own, seems at first glance to signal a loosening up of racial boundaries that have been rigorously policed historically.[18] However, this dismantling of traditional racial and ethnic identities and affiliations signals neither the happy eradication of racism nor a simple reiteration of white privilege. Instead the current situation is much more complex, with mixed-race bodies blurring the boundaries between whiteness and nonwhiteness even as they receive certain privileges that historically have been conferred upon those with white bodies.

It is important to note that the concentration of nonwhite characters and motifs in recent years has been found in various hybrid action genres—horror, thriller, and urban action as well as science fiction—which, with their emphasis on the visual and the visceral, fit the requirements of the high-concept blockbuster film. What Yvonne Tasker observed of Hollywood action films in the early 1990s continues to hold in contemporary action movies, with the modification that other nonwhite performers have begun to appear, especially those of Asian, Latino/a, and mixed-race descent. As Tasker wrote:

> Action heroes and heroines are cinematically constructed almost exclusively through their physicality, and the display of the body forms a key part of the visual excess that is offered in the muscular action cinema. Such an emphasis on physicality has . . . opened up a space in the action cinema for black performers who have been almost totally excluded from other Hollywood genres.[19]

The science-fiction action film, which became a generic staple in the blockbuster era, draws on the spectacle of special effects and, increasingly, of racial and cultural difference to dramatize the conflict between self and other, human and alien (in the form of extraterrestrials or technology) so central to the genre. As our relationship to technology has become more ambivalent, so has our relationship to the other in science-fiction cinema, as Vivian Sobchack, Scott Bukatman, and others have argued.[20]

Also, the body has functioned as the primary site upon which the instability between the self/other boundary has been played out, from early films such as *The Thing from Another World* (1951) and *The Invasion of the Body Snatchers* (1956) to later ones such as *RoboCop* (1987) and *eXistenZ* (1999). The fact that in a number of contemporary science-fiction action films the bodies of the key characters are racially ambiguous is particularly significant within this generic context. These characters literally embody the racial and ethnic diversity of the mise-en-scène and supporting characters in the films in which they star, appearing to signify the end of racial boundaries. Not surprisingly, as nonwhite, racially ambiguous, and mixed-race characters have become more visible and been further developed on the big screen, whiteness seems to have lost much of its former social and cultural cachet.

These developments are expressed in *The Matrix* in its depiction of marginal identities and groups and in the protagonist's relationship to them. Throughout the film, racial, gender, and sexual differences are reduced and spectacularized to virtually orientalized bodies that move in concert—and sometimes merge—with orientalized virtual spaces. In the next several pages I examine how this process of spectacular reduction occurs and consider the ideological implications of the racialized styles that result.

Critical Response

As in the case of *Blade Runner,* critics tended to fixate on the nonnarrative elements of *The Matrix,* especially the special effects and action sequences. This sentiment was reflected at the 2000 Academy Awards, where *The Matrix* took Oscars for editing, visual effects, sound, and sound effects editing. Also, most reviewers praised the film's relentless recycling of ideas and styles from cinema, popular culture, philosophy, religion, and the sciences. In some cases, these allusions were enumerated in list form for less culturally literate viewers. For instance, an article in *Time* magazine provided a compilation of source notes for the film that included The Bible, Greek mythology, *Alice's Adventures in Wonderland,* cyberpunk novels, theoretical mathematics, Jungian psychology, anime, and the martial arts.

Unlike their responses to *Blade Runner,* however, critics were neither negative nor ambivalent about the Wachowskis' aesthetic and cultural scavenging. Instead the directors' privileging of mise-en-scène was considered complementary rather than antithetical to the film's narrative trajectory. Critics applauded the creativity with which the Wachowskis deployed multiple cultural signifiers to tell a story that struck a chord with its ostensibly techno-savvy audiences. Consider, for instance, Janet Maslin's comments in her *New York Times* review:

> The most salient things any prospective viewer need know is Keanu Reeves makes a strikingly chic Prada model of an action hero, that the martial arts dynamics are phenomenal and that anyone bored with the notably pretentious plotting can keep busy toting up this

film's debts to other futuristic science fiction. . . . Nonetheless whatever recycling the brothers do here is canny enough to give "The Matrix" a strong identity of its own.[21]

A couple of unkempt college dropouts with a yen for comics and kung fu movies had realized Ridley Scott's earlier desire to make a dark, comic-book action film about the future. How were the Wachowski brothers able to pull off this major feat? What formal and cultural elements made their particular form of cinematic pastiche so "canny"—just smart enough to establish *The Matrix* as the new *Star Wars* for the digitally advanced youth of the impending millennium?

Maslin's review provides a clue to the secret ingredient that appears to have made *The Matrix* so appealing to these audiences: "the martial arts stunts . . . are its [the film's] strongest selling point. As supervised by Yuen Wo Ping, these airborne sequences bring Hong Kong action style home to audiences in a mainstream American adventure with big prospects as a cult classic and with the future very much in mind."[22] The suggestion here is that the originality of *The Matrix* stemmed from its ability to combine Eastern and Western popular culture through particular visual idioms.

Jeffrey Ressner made that connection even clearer in his enthusiastic review in *Time:*

> *[The Matrix]* invokes the kung furiosity of prime Jackie Chan and the heroic bloodshed and long coats of John Woo movies; the Hollywood–Hong Konglomeration has never meshed so suavely as in this film's fight scenes and wire-work aerobatics. Never seen the mega-imaginative, ultraviolent Japanese cartoons known as *anime (Akira, Ghost in the Shell)?* Now you have—in whirling live action.[23]

In their 1999 *Newsweek* review, N'gai Croal and Devin Gordon quoted Hong Kong director Stanley Tong, lending cultural authenticity to the idea that the film epitomizes the melding of Eastern and Western cinematic strengths: "Even veteran Hong Kong directors are blown away. 'The combination of Chinese martial arts and American special effects is something I've wanted to do for a long time,' says Stanley Tong, who directed several Jackie Chan movies."[24]

What such reviews failed to point out is that East Asian filmmakers—Tsui Hark in particular—already had blended the "magic" of special effects with that of the martial arts. However, science-fiction and swordplay films such as *Zu: The Warriors of Magic Mountain* (1983), *Invincible Asia 2* (1992), *The Wicked City* (1992), and *The Bride with White Hair* (1993) remained inaccessible to most mainstream American audiences. It took Hollywood blockbusters such as *The Matrix* in 1999 and *Crouching Tiger, Hidden Dragon* a year later to popularize this stylistic blend of Eastern martial arts and ostensibly Western special effects.

I say "ostensibly" because the special effects highlighted in both films, especially in *The Matrix,* though developed in U.S. laboratories, are no longer exclusively Western products. Techniques such as digital editing, motion capture, and other forms of computer-generated effects are being used to create the aesthetic template for video games, commercials, music videos, television programs, and action films around the world. Additionally, anime—especially of the *mecha* genre—had anticipated such technologies thematically and visually since at least the time of Katsuhiro Ôtomo's *Akira* (1986).

Orientalism Redux

Andy and Larry Wachowski, like their compatriots Quentin Tarantino, Guillermo del Toro, McG, Robert Rodriguez, and others, no doubt were familiar with these developments. In *The Matrix Revisited,* a DVD documentary about the making of the film, the Wachowskis acknowledge their debt to Hong Kong cinema and Japanimation. Indeed, an entire chapter of the DVD is devoted to action choreographer Yuen Wo Ping's collaboration with the directors and his grueling training sessions with the principal actors. Although anime influences receive less attention in the documentary, the Wachowskis paid homage to the Japanese medium in 2003 with *The Animatrix,* a DVD compilation of nine original anime shorts loosely based on *The Matrix.* According to press coverage and the official Warner Bros. website, the Wachowskis actively participated in the *Animatrix* project, writing three of the pieces, directing two, and personally supervising the completion of the rest.[25]

Commenting on the *Matrix* oeuvre of which the documentary and *The Animatrix* are a part, producer Joel Silver declared, "This isn't just merchandising or advertising. The animes, the Web site, the game and the movie work together to tell the story."[26] Silver's comment sums up the ways in which *The Matrix* exemplifies the model of the New Hollywood blockbuster with its synergistic blurring of text and context, narrative and economics. Indeed the multiple manifestations of the film across various entertainment platforms demonstrates how tightly creative conception and execution are tied to marketing, distribution, and exhibition in today's entertainment market. Furthermore, it is telling that these horizontal marketing practices drew heavily on the subcultural fan base around anime and martial arts movies to produce a film that seemed fresh and new to mainstream viewers, many of whom might not have been familiar with these East Asian popular media.

Although the Wachowskis' contribution is in some ways groundbreaking, I wish to stress again that *The Matrix* does not exist in a stylistic or cultural vacuum. Rather, the film and its spin-offs belong to a larger tendency in U.S. cinema of alluding to East Asian culture and imagery to project a particular picture of the future on the big screen. In other words, the supposedly innovative aspects of the film were recognized and applauded precisely because they drew on familiar orientalist tropes and attitudes that *Blade Runner* had introduced two decades earlier—Asiatic allusions that in the 1980s and 1990s became a part of the cinematic vocabulary of media producers not only in the United States but also in Japan.

As Susan Napier has noted, prominent Japanese animators such as Mamoru Oshii and Katsuhiro Ôtomo were influenced by stylistic elements of *Blade Runner,* which they incorporated into their own work.[27] These Japanese iterations of U.S. cyberpunk were then, in turn, pleasurably (mis)translated by anime fans Larry and Andy Wachowski. The cinematic and cultural feedback loop demonstrated here through forms of homage among fans and filmmakers across time and space structured not only the stylistic framework of this film but also its thematic preoccupation with the idea of authenticity, which played out in its treatment of race, gender, sexuality, and technology.

In chapter 2 I pointed out the ways in which *Blade Runner,* by revealing the empty emotional lives of the human characters and the potential for emotional development of the replicants, seems to question the validity of the human/machine binary as analogous to that of the self/other. In this sense, that film exposes the permeability of the border between human and nonhuman as characters' perceptions of and actions toward their respective others change. Narratively, Roy Batty and Rachael *become* human as dramatic foils for Deckard. Visually, however, the replicants are *already* human from the moment they appear onscreen by virtue of their light, individuated bodies, which register as white against the dark, undifferentiated bodies that comprise the dirty, dystopic spaces of the near future. In this way, even as they symbolically perform the plight of the economically abject, the white bodies of the replicants limn the cinematic objectification of racial others in *Blade Runner*, aestheticizing racial difference and, in the process, depoliticizing it.

In contrast, *The Matrix* thematically promulgates an anti-technological humanism through its foregrounding of stylistically racialized bodies. In this sense, it reiterates the racial and ontological boundaries in *Blade Runner* but also raises new questions about border crossing in more recent contexts of racial formation. I now turn to these questions and to the multiracial hero played by Keanu Reeves, the figure that prompts them.

Neo as the "Dark White Man"

Unlike Gaff, the multiracial character in *Blade Runner*, Neo, the less discernibly mixed-race protagonist in *The Matrix*, carries the film's narrative. The Eurasian hacker destined to save humanity from slavemaster machines presents a cross-marketable composite of Gaff's foppish racial pastiche and Deckard's blank-faced existentialism. Whereas Olmos is distinctly non-white, Reeves passes as white for most non–Asian American audiences, as several scholars have pointed out.[28] Consider, for instance, Wu's description of Reeves's ambiguous racial status: "To the extent that Reeves has not selected whiteness but has stumbled into it, he indicates how whiteness is the default mode. Unless he deviates blatantly from the norm, he is assumed to be white. Even though Reeves is essentially white, the uniformly negative commentary of film critics on his work unwittingly echoes the classic line about Asians. To many reviewers, ironically, he is inscrutable."[29] As Wu suggests, Reeves and the characters he plays are read as default white because their racial identities are not made explicit. At the same time, however, an unconscious acknowledgment of the actor's Asiatic roots curiously underscores reviewers' assessment of his on- and offscreen personae.

We see this paradox at work in *The Matrix*, in which Neo assumes the iconic role of the young, white male hero through his juxtaposition with

Trinity and Morpheus along the lines of gender and racial difference, respectively. Neo also fulfills audience expectations of the action adventure hero, a role that until recently men of color have seldom been allowed to play in Hollywood. In the film he evolves from a passive, feminized object violated by technology to an active, masculinized subject capable of beating the machines at their own game. This transformation is shown primarily through Neo's relationship to his body and through his control over its movements in various spaces.

Ultimately, it is only when he can enter and *become* the body and mind of Agent Smith—namely, when Neo masters the technology behind the Matrix—that we are able to recognize him as the One. Like the hacker cowboys of cyberpunk novels, Neo becomes a (white, masculine) subject by taking on the racial, gendered, and technological traits of others—Morpheus's strength, discipline, and faith, qualities inscribed in his large, black, masculine body; Trinity's abilities to fight and nurture, likewise expressed through her androgynously feminine body—and finally the knowledge of the Matrix itself, information embedded in esoteric computer code that, expressed in Chinese and Japanese script, is culturally coded East Asian.

Neo achieves apotheosis as the One through the help of his strikingly unconventional friends, whose various differences and camera time noticeably diminish as his own powers and confidence increase. Morpheus morphs from a dangerous cyber terrorist, kung fu master, and poststructuralist professor to a battered Rodney King in need of rescue. A cool, sexually ambiguous Trinity opens the film with one of its most stunning action sequences. By the end of the film she has become both girlfriend and mother to the One and sealed this new position in soft romantic lighting with the perfunctory heteronormative kiss—albeit in a gender inversion of the climatic scene in *Sleeping Beauty*. Tank (Marcus Chong), the Nebuchadnezzar's multiracial pilot, is wounded but resurrected to save Neo from the traitorous Cypher (Joe Pantoliano). And his brother (Anthony Ray Parker) is killed, along with the other minor characters, including the only other female in the group, the very butch and Nordic Switch (Belinda McClory), who initially is paired visually with Trinity.

No doubt this racially and sexually diverse crew appeals to a wide spectrum of viewers in various ways. That such difference appears among the principal characters can be seen as politically progressive. That it remains contained within the rules of the Hollywood narrative formula is perhaps not as much so.

A similar paradox is reflected in Neo's fluid sexual and racial identity. The protagonist appears at first glance to be an average, All-American white dude. However, it is important to note the trace of otherness that remains perceptible, if not wholly definable, in this dude. According to Nishime, Neo's otherness is expressed through his metaphorical biraciality, which she describes thus:

> Reeves as Neo, occupies a liminal space within the film. He is the only character who we see move from the world of the matrix into the "real world." Yet he never is at home in either world. More telling are the two re-births in the film. The first comes as he regains consciousness in the "real" world. He barely survives the process and must be brought to life, Frankenstein style, by Morpheus. At the end of the movie . . . he is reborn, or maybe resurrected, by the love of a white woman, Trinity. Thus, within the film's metaphoric logic, Neo is the child of a black father and white mother, doubly re-inforcing a sense of Neo as biracial.[30]

In the next section, following Nishime, I explore how Neo, coded on surface as straight and white, can also be read as queer and nonwhite through his association with the other primary characters in the film, Trinity and Morpheus.

The Hero as Feminized Infant

Neo's love interest is white but with the dark features common to orientalized white women (i.e., pale skin and dark hair and eyes). Neo's phenotypical twinning with Trinity, coupled with his generally passive demeanor and her generally active one, serve to effeminize Neo in ways that differ from Deckard's emasculation in *Blade Runner*. As I discussed in chapter 2, Deckard's appearance and actions recall the hard-boiled detectives of film noir and the stoic loners of the Western, both antihero types working within their own rules, which often contradict those of the societies in which they are confined. External castrating forces (women, technology, corporations, people of color, the law) constantly threaten the masculinity of these types. Here I want to stress that for one's masculinity to be perceived as under threat, it (or the desire to have it) must have existed in the first place. Hence my reference to Deckard as "emasculated."

In contrast, I read Neo as "effeminized" because he does not seem compelled to perform the hard, Anglo-American masculinity Decard tries to pull off, embodied in iconic action characters played by such stars as Kurt Russell, Clint Eastwood, Arnold Schwarzenegger, Sylvester Stallone, and Bruce Willis. Instead Neo, played with Reeves's characteristic minimalism, strongly resembles the male protagonists of anime, which Mary Kittleson describes in the following way: "Heroism in most *manga* and *anime* is internal: heroes must be sincere and they must be selfless, at least at the moment of heroism. It is not necessary for a *manga* or *anime* hero to be an [sic] saint, to fight for the right side, or even to be successful. Anyone who sincerely gives his or her best efforts to almost any task can be a hero."[31]

According to Kittleson, the more ambivalent, internalized representation of the hero in Japanese popular media appeals to North American twenty-something youth in ways that the clear-cut Hollywood action hero cannot. As she explains, "The American heroic ideal often leaves them [members of Generation X] with a choice between denouncing the actions of those they love or finding a rationalization for causes they might find more than slightly questionable. Japan's flawed warrior-heroes offer them an alternative to that choice."[32]

When we are introduced to Neo, he reflects the passivity, ennui, and confusion of these youth: a computer programmer by day and a hacker by night, Thomas Anderson/Neo leads a somnolent existence with no apparent meaning or larger purpose. When his abilities are initially tested, he demonstrates the mixed emotions and actions of most anime heroes. Too scared to follow Morpheus's phone orders to escape using a high-rise scaffold, Neo is captured by the agents while Trinity watches using her motorcycle mirror. Later Neo fails again when he is unable to jump from one roof to another, disappointing the crew and questioning their faith in him as a potential savior. It is only at the end of the film, when Neo acts out of altruistic love for his mentor, friend, and surrogate father, that he proves himself a hero. Even then, his heroism has a certain kind of receptive humility. Reeves's softer, pansexual appeal differs noticeably from that of Hollywood male heroes of the 1980s and the darker, mixed-race heroes of the present, such as Vin Diesel and Dwayne "the Rock" Johnson, characterized by hard bodies and hard actions.

Neo's divergence from action heroes such as Superman, Rambo, and the Terminator is emphasized through his relationship with Trinity. Regardless of Trinity's ultimate containment, she opens the film as a tough, controlled, and utterly empowered woman. With her short, black, slicked-back hair; her tight, muscular body encased in and accentuated by a black vinyl body suit; and dark sunglasses obscuring her soft eyes, Trinity visually defies the "little girl" label of the police supervisor, whose unit she proceeds to pummel with sophisticated "wire fu" punches and kicks. Whereas Reeves resembles the insecure male characters of so many anime films, Moss resembles the stoic, androgynous, dominatrixlike female characters that populate this medium.

In marked contrast to Trinity's stunning, action-filled introduction, in our first encounter with Neo he is sleeping in front of his computer screen, which flashes virtual news reports of terrorism in Chinese, Arabic, and English. The following passage from the shooting script reveals how mired Neo is in technology. Note especially the references to animal and plant bodies in the description of the computer equipment, which grotesquely melds

Carrie-Anne Moss in *The Matrix* (1999). Trinity downloads helicopter piloting skills and prepares to rescue Morpheus with Neo.

the synthetic with the organic, the artificial with the natural: "It is a studio apartment that seems overgrown with technology. Weed-like cable coils everywhere, duct-taped into thickets that wind up and around the legs of several desks. Tabletops are filled with cannibalized equipment that lay open like an autopsied corpse. At the center of this technological rat-nest is NEO, a man who knows more about living inside a computer than outside one."[33]

Throughout the first act of the film and until the second turning point (when Neo and Trinity, wielding "guns, lots of guns," storm the office building where Morpheus is being held captive), Neo's relationship to technology is primarily a receptive, unquestioning one. This characterization of Neo helps set up the thematic thrust of the film and the developmental trajectory of the protagonist from ordinary Everyman to extraordinary Hero. Meanwhile, Neo's physical and emotional passivity also suggests a different form of masculinity, which is somewhat childlike and dependent on a stronger, more active female counterpart.

Until the training scene, we see Neo in physically vulnerable positions relative to the camera that demonstrate his defenseless exposure to a highly technologized environment. This vulnerability becomes most apparent in three scenes during the exposition. In the first scene Neo, representing all rebellious, antiestablishment youth, responds to the agents' request for his cooperation by giving them the finger. As punishment, a layer of skin grows, like mucus, over his mouth, literally rendering him speechless, before the agents implant a techno-organic bug in his stomach. In the second scene Trinity uses a device described as "a cross between a rib separator, speculum, and air compressor" to extract this bug.[34] And in the third scene mercury swiftly crawls up Neo's skin after he touches a mirror while waiting to enter the Matrix. Neo panics as the mercury reaches his face and threatens to transform him into a shiny, technological object—pure surface, like the mirror itself. This image is followed by a sharp cut of Neo waking up, connected to various tubes and types of apparatus, in his pod, where he has been dreaming what he thought was his life.

In all three scenes Neo loses control over his body when it is violated and taken over by alien objects and substances. A certain kind of mind/body split occurs here. Neo, who has considered himself a human subject with free will, suddenly finds himself trapped in his own body, which has been rendered foreign through the intervention of technology. Neo's body is paralyzed and

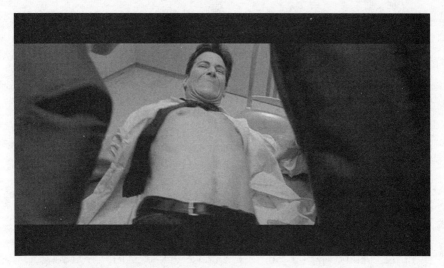

Keanu Reeves in *The Matrix*. Matrix agents literally render Neo speechless as they implant a bug in his stomach.

his subject position threatened when he loses his ability to speak in the first scene and his ability to act in the second and third scenes. The first scene ends with Neo cornered against the wall, sans mouth, by two agents, who throw him shirtless on an examination table to insert the bug through his navel in a clear simulation of gang rape.

In the second scene Neo is forced again to take off his shirt and lie down while Trinity extracts the bug from his stomach with a huge, phallic instrument—half laser syringe and half microscope. The scene recalls the *Alien* movies, not only in the specific way that the alien survives and reproduces (as a parasite in the stomach of a human host) but also in its rare depiction of a tough and capable female leader. Trinity performs what amounts to an abortion on Neo, who unwittingly has functioned as a passive vessel and mediator for agents of the Matrix.

In the third scene Neo's passivity is overtly gendered through the appellations conferred on him by Morpheus and Cypher—Alice in *Alice in Wonderland* and Dorothy in *The Wizard of Oz* (1939), respectively—both lost young girls trying to get back home. Home, for Neo, appears at the end of the symbolic rabbit hole into which he falls after choosing to take the red pill offered by Morpheus, which would give him access to the truth of the Matrix, over the blue one, which would keep him from that truth. Again the abortion trope frames Neo's nightmarish descent into reality. This time Morpheus, playing both doctor and midwife, aborts Neo from the Matrix in order to birth him into the Real World. Unlike the earlier abortion scene, this one is framed in the terminology and iconography of rebirth, as A. Samuel Kimball notes:

> Until Neo is "snatched from the flow of waste" by Morpheus's machine "hovering inside the sewer main," Neo's birth threatens to be an abortion. Indeed, the scene thoroughly intermixes an imagery of intestinal evacuation with the imagery of parturition. If this imagery contaminates the very birthing that releases Neo from the matrix, the action of Morpheus and his crew in saving Neo from excremental oblivion purifies it, refiguring an abortion as a rebirthing.[35]

Neo is reborn when he is unplugged from the Matrix and wakes up to the reality that he has literally been a slave to technology. It is telling here that his chief rescuer is a dangerous black criminal, a hacker–terrorist shaking up the white-dominated world of the Matrix. As mentioned earlier, Morpheus's physical blackness functions as a foil to Neo's ostensible whiteness. At the same time, however, Neo is associated with Morpheus to the extent that he identifies with and desires to be more like him. In *The Matrix* the color black—whether displayed on one's skin or on one's clothing—signifies radical difference from the simulated, false, and emotionless world of the Matrix.

More specifically, the mise-en-scène of the film connects the rebellious, countercultural connotations associated with black skin, black history, and black style to those of the black clothing preferred by working-class anarchists and punks as well as by the avant-garde and the fashion industry, which embraced the color following its popularization by Japanese designers in the 1980s.[36] Alluding and appealing to these various subcultures, blackness as a trope provides a more attractive alternative to the sterile and artificial whiteness of the agents, which stand for the dominant culture. Inasmuch as Morpheus's black body and fly fashion sense define him as a romantic symbol of youth rebellion, Agent Smith's (Hugo Weaving) "organization man" image, completely identical with the images of the other agents, constitutes him as the unromantic icon of the government and corporate status quo.

Hugo Weaving in *The Matrix*. Agent Smith denounces the human race to a chained and tortured Morpheus.

Throughout the film, Neo falls between these two stylized racial poles. The following description of Neo's double life, uttered by Agent Smith during the interrogation scene, sums up the protagonist's liminal position between computer programmer and hacker, dominant culture and subculture, white and black:

> It seems that you have been living two lives. In one life, you are Thomas A. Anderson, program writer for a respectable software company. You have a social security number, you pay your taxes, and you help your landlady carry out her garbage. The other life is lived in computers where you go by the hacker alias Neo, and are guilty of virtually every computer crime we have a law for. One of these lives has a future. One of them does not.[37]

Rather than marginalizing him, as one might expect, Neo's double life (and, to some extent, his double consciousness) paradoxically serves to universalize his plight in the film's overtly multicultural logic.

In this sense, Reeves's embodiment of Neo extends the category of the "dark white male" that Richard Dyer posits in *White*. If, as Dyer suggests,

Blade Runner's Deckard epitomizes the "dark white man," the white male figure whose universality stems from his possessing a tinge of darkness, Neo suggests a reworking of this type in his projection of what one might call the "white dark man." According to Dyer, the darkness in the "dark white man" is manifested physically in a darker skin complexion, eyes, and/or hair color and morally in ambivalent, not so virtuous, thoughts and actions. Furthermore, this coded darkness represents the sexualized racial other that threatens to overwhelm our less than perfect white male hero and, at the same time, endows him with his necessary hetero-masculine edge: "[The darkness] furnishes the heterosexual desire that will rescue whites from sterility while separating such desire from what whiteness aspires to. Dark desires are part of the story of whiteness, but as what the whiteness has to struggle against. Thus it is that the whiteness of white men resides in the tragic quality of their giving way to darkness and the heroism of their channeling or resisting it." Indeed, it is precisely the fatal flaw of the sexualized racial darkness in the protagonist that draws us to him: "The presence of the dark within the white man ... enables him to assume the position as the universal signifier for humanity."[38]

From the beginning of the film we are led to understand that Neo is different from those around him. Neo follows the text instructions on his computer and the tattooed white rabbit to the S&M cyber club where he meets Trinity. She articulates his difference as a desire for something he has not experienced but feels: "I know why you're here, Neo. . . . I know why you hardly sleep, why you live alone and why, night after night, you sit at your computer. . . .The answer is out there, Neo. It's looking for you and it will find you, if you want it to."[39] Later Morpheus tells Neo, "You have come because you know something. What you know you can't explain but you feel it. You've felt it your whole life, felt that something is wrong with the world."[40] The vague sense of discontent that Trinity and Morpheus describe constitutes the internal, invisible tinge of "darkness" in Neo, which draws him to Morpheus and consequently to his destiny.

In the shock of being unplugged from the Matrix and waking up from the dream of false consciousness, Neo is rendered a "free" human subject. Through his physical senses he becomes aware of his individual enslavement and the collective enslavement of humankind by the artificial intelligence that has taken over. However, Neo is not able to fully accept his subject position and its responsibilities until he can translate his awareness into action. It is only when he consciously accepts and embraces his internal difference (which is externalized through the gender and racial differences embodied by Trinity and Morpheus, respectively) that Neo becomes truly free, truly human.

Importantly, freedom also requires Neo's repudiation of the technological other represented by the Matrix and its chief representative, Agent Smith. Neo does not realize his potential as the One until he renames himself in his final fight with Smith. As my later reading of this scene will show, Neo's rejection of Smith ironically requires an identification and subsequent doubling between the two characters—a doubling that demonstrates the complex relationship between race and technology in the film as articulated through oriental style.

Race and Technology in *The Matrix*

A product of new filmmaking technologies—from its bullet-time sequence to its green-screened backgrounds—*The Matrix* ironically promulgates a distinctly anti-technological and politically prophylactic message. The new technology represented explicitly in props and implicitly in special effects grounds the story materially, but the reliance of the storytelling process on technology is erased at the narrative level. At no point in the film is the audience supposed to cheer for the sentinels or the agents, which are merely patrolling computer programs—virtual (unreal) police keeping (real) human slaves contained in the prison of the Matrix.

Although *Blade Runner* thematically suggests the potential for communication and understanding between humans and nonhumans, *The Matrix* celebrates the borders between human and machine as natural and necessary for distinguishing the good (self/human) from the bad (other/technology). After learning that the world as he knows it is not real, Neo is exposed to another, bleaker world that is presented as most definitely real; the two spaces are connected through a liminal training space appropriately called the construct. Divisions between real and unreal spaces are clearly delineated, leaving the ways in which these spaces inform each other unexplored. The same goes for divisions between the humans and the nonhumans. The film never questions the humanity of the ostensibly human subjects who are trapped in the Matrix. To put it a bit differently, the film leads one to assume that there is an essential human being, extricable from the technological web that constitutes his or her sociohistorical contexts.

However, this humanist theme is repeatedly contradicted by the film's mise-en-scène. Along with the overwhelming presence of computer-generated imagery effects and the reliance of the principal characters on various forms of advanced technology, the biological humanity of those characters is never totally established. For example, a certain irony lies in the audience's acceptance of the protagonists as human because most members of Morpheus's crew, including Neo, do not strictly qualify as such. We are told that except for Tank and Dozer, the two black brothers who were born "naturally" of a mother in Zion, the last human city, all of the principal human characters are actually products of genetic engineering. The shocking image of a white fetus being fed human remains intravenously, which Morpheus shows Neo during his TV history lesson, makes it apparent that the bodies of these humans are food made to be consumed by the machines.

The appearance, attitudes, and actions of Morpheus and his crew must differ noticeably from those of the beings trapped in the Matrix in order to counter their own cyborgian status. In this context, the racial diversity of the crew contrasted with the predominantly white racial composition of the agents and those trapped in the Matrix takes on new significance. Again, following Nishime's formulation of Neo as metaphorically biracial, one could posit that as "Thomas Anderson" he is white in the Matrix and as "Neo" he is black in the "real world." After Neo chooses the red pill and learns to distinguish between truth and appearance, he enters a rigorous training period in which Morpheus tries to reprogram his mind to follow suit. Here it is significant that a stately black male leader educates Neo and the audience on the historical roots of humankind's current oppressed state. The figure—and later the body—of this particular character links mass technological subjugation in the future with the historical experience of black slavery in the United States, a specific form of racialized subjugation consigned to the past.

Ideologically, then, both *Blade Runner* and *The Matrix* reflect a dominant white liberal perspective of racial difference. Both films appropriate the moral power of the slave position without acknowledging or dealing with its historical baggage. And they reduce the brutal colonialist roots of slavery to an easy affective strategy whose purpose is to secure audience identification with certain characters. The difference is that in *The Matrix* the specter of African enslavement is embodied in and directly addressed by black actors. Along with Morpheus, the Oracle and the two "homegrown" brothers embody the symbolic blackness that *Blade Runner* rendered metaphorically through the hyperwhite, artificial bodies of the replicants.

What role, then, does oriental style play in this world of black bodies and white technology? In the previous chapter I traced the evolution of this style by looking at its roots in the U.S. reception of anime and martial arts movies. I discussed the ways in which the incorporation of these media in Hollywood cinema has resulted in action films that simultaneously technologize and orientalize nonwhite bodies, spaces, and cultures. In the rest of this chapter I look at two key action scenes in *The Matrix* that illustrate this particular mode of representing racial difference. The first is Neo's sparring session with Morpheus after martial arts combat programs have been downloaded into his brain. The second is his showdown with Agent Smith in the subway station where he dies and is reborn a second time, this time as the One. I focus on the implicitly and explicitly racialized ways in which the characters interact in these scenes in order to arrive at some conclusions about how Asian, African, and Anglo-American identities in the film are constructed through the popular discourse of multicultural Orientalism.

Turning Black: Neo Fights Morpheus

The first scene opens with Neo lying in his chair in the *Nebuchadnezzar* hovercraft, eyes moving rapidly under their lids, as he learns combat skills through a training program that Tank downloads into his brain. The computer screen flashes titles such as Savate, Jujitsu, Ken Po, and Drunken Boxing. When Morpheus asks how Neo is doing, Tank responds, "Ten hours straight. He's a machine." When Neo wakes up, he looks more awake than he has so far in the film. According to the description in the shooting script, "Neo's body spasms and relaxes as his eyes open, breath hissing from his lips. He looks like he has just orgasmed."[41]

Morpheus initiates Neo into his new body and self in a virtual Japanese dojo that resembles similar spaces in video games such as *Virtua Fighter* and *Tekken*. Both characters are dressed in traditional *gi*, Morpheus in black and Neo in white with a black belt. The lighting is soft and serene; after medium close-ups of the characters in shot reverse shot, the camera cuts to a still long shot of the figures in profile as they assume their stances. In its spare and static composition, the image resembles still, blocked scenes from noh theatre.

The effect is broken by the sound of a gong, which is followed by New Age–influenced Asiatic music. Neo warms up like a boxer, looking cocky in response to Morpheus's "Hit me, if you can." Neo's fast and intense moves, which look "like a Jackie Chan movie at high speed," contrast with Morpheus's smooth and graceful ones as he effortlessly blocks the protégé's strikes.[42] Morpheus throws Neo to the ground. As he gets back up, the music shifts to loud industrial; the camera cuts to the ship where the crew members have left dinner to watch the fight on the screen. During the fight, the camera cuts in closely and frequently to Neo's movements, illustrating his neophyte speed and energy. Despite his technical skills, however, Neo loses to Morpheus after both engage in some spectacular slow-motion "wire fu."

Where is the Orient in this scene? Everywhere and nowhere. Here I return to the idea of yellowface, which Robert Lee defines as follows:

Yellowface marks the Asian body as unmistakably Oriental; it sharply defines the Oriental in a racial opposition to whiteness. Yellowface

Laurence Fishburne and Keanu Reeves in *The Matrix*. Morpheus and Neo spar in the virtual dojo training program.

exaggerates 'racial' features that have been designated as 'Oriental,' such as 'slanted' eyes, overbite, and mustard-yellow skin color. Only the racialized Oriental is yellow; Asians are not. . . . What does Yellowface signify? Race is a mode of placing cultural meaning on the body. Yellowface marks the Oriental as *indelibly alien*.[43]

Here Lee draws an implicit parallel between blackface and yellowface by stressing the role of the excessively racialized physical body in these performances. Asian American scholars such as Joseph Won and Jeffrey Ow have noted that although blackface is no longer socially tolerable in the post–civil rights United States, yellowface continues to be an acceptable mode of representing people of Asian descent.[44] For instance, the buck-toothed caricatures of Chinese laundrymen featured in the 2002 line of Abercrombie & Fitch tee shirts and the 2003 Wal-Mart Halloween costumes of Filipina mail-order brides typify contemporary yellowface as a form of anti-Asian racism that attempts to masquerade as supposedly harmless entertainment.

It is important, however, to distinguish between the kind of cultural interpretation, translation, and disidentification at work in these yellowface representations and the yellowface that Reeves and Fisburne are performing in this scene. The serious manner in which the characters execute their kung fu moves, the self-consciously virtual nature of the dojo in which the scene is set, and the important narrative function of the scene in the film's plot and the development of Neo's character all suggest a more complex blend of cultural and racial appropriation and homage than allowed by present definitions of yellowface.

How does racial difference signify, then, in the orientalized virtual space of this particular scene? On one level, the fight sequence reiterates the mentor–student relationship of such cinematic bildungsromans as *Star Wars* and *The Karate Kid*, where the student is a young white male and the teacher some kind of racial or alien other. As discussed in chapter 3, the teacher in this formula functions both as a surrogate parent and as a kind of technological prosthetic; his exotic, esoteric knowledge is transferred to the student, who, we know, ultimately will surpass the teacher by fulfilling his preordained destiny using that knowledge.

Although the idea of the mentor as prosthetic/parent generally holds in this instance, it is challenged slightly by alternative interpretations of the scene by those Asian American viewers (and dedicated Keanu Reeves fans of all races) who are aware of Reeves's mixed Asian ancestry. In this case, Neo might be seen as both white and nonwhite. His phenotype hints at the trace of Asian blood, while his narrative and symbolic role as the slacker hacker codes him as white in dominant cinematic circles. In either case, the scene shows Neo shaking off his old self and poised at the brink of becoming something different and better.

Here Neo becomes symbolically black in two ways: first, *through* his close association with Morpheus as mentor and surrogate father, and second, *against* his former identity, coded white through its association with the Matrix. In the process of sparring with Morpheus, Thomas Anderson of the predominantly white establishment of the Matrix is replaced by Neo of the predominantly black underground resistance. This racial and political conversion occurs significantly through virtual, orientalized objects, spaces, and performances—from costumes and props to music and setting to martial arts action sequences and *manga*-inspired storyboarding.

Containing the Virtual Orient: Neo Fights Agent Smith

In the second scene, Neo has matured considerably: he has risked his life to save Morpheus even after the Oracle has told him he is not "the One." Both Morpheus and Trinity have escaped the Matrix safely, and Neo is about to follow suit when Agent Smith stops him in a subway tunnel. Instead of running, Neo decides to stay and fight: "In his eyes we see something different, something fixed and hard like a gunfighter's resolve. There is no past or future in these eyes. There is only what is."[45] The camera looks up at Neo, reflecting his increased power and confidence, and cuts to a close-up of Smith before reverting to a setup that clearly alludes to the spaghetti Westerns of Sergio Leone.

We get an extreme close-up of Neo's hand on his gun at hip level, which cuts to a long shot of Smith and Neo facing each other in the classic setup of the Western duel. Western composition meets Eastern action as the characters rush at each other in slow motion bullet time, firing their guns simultaneously. The shot ends in an obvious homage to John Woo referencing Leone, with each character pressing his gun to the other's head. The sadistic homoerotic undertones of the fight are spelled out in the following description of this pose: "They freeze in a kind of embrace; *Neo sweating, panting, Agent Smith machine-calm.* Agent Smith smiles."[46]

Smith's smile fades as it becomes clear that both men are out of bullets. Smith throws his gun to the side; Neo follows. The two fight hand to hand, displaying the cinematic kung fu of choreographer Yuen Wo Ping. Neo delivers a high kick to Smith, breaking his sunglasses. We see Smith's eyes, "ice blue."[47] Smith rises and fights Neo with more fervor; soon Neo is hurt, his mouth spouting blood. In another obvious homage—this time to Bruce Lee—he gets up, wipes the blood away, assumes his stance, and repeats the famous "come hither" hand signal that Morpheus used earlier in the construct. The fight resumes. Neo appears to have lost as Smith pummels him against the wall with blurred fists and throws him onto the subway tracks as a train is about to arrive. We hear its sound, "like an animal cry, a burst of high-speed metal grinding against metal."[48] The train functions as a symbol of technology, another extension of the Matrix, which threatens to kill Neo. In response to Smith's prediction of Neo's (and humankind's) death to the machines ("Good-bye, Mr. Anderson"), Neo rises up, declares his new identity ("My name is Neo"), and throws Smith on the tracks instead.

Like a monster in a horror movie, however, Smith refuses to die. Instead another chase sequence, this time through Chinatown—a not-so-explicit reference to a similar scene in *Ghost in the Shell* (1996)—ensues before the final showdown between protagonist and antagonist, "black" racial other and white technological other. The chase ends when Neo opens the door in an abandoned apartment to face Smith, who shoots him, first in the stomach and then successively in the chest and the head as the camera cuts to a long shot. Neo's monitor goes flat in the ship, signaling his death. Trinity, however, refuses to believe he is dead, using the solipsistic logic that the One she loves cannot be dead. And of course it is her faith in her love for Neo, and his reciprocal love for her, that brings him back to life a second time, this time as the all-powerful One.

The One has some pretty amazing powers: he can stop a stream of bullets in midair and effortlessly block the agents' mechanical punches, all through his newfound ability to see the "real" world of the Matrix, which is comprised of computer code: "Neo looks out, now able to see through the curtain of the Matrix. For a moment, the walls, the floor, even the Agents become a rushing stream of code."[49] Later the One destroys Smith by entering his body through his navel as a streak of blinding white light and shattering him from the inside. Lumps move under Smith's skin, followed by an implosion that sends bits of the former Agent flying, leaving the One standing calmly, flexing his new muscles. The scene reenacts the earlier violation of Neo's body in the interrogation room when the Agents slipped the grisly techno-organic bug into Neo, again through his navel. This time, however, the roles are reversed. Neo, the human, has defeated the Matrix, the machine.

Or has he? Even as this sequence references and replays the narrative convention of man overcoming monster, it also hints that the man himself is part of the monster, and vice versa. In the subway fight the script describes Smith as "machine-calm."[50] A similar kind of calm settles over Neo after he has reawakened as the One. Meanwhile, Smith, whose machine qualities have started degenerating through his contact with Morpheus, becomes increasingly emotional, and indeed he is hysterical by the time the One enters and kills him (at least until he is resurrected for the sequels). Reinforcing the link between the natural and the technological worlds, hybrid imagery is used not only to describe the train that almost kills Neo (its sound that of an "animal cry") but also the bullets that Neo stops in midair (like "a cloud of obedient bees").[51] In this light, not much seems to have changed: the world

Paul Goddard, Hugo Weaving, and Robert Taylor in *The Matrix*. Neo sees the agents in and as computer code after his transformation into the One.

has not become a Luddite utopia with the coming of the One. The terms of the game remain the same. Technology remains an integral part of the fight. The difference is that the One exercises control over the technological other in a way that his previous incarnations, Thomas Anderson and Neo, could not.

Neo's ability to defeat the machines *by thinking and acting like them* epitomizes techno-orientalist stereotypes that have historically been associated with Asian Americans, aimed, for instance, at Chinese American immigrants in the nineteenth century and Japanese Americans during World War II. The stereotype, however, seems to work somewhat differently here. Like earlier Hollywood representations of Chinese coolies and Japanese kamikaze pilots, Neo is a hybrid of human and machine. Existing initially as "food" for the machines, he is inextricably inked to them through the plugs that remain in the back of his head, his extraordinary hacker skills, and his doubling with Agent Smith, which plays out further in the sequels. However, unlike past techno-orientalist representations of Asian American masculinity, Neo comes to stand in for the very figure of the human, in large part *due to*—rather than despite—his racially (both black and white) and ontologically (both human and machine) hybrid status. To be more specific, what distinguishes Neo from Morpheus and the other rebels—and ultimately convinces everyone that he is the One—is his ability to see the world of the Matrix for what it is, namely, a virtual fantasy composed of computer code.

This requires an ability to mimic and pass as the enemy other—a character trait central to many racial stereotypes specific to Asian Americans. Once he is able to *experience* the code as mere data, Neo, the consummate hacker, can control and contain his enemies effortlessly, a position of power usually given to white male protagonists. In other words, according to the film, it is precisely the trait of mutability—the ability to move across racial, social, and ontological boundaries via the conditional status of the racially ambiguous model minority—that will save the human race.

Conclusion

The scenes discussed here from *The Matrix* demonstrate the dialectical movement between West and East, between whiteness and nonwhiteness, that has always existed in American Orientalism. They also exemplify increasingly complex modes of representing the relationships among oriental, racial, and technological others in popular media culture.

Forms of Orientalism currently appearing in Hollywood derive from and reproduce, but also rework, some of the imperialist tendencies of the West, which have been well documented in postcolonial, ethnic, and Asian American studies. This study supplements existing postcolonial scholarship by addressing a critical silence around the ambivalences that fundamentally structure and shape orientalist discourse. Here I am referring primarily to two modes of orientalist expression present in Asian set and themed films such as *Crouching Tiger, Hidden Dragon, Lost in Translation, The Last Samurai,* and *Memoirs of a Geisha* as well as in other contemporary movies that incorporate Asian signifiers in the vein of *The Matrix,* such as the hip-hop kung fu movies discussed earlier.

The first mode occurs when imperialist tendencies are expressed in the clothing of liberal multiculturalism, the second when such tendencies are unacknowledged or acknowledged with an ironic wink. It is important to note the connection between the two modes: namely, the references to East Asia in contemporary Hollywood films continue to be expressed through a Western perspective—whether oriental style is used to express the desire of the viewer for an exoticized locale or to indicate the viewer's familiarity with East Asian cultures.

The Matrix illustrates the eminent marketability of both kinds of popular cinematic Orientalism. The movie appealed to a broad audience base, from college youth, who were drawn to the fast-paced action video game template, to their professors, who were excited to see Baudrillard, Plato, and Lao Tzu referenced on the big screen. Its originality, to a large extent based on its appropriation of East Asian popular media and culture, was primarily attributed to the filmmakers' ability to translate this mediated Orient for the Hollywood audience. In the past several years, *The Matrix* and subsequent science-fiction and action films, television programs, and new media aimed at older youth, have popularized what I have been calling oriental style. Although this increased visibility of hybridized East Asian popular culture suggests greater opportunities for artistic and commercial exchange between East Asia and the United States through visual culture, it also limits the ways in which the former is perceived.

After listening to a condensed version of this chapter, an undergraduate Asian American student at the University of Oklahoma asked me if I thought *The Matrix* signaled a positive step for Asian American representation. When I deflected the question back at him, the student responded that since the film and others like it have come out, he has been asked more than ever by non-Asian peers if he knows kung fu. He did not think *The Matrix* was such a good thing because, even as it rendered him visible—and some might say in a not necessarily negative way—this visibility was limited to the question "Do you know kung fu?"

Filmmakers such as, Tarantino, and others may be reflecting and constructing new, perhaps more positive, modes of relating to East Asia for Americans. Yet it is telling that the representations of Asia they privilege derive from anime and martial arts, which emphasize violence, technology, and a rather inhumane (if ultrahip) future. Such oriental styles influence not only how Americans of all races perceive Asia but also how people of Asian descent are led to see themselves, as my student's question made clear. Although in *The Matrix* the Wachowski brothers made a laudable attempt to show a world without boundaries, they were unable to do so in the film's sequels, its video game, its toys, and its comics.

What may be needed instead, as I suggested in my response to the student's question, is the production and distribution of more films in which racial and ethnic styles emerge from a deep knowledge of and respectful engagement with the histories, cultures, and peoples they showcase. Perhaps when the stories behind such styles are told with the right amount of precision and passion, they will give all of us a much-anticipated glimpse into past, present, and future worlds that *The Matrix* can ultimately neither see nor imagine.

Afterword

Imagination is the politics of dreams.

—Sherman Alexie, "Imagining the Reservation," in *The Lone Ranger and Tonto Fistfight in Heaven*

A decade after the release of *The Matrix,* Asiatic tropes and imagery permeate the popular culture of a nation that, on the surface, seems devoted to acknowledging and celebrating its racial and ethnic diversity. Most nonwhite Americans, meanwhile, know the limitations of this mediated multiculturalism, which falsely advertises the achievement of a colorblind meritocracy wherein people of color have come to possess the social and political privileges taken for granted by the majority of white Americans.

Yet these limitations do not wholly diminish the impact of the growing presence of nonwhite bodies, cultures, and spaces in U.S. popular media generally and film specifically. Although the commercial visibility of historically marginalized groups does not directly translate to an increase in their political power, it functions as a broad cultural barometer of current and future attitudes about those groups in the popular imaginary. Furthermore, as technologies in various fields become ever more advanced, these commodified images of difference and the collective narratives attached to them will undoubtedly come to play an even more prominent role in forming our common perceptions of ourselves.

In *Yellow Future* I have examined the shifting political dynamics around the presence of the marginalized in the stories and spectacles of contemporary Hollywood cinema. More precisely, I have traced Hollywood's fascinated gaze upon East Asian cities, peoples, and cultures and tried to show the complex ways in which that gaze transforms them into virtual projections of a technologized and dystopic near future—the not-so-bright "yellow future" toward which the United States, according to the orientalist logic of the films discussed, seems to be headed.

What I have not addressed and what subsequent research might illuminate is the countering gaze, namely, Asian and Asian American movies that return and resist, reproduce and rework the elements of Hollywood-manufactured oriental style. Examples of such movies include, among many others, Taiwanese American filmmaker Justin Lin's cross-over film about delinquent Asian American youth, *Better Luck Tomorrow* (2002); Thai filmmaker Prachya Pinkaew's postcolonial martial arts movie, *Ong-bak* (2003/2004); Korean filmmaker Park Chan-wook's clever and controversial thriller, *Oldboy* (2003/2005); and Hong Kong filmmaker Stephen Chow's generically enigmatic comedy, *Kung Fu/Kung Fu Hustle* (2004/2005), which humorously alludes to action scenes and special-effects techniques from the *Matrix* movies.[1] Well received in the United States for Asian and, in Lin's case, Asian American productions, all four films draw on the same kinds of East Asian popular media—*manga,* anime, and martial arts movies—which stylistically characterize an ever-growing variety of current popular media, from music videos to TV cartoons to videos on YouTube.

What, then, differentiates Asian-produced media that reference oriental style from the celebratory yellowface of non-Asian-produced media, which may seem, at least to non-Asian viewers and consumers, to be engaged in similar forms of appropriation and homage? One could respond that people of Asian descent bring a distinctly Asian sensibility to their performance of this style because they are intimately familiar with Asian culture. They speak Asian languages, eat Asian foods, and have a firm grasp of Asian histories, aesthetics, and etiquette. Although this kind of essentialist response would make the act of authenticating certain kinds of representations over others much easier, it fails to hold when one takes into account recent developments in the two realms on which I have centered: Hollywood filmmaking with regard to its representations of the Asiatic and the racial and cultural politics underlying the continual evolution of Asian America.

As I discussed in earlier chapters, Hollywood is more explicitly interconnected with other entertainment media and foreign countries than ever before, because the majority of its revenue now comes from ancillary and foreign markets. Such economic factors must be acknowledged when trying to make sense of Hollywood's present enthrallment with Asia, as reflected in the increasing number of North American, Asian, and European co-productions; Hollywood remakes of Asian films; and Asian filmmakers, such as Gurinder Chadha, Ang Lee, and Justin Lin, helming transnational film properties.

Asian and Asian diasporic filmmakers, producers, and distributors adopt and adapt various modes of strategic essentialism to achieve theatrical release and distribution for their films in the United States, thereby gaining international recognition for these films. At the same time, Hollywood filmmakers, producers, and distributors, on the constant lookout for new ideas to satiate an ever more diverse (and diverse-minded) U.S. audience, not only borrow freely from but also actively collaborate with their counterparts in Asia. The result is a cultural and economic feedback loop that is exemplified in the previously mentioned Asian and Asian American films along with U.S. films such as the *Matrix* series and the *Kill Bill* movies. This kind of cultural mixing, expressed through shared aesthetic styles, tastes, and sensibilities, strongly questions the notion of unadulterated authentic Asiatic subjectivities on the big screen.

Purist notions of racial, ethnic, and cultural authenticity also break down offscreen, within the fissures and contradictions that define Asian American identity in the early twenty-first century. Here I return, once again, to Palumbo-Liu's notion of "Asian/American," which neatly corresponds to the immense diversity that has come to characterize this particular racialized identity in the United States. "Asian/American," always already transnational, diasporic, and virtual, has grown even more so in recent years due to the increased visibility of differences within the community regarding race and ethnicity, sexual orientation, political affiliation, class, generation, and region and to the increasing presence of Asiatic representations in the dominant popular media, especially the Internet. Scholars such as Lisa Lowe, David Eng, Lisa Nakamura, Wendy Chun, Rachel Lee, and Cynthia Sau-ling Wong have eloquently discussed various aspects of these developments and considered their consequences for the future of the Asian American community and the discipline of Asian American studies.[2]

In her landmark essay "Heterogeneity, Hybridity, and Multiplicity: Marking Asian American Differences," Lowe proposes that recognition of the many differences within Asian American groups in the United States can provide a more fluid identity position for its members, at once ethnically specific yet open enough for them to identify with other groups. Her theoretical model challenges the binary of nationalism and assimilation seen in earlier Asian American activist literature and scholarship by suggesting we take elements of Asian American identity and experience that have been denigrated by the dominant culture as nonhuman or not quite human—elements such as fragmentation, division, contradiction, multiplicity, and adaptability—using them instead to develop alternative definitions for such concepts as nation and human, community and solidarity. Instead of following vertical models of community formation that emphasize a cohesive, unified, and static self linked to others through fixed genealogical ties, Lowe imagines Asian Americans as members of a horizontal network of multiple, constantly changing selves for whom blood lines matter less than common interests, politics, and goals.[3]

Lowe's emphasis on the horizontal to rethink Asian American recalls Benedict Anderson's use of the horizontal in his idea of the imagined community as a blueprint for the modern nation and contemporary forms of nationalism, which emerged in part through the wide dissemination and consumption of print media such as newspapers and novels.[4] Our shift to an ever-growing emphasis on electronic and digital media has taken the connection between horizontality and community discussed by Lowe and Anderson a step further. More to the point, the horizontal practices of film production and consumption that characterize contemporary Hollywood within a web of globally interconnected entertainment media promote and sustain a postmodern transnational system of cultural exchange. This system—a new kind of imagined and imagining audience—is maintained less through the textual language of linear print narratives and more through the visual and visceral language of style, affect, and performance, epitomized in the notion of oriental style.

Rather than condemning this sometimes unabashedly commercial lingua franca, which is spoken predominantly by younger media audiences and producers, we need to develop more sophisticated critical ways to examine the relationship between the formal terms of this language and its ideological messages, especially with regard to representations of race and ethnicity. In my mind, this goal is crucial if our work in ethnic studies, media studies, and cultural studies is to have use value outside the academy—that is, to provide those who consume and produce popular media with the critical tools necessary not just to analyze but to actively shape changing attitudes about difference in an increasingly unstable and virtual world.

Acknowledgments

As anyone who has done it knows, writing an academic book is hard work. I feel lucky to have stumbled across a topic that still interests me and to have received the institutional support to develop that topic into a book. I have many people to thank and apologize in advance for any unconscious omissions.

First and foremost, I thank Richard Morrison at the University of Minnesota Press, who has been unfailingly encouraging through the evolution of this project, and Adam Brunner, who patiently answered all my nervous e-mails and shepherded the final manuscript to completion. Deep thanks as well to the anonymous readers who provided excellent, spot-on criticism; I tried to incorporate their suggestions in the following pages.

The idea for *Yellow Future* grew out of my dissertation in the Department of Radio–TV–Film at the University of Texas at Austin. My dissertation was made possible through the William T. Livingston Dissertation Fellowship, and I am grateful to my advisers, John D. H. Downing and S. Craig Watkins, as well as my committee members, Charles Ramírez Berg, Mia Carter, James Kyung-Jin Lee, and Thomas G. Schatz. I thank all my teachers at the University of Texas, in particular John for constantly reminding me through his intellectual openness, warmth, and humor that a "life of the mind" is still possible; Craig for demonstrating how to represent with grace and generosity; Tom for showing me how to write both critically and passionately about movies; and Jim for nurturing my academic and political investment in Asian American studies. I also thank Karin Wilkins and Richard Lewis, teachers who became wonderful friends; the lovely ladeez of the Austin Project for witnessing and helping me find voice; and my friends in graduate school, who helped me pull through and get out, especially Carlos Beceiro, Mary Beltrán, Rana Emerson, Justin Garson, Mocha Jean Herrup, Rebecca Lorins, Casey McKittrick, Rosanna Brillantes Meyer, Doug Norman,

Scott Nyerges, Henry Puente, P. J. Raval, Aimee Roundtree, and Lee Sparks, as well as my former students Robert Chu, Jennifer Malone, and Vanat Sermpol, who have since become good friends.

Along with what I learned in my doctoral program, much of my education has come from presenting papers and attending panels at academic conferences, including meetings of the American Studies Association, the Association for Asian American Studies, the Society for Cinema and Media Studies, the International Communication Association, MIT2, and Traffic and Diaspora at Wesleyan University. I am intellectually indebted to the generous scholars I met at these academic forums and others, including Kim Alidio, Lisa Brooten, Anne Soon Choi, Sylvia Chong, Shilpa Davé, David Desser, Peter Feng, Camilla Fojas, Neville Hoad, Lynn Itagaki, Marilyn Ivy, L. S. Kim, Christina Klein, Robert Ku, Glenn Man, Anita Mannur, Glen Mimura, Lisa Nakamura, Susan Napier, LeiLani Nishime, Tasha Oren, Kent Ono, Lynn Schofield and Celine Parreñas Shimizu.

I presented versions of this book at Southern Illinois University as part of the Global Media Research Center Speaker Series in 2007 and in 2008 as part of the U.S. Studies Centre lecture series and the Department of Gender and Cultural Studies seminar series at the University of Sydney. I thank the audience members at these talks for their helpful comments, questions, and advice.

I wrote most of *Yellow Future* while an assistant professor in the Honors College at the University of Oklahoma, where I received research support through the Reach for Excellence endowment and a Junior Faculty summer fellowship in 2004. I thank the University of Oklahoma, the Honors College, and the deans of the college during my time there, Robert Griswold and Robert Con Davis-Undiano. I am grateful to my former colleagues Julia Ehrhardt, Randy Lewis, and Circe Strum and to my third-year reviewers, Clemencia Rodriguez and Robert Warrior, for reading and providing terrific comments on various drafts of the manuscript. My students were a joy to teach, and I thank them for engaging so passionately in the classroom and compelling me to rethink many of my own intellectual and political assumptions.

Deep gratitude goes to the friends who supported and inspired me during my time in Norman, Oklahoma: Carlos Beceiro, Ray Canoy, Anne Choi, Julia Ehrhardt, Yoshiko Fukushima, Andy Horton, Catherine John, Randolf

Lewis, Heidi Mau, Carolyn Morgan, Chris Nichols, Doug Norman, Joanna Rapf, Tara Rodgers, Clemencia Rodriguez, Geoboo Song, and Brian Thompson. In particular I thank Tara for the brilliant and cathartic long-distance conversations; Brian and Chris for stimulating discussions about movies and many other things; Julia and Randy for being great colleagues and coteachers; and Catherine for being such a wonderful "big sister," reminding me always that I am so much more than my work.

The decision to move halfway around the world for a position at the University of Sydney was not an easy one, but I am glad that I made it. I thank my former head of school, Duncan Ivison, and my chair, Catherine Driscoll, as well as my amazing colleagues and the talented honors and postgraduate students in Gender and Cultural Studies for welcoming me into an intellectual community that is lively, nurturing, and fun. I especially thank Gilbert Caluya, Natalya Lusty, Elspeth Probyn, Kane Race, and Rebecca Suter for reading various drafts of a seemingly never-ending introduction and my new friends here for supporting me as I sought closure and transformation in another hemisphere.

Finally, I thank from the bottom of my heart the two most important people in my life, my mother, June Park, and my brother, Herbert Park, for their tough love, constant laughter, and unwavering faith in me.

Notes

Introduction

1. Thomas Foster, *The Souls of Cyberfolk: Posthumanism as Vernacular Theory* (Minneapolis: University of Minnesota Press, 2005), xvi.

2. Seminal studies on Asian stereotypes in Hollywood cinema include Eugene Franklin Wong, *On Visual Media Racism: Asians in the American Motion Pictures* (New York: Arno Press, 1978), and Gina Marchetti, *Romance and the "Yellow Peril": Race, Sex, and Discursive Strategies in Hollywood Fiction* (Berkeley: University of California Press, 1994). The following books touch on the topic in larger studies on Asian American film and culture: Russell Leong, ed., *Moving the Image: Independent Asian Pacific American Media Arts 1970–1990* (Los Angeles: UCLA Asian American Studies Center Press, 1992); Dorinne Kondo, *About Face: Performing Race in Fashion and Theater* (New York: Routledge, 1997); Jun Xing, *Asian America through the Lens: History, Representations, and Identities* (Lanham, Md.: AltaMira Press, 1998); Traise Yamamoto, *Masking Selves, Making Subjects: Japanese American Women, Identity, and the Body* (Berkeley: University of California Press, 1999); Darrell Hamamoto and Sandra Liu, eds., *Countervisions: Asian American Film Criticism* (Philadelphia: Temple University Press, 2000); Peter Feng ed., *Screening Asian Americans* (New Brunswick, N.J.: Rutgers University Press, 2002); Peter Feng, *Identities in Motion: Asian American Film and Video* (Durham, N.C.: Duke University Press, 2002); Celine Parreñas Shimizu, *The Hypersexuality of Race: Performing Asian/American Women on Screen and Scene* (Durham, N.C.: Duke University Press, 2007); and Glen Mimura, *Ghostlife of Third Cinema: Asian American Film and Video* (Minneapolis: University of Minnesota Press, 2009).

3. Lisa Nakamura, *Cybertypes: Race, Ethnicity, and Identity on the Internet* (New York: Routledge, 2002), 14–22.

1. Style, Visibility, Future

1. Edward Said, *Orientalism* (New York: Pantheon Books, 1978), 12.

2. Ibid., 49–53, 207.

3. Lisa Lowe, *Critical Terrains: French and British Orientalisms* (Ithaca, N.Y.: Cornell University Press, 1991), 3, note 3.

4. Michel Foucault, *Discipline and Punish: The Birth of the Prison*, trans. Alan Sheridan (New York: Vintage Books, 1995), 182–84.

5. Said, *Orientalism*, 205–22.

6. See Gayatri Spivak, *In Other Worlds: Essays in Cultural Politics* (New York: Routledge, 1988); Reina Lewis, *Gendering Orientalism: Race, Femininity and Representation* (London: Routledge, 1996); David Eng, *Racial Castration: Managing Masculinity in Asian America* (Durham, N.C.: Duke University Press, 2001); and Sara Ahmed, *Queer Phenomenology: Orientations, Objects, Others* (Durham, N.C.: Duke University Press, 2006).

7. Said, *Orientalism*, 6–7, 14, emphasis in original.

8. See Robert G. Lee, *Orientals: Asian Americans in Popular Culture* (Philadelphia: Temple University Press, 1999); John Kuo Wei Tchen, *New York before Chinatown: Orientalism and the Shaping of American Culture 1776–1882* (Baltimore: Johns Hopkins University Press, 1999); Sheng-mei Ma, *The Deathly Embrace: Orientalism and Asian American Identity* (Minneapolis: University of Minnesota Press, 2000); Henry Yu, *Thinking Orientals: Migration, Contact, and Exoticism in Modern America* (New York: Oxford University Press, 2001); Christina Klein, *Cold War Orientalism: Asia in the Middlebrow Imagination, 1945–1962* (Berkeley: University of California Press, 2003); Mari Yoshihara, *Embracing the East: White Women and American Orientalism* (New York: Oxford University Press, 2003); Karen Leong, *The China Mystique: Pearl S. Buck, Anna May Wong, Mayling Soong, and the Transformation of American Orientalism* (Berkeley: University of California Press, 2005); Colleen Lye, *America's Asia: Racial Form and American Literature, 1893–1945* (Princeton, N.J.: Princeton University Press, 2005); Shilpa Davé, LeiLani Nishime, and Tasha Oren, eds., *East Main Street: Asian American Popular Culture* (New York: New York University Press, 2005).

9. Said, *Orientalism*, 16–19.

10. David Palumbo-Liu, *Asian/American: Historical Crossings of a Racial Frontier* (Stanford, Calif.: Stanford University Press, 1999), 1, emphasis in original.

11. Aiwa Ong, *Flexible Citizenship: The Cultural Logistics of Transnationality* (Durham, N.C.: Duke University Press, 1999), 6–7.

12. See Hamid Naficy, ed., *Home, Exile, Homeland: Film, Media, and the Politics of Place* (New York: Routledge, 1998); Hamid Naficy, *An Accented Cinema: Exilic and Diasporic Filmmaking* (Princeton, N.J.: Princeton University Press, 2001); and Ella Shohat and Robert Stam, eds., *Multiculturalism, Postcoloniality and Transnational Media* (New Brunswick, N.J.: Rutgers University Press, 2003).

13. Benedict Anderson, *Imagined Communities: Reflections on the Origin and Spread of Nationalism* (London: Verso, 1991), 1–46.

14. David Morley and Kevin Robins, *Spaces of Identity: Global Media, Electronic Landscapes and Cultural Boundaries* (London: Routledge, 1995), 147–73.

15. William Wu, *The Yellow Peril: Chinese Americans in American Fiction 1850–1940* (Hamden, Conn.: Archon Books, 1982), 1.

16. Richard Thompson, *The Yellow Peril: 1890–1924* (New York: Arno Press, 1978), 1–62.

17. Ibid., 153, 160.

18. Morley and Robins, *Spaces of Identity*, 152–53.

19. Paul Kennedy, *The Rise and Fall of the Great Powers: Economic Change and Military Conflict from 1500 to 2000* (New York: Random House, 1987), 462–63.

20. Thomas Foster, *The Souls of Cyberfolk: Posthumanism as Vernacular Theory* (Minneapolis: University of Minnesota Press, 2005), xiii–xvi, 1–48.

21. Pam Rosenthal, "Jacked In: Fordism, Cyberpunk, Marxism," *Socialist Review* 21 (1991): 85.

22. Wendy Chun, *Control and Freedom: Power and Paranoia in the Age of Fiber Optics* (Cambridge, MA: MIT Press, 2006), 172–77.

23. Mike Featherstone and Roger Burrows, eds., *Cyberspace/Cyberbodies/Cyberpunk: Cultures of Technological Embodiment* (London: Sage, 1995), 7.

24. Ibid., viii–ix.

25. Istvan Csicsery-Ronay Jr., "Cyberpunk and Neuromanticism," in *Storming the Reality Studio: A Casebook of Cyberpunk and Postmodern Science Fiction*, ed. Larry McCaffery (Durham, N.C.: Duke University Press, 1991), 183.

26. See Nicola Nixon, "Cyberpunk: Preparing the Ground for Revolution or Keeping the Boys Satisfied?" *Science-Fiction Studies* 19 (1992): 224; Mimi Nguyen, "Tales of an Asiatic Geek Girl: *Slant* from Paper to Pixels," in *Technicolor: Race, Technology, and Everyday Life*, ed. Alondra Nelson and Thuy Linh N. Tu (New York: New York University Press, 2001), 177–91; Rachel C. Lee and Sau-ling Cynthia Wong, eds., *AsianAmerica.Net: Ethnicity, Nationalism, and Cyberspace* (New York: Routledge, 2003).

27. Chun, *Control and Freedom*, 192.

28. Ibid., 187–188.

29. William Gibson, *Neuromancer* (New York: Ace Books, 1984), 4–5, 51–52.

30. Ibid., 191, emphasis in original.

31. Lisa Nakamura, *Cybertypes: Race, Ethnicity, and Identity on the Internet* (New York: Routledge, 2002), 61.

32. Ibid., 14.

33. Ibid., 61–85; Lisa Nakamura, *Digitizing Race: Visual Cultures of the Internet* (Minneapolis: University of Minnesota Press, 2008), 95–130.

34. Nakamura, *Digitizing Race*, 96.

35. Nakamura, *Cybertypes*, 62, 80–83.

36. See Donna Haraway, *Simians, Cyborgs, and Women: The Reinvention of Nature* (New York: Routledge, 1991); Allucquère Rosanne Stone, *The War of Desire and Technology at the Close of the Mechanical Age* (Cambridge, Mass.: MIT Press, 1995); Ann Balsamo, *Technologies of the Gendered Body: Reading Cyborg Women* (Durham, N.C.: Duke University Press, 1996); Sherry Turkle, *Life on the Screen: Identity in the Age of the Internet* (New York: Simon & Schuster, 1997).

37. Michael Omi and Howard Winant, *Racial Formation in the United States: From the 1960s to 1980s* (New York: Routledge, 1989), 61–62.

38. Ibid.

39. Sara Ahmed, *Queer Phenomenology: Orientations, Objects, Others* (Durham, N.C.: Duke University Press, 2006), 112, 126.

40. Etienne Balibar and Immanuel Wallerstein, *Race, Nation, Class: Ambiguous Identities* (New York: Verso, 1991), 17–18.

41. Homi Bhabha, *The Location of Culture* (London: Routledge, 1994), 66.

42. Ibid., 75.

43. Ibid., 81.

44. Richard Dyer, *White* (London: Routledge, 1997), 207.

45. Ibid., 45.

46. Ibid., 207.

47. See Nina E. Lerman, Ruth Oldenziel, and Arwen P. Mohun, eds., *Gender and Technology: A Reader* (Baltimore: Johns Hopkins University Press, 2003); Ruth Oldenziel, *Making Technology Masculine: Men, Women, and Modern Machines in America, 1870–1945* (Amsterdam: Amsterdam University Press, 2004); and Judy Wajcman, *TechnoFeminism* (Cambridge, England: Polity Press, 2004).

48. Foster, *The Souls of Cyberfolk*, 171–202.

49. Ibid.

50. See Gary Okihiro, *Margins and Mainstreams: Asians in American History and Culture* (Seattle: University of Washington Press, 1994); George Lipsitz, *The Possessive Investment in Whiteness: How White People Profit from Identity Politics* (Philadelphia: Temple University Press, 1998); Vijay Prashad, *Everybody Was Kung Fu Fighting: Afro-Asian Connections and the Myth of Cultural Purity* (New York: Beacon Press, 2002); Claire Jean Kim, *Bitter Fruit: The Politics of Black–Korean Conflict in New York City* (New Haven, Conn.: Yale University Press, 2003); James Kyung-Jin Lee, *Urban Triage: Race and the Fictions of Multiculturalism* (Minneapolis: University of Minnesota Press, 2004); and Bill Mullen, *Afro Orientalism* (Minneapolis: University of Minnesota Press, 2004).

51. Audre Lorde, *Sister Outsider: Essays and Speeches* (Freedom, Calif.: Crossing Press, 1984), 110–13.

52. See, for instance, Chon Noriega, ed., *Chicanos and Film: Representation and Resistance* (Minneapolis: University of Minnesota Press, 1992); Michele Wallace, *Black Popular Culture* (Seattle: Bay Press, 1992); Rey Chow, *Writing Diaspora: Tactics*

of Intervention in Contemporary Cultural Studies (Bloomington: Indiana University Press, 1993); Kobena Mercer, *Welcome to the Jungle: New Positions in Black Cultural Studies* (London: Routledge, 1994); Herman Gray, *Watching Race: Television and the Struggle for "Blackness"* (Minneapolis: University of Minnesota Press, 1995); Robyn Wiegman, *American Anatomies: Theorizing Race and Gender* (Durham, N.C.: Duke University Press, 1995); Fatimah Tobing Rony, *The Third Eye: Race, Cinema, and Ethnographic Spectacle* (Durham, N.C.: Duke University Press, 1996); Ien Ang, *On Not Speaking Chinese: Living between Asia and the West* (London: Routledge, 2001); and Charles Ramírez Berg, *Latino Images in Film: Stereotypes, Subversion, and Resistance* (Austin: University of Texas Press, 2002).

53. bell hooks, *Black Looks: Race and Representation* (Boston: South End Press, 1992), 21.

54. Ibid.

55. Bruce Schulman, *The Seventies: The Great Shift in American Culture, Society, and Politics* (Cambridge, Mass.: Da Capo Press, 2001), 62–72.

56. Ibid., 25.

57. Stuart Hall, "New Ethnicities," in *Stuart Hall: Critical Dialogues in Cultural Studies,* ed. David Morley and Kuan-Hsing Chen (London: Routledge, 1996), 444.

58. Ellis Hanson, "Introduction," in *Out Takes: Essays on Queer Theory and Film,* ed. Ellis Hanson (Durham, N.C.: Duke University Press, 1999), 8.

59. Ibid., 4.

60. See Patricia Williams, *Seeing a Color-Blind Future: The Paradox of Race* (New York: Noonday Press, 1998); Michael Warner, *The Trouble with Normal: Sex, Politics, and the Ethics of Queer Life* (New York: Free Press, 1999); Sara Ahmed, *The Cultural Politics of Emotion* (London: Routledge, 2004); and Howard Winant, *The New Politics of Race: Globalism, Difference, Justice* (Minneapolis: University of Minnesota Press, 2004).

61. Geoff King, *Spectacular Narratives: Hollywood in the Age of the Blockbuster* (London: I. B. Tauris, 2000), 3–4.

62. See Sumi K. Cho, "Korean Americans vs. African Americans: Conflict and Construction," in *Reading Rodney King, Reading Urban Uprising,* ed. Robert Gooding-Williams (New York: Routledge, 1993), 196–214; Elaine H. Kim, "Home Is Where the Han Is: A Korean-American Perspective on the Los Angeles Upheavals," in *Reading Rodney King,* 215–35; Wen Ho Lee and Helen Zia, *My Country versus Me: The First-Hand Account by the Los Alamos Scientist Who Was Falsely Accused of Being a Spy* (New York: Hyperion Books, 2003); Sylvia Chong, "Look an Asian! The Politics of Racial Interpellation in the Wake of the Virginia Tech Shootings," *Journal of Asian American Studies* 11, no. 1 (2004): 27–60.

63. Teresa de Lauretis, *Technologies of Gender: Essays on Theory, Film, and Fiction* (Bloomington: Indiana University Press, 1987), 26.

64. Ibid., emphasis added.

65. de Lauretis, *Technologies of Gender,* 25, emphasis in original.

66. Ibid., emphasis in original.

67. Elspeth Probyn, "Technologizing the Self: A Future Anterior for Cultural Studies," in *Cultural Studies,* ed. Lawrence Grossberg, Cary Nelson, and Paula Treichler (New York: Routledge, 1991), 511.

68. Ibid., 508.

2. An Oriental Past

1. Geoff King, *New Hollywood Cinema: An Introduction* (New York: Columbia University Press, 2002), 11–48. The 180-degree rules states that two characters in the same scene should always have the same left–right relationship to each other.

2. Thomas Schatz, *Old Hollywood/New Hollywood: Ritual, Art, and Industry* (Ann Arbor, Mich.: UMI Research Press, 1983), 218.

3. Ibid., 236, emphasis in original.

4. Thomas Schatz, "The New Hollywood," in *Film Theory Goes to the Movies,* ed. Jim Collins, Hilary Radner, and Ava Preacher Collins (New York: Routledge, 1993), 17–25.

5. Justin Wyatt, *High Concept: Movies and Marketing in Hollywood* (Austin: University of Texas Press, 1994), 8–20.

6. Fredric Jameson, "Postmodernism, or the Cultural Logic of Late Capitalism," *New Left Review* 146 (1984): 52–96.

7. Thomas Elsaesser, "The Blockbuster: Everything Connects, but Not Everything Goes," in *The End of Cinema as We Know It: American Film in the Nineties,* ed. Jon Lewis (New York: New York University Press, 2001), 11–22.

8. Tino Balio, "'A Major Presence in All of the World's Important Markets': The Globalization of Hollywood in the 1990s," in *Contemporary Hollywood Cinema,* ed. Steve Neale and Murray Smith (London: Routledge, 1998), 58–71.

9. David Harvey, *The Condition of Postmodernity: An Enquiry into the Origins of Cultural Change* (London: Blackwell, 1991), 54.

10. Gary Okihiro, *Margins and Mainstreams: Asians in American History and Culture* (Seattle: University of Washington Press, 1994), 31–63.

11. John Kuo Wei Tchen, *New York before Chinatown: Orientalism and the Shaping of American Culture, 1776–1882* (Baltimore: Johns Hopkins University Press, 1999), xv–xxiv, 191–92.

12. Claire Jean Kim, "The Racial Triangulation of Asian Americans," *Politics and Society* 27 (1999): 109.

13. Robert G. Lee, *Orientals: Asian Americans in Popular Culture* (Philadelphia: Temple University Press, 1999), 31–32. See also Noel Ignatiev, *How the Irish Became White* (New York: Routledge, 1995); David Roediger, *The Wages of Whiteness: Race and*

the Making of the American Working Class (London: Verso, 1996); and George Lipsitz, *The Possessive Investment in Whiteness* (Philadelphia: Temple University Press, 1998).

14. Lee, *Orientals*, 15–82.

15. Sucheng Chan, *Asian Americans: An Interpretive History* (New York: Twayne, 1991), 54–61.

16. Lisa Lowe, *Immigrant Acts: On Asian American Cultural Politics* (Durham, N.C.: Duke University Press, 1996), 7, and Kim, "The Racial Triangulation of Asian Americans," 115–16.

17. Kim, "The Racial Triangulation of Asian Americans," 106–7.

18. Ibid., 107, 115.

19. Christina Klein, *Cold War Orientalism: Asia in the Milldlebrow Imagination, 1945–1961* (Berkeley: University of California Press, 2003), 9–12.

20. Glenn Omatsu, "The 'Four Prisons' and the Movements of Liberation: Asian American Activism from the 1960s to the 1990s," in *The State of Asian America: Activism and Resistance in the 1990s*, ed. Karin Aguilar–San Juan (Boston: South End Press, 1994), 19–70.

21. For details on the Chin case see the 1989 documentary film *Who Killed Vincent Chin*, directed by Renee Tajima and Christine Choy; for details on the Lee case see Wen Ho Lee, *My Country versus Me: The First-Hand Account by the Las Alamos Scientist Who Was Falsely Accused of Being a Spy* (New York: Hyperion, 2003).

22. Okihiro, *Margins and Mainstreams*, 141–43.

23. Colleen Lye, *America's Asia: Racial Form and American Literature, 1893–1945* (Princeton, N.J.: Princeton University Press, 2004), 5.

24. For instance, see David Brand, "The New Whiz Kids," *Time* (August 31, 1987), available at http://www.time.com/time/magazine; and David A. Bell, "The Triumph of Asian-Americans," *The New Republic* (July 15–22, 1985): 24–32.

25. Bill Ong Hing, *Making and Remaking Asian America through Immigration Policy, 1850–1990* (Stanford, Calif.: Stanford University Press, 1993), 79–120.

26. Christopher Connery, "Pacific Rim Discourse: The U.S. Global Imaginary in the Late Cold War Years," *boundary 2* 21 (1994): 31–33.

27. Ibid., 33.

28. Harvey, *The Condition of Postmodernity*, 147.

29. Connery, "Pacific Rim Discourse," 42.

30. Ibid., 31–32.

31. Min Zhou and James Gatewood, "Introduction: Revisiting Contemporary Asian America," in *Contemporary Asian America: A Multidisciplinary Reader*, ed. Min Zhou and James Gatewood (New York: New York University Press, 2000), 13–14.

32. Hing, *Making and Remaking Asian America*, 37–38.

33. Paul Ong and John Liu, "U.S. Immigration Policies and Asian Migration," in *Contemporary Asian America*, 159.

34. Lee, *Orientals*, 187–188.

35. Hing, *Making and Remaking Asian America*, 38–41.

36. Ong and Liu, "U.S. Immigration Policies and Asian Migration," 60.

37. Paul Ong, Edna Bonacich, and Lucie Cheng, *The New Asian Immigration in Los Angeles and Global Restructuring* (Philadelphia: Temple University Press, 1994), 8–17.

38. Ibid., 26–29.

39. Lowe, *Immigrant Acts*, 14–16.

40. Examples of such legislation include the 1986 Immigration Reform and Control Act, the 1990 Immigration Act, and California's Proposition 186 in 1994. Ibid., 15.

41. Ibid., 16.

42. Lee, *Orientals*, 11.

43. Palumbo-Liu, *Asian/American*, 174–81.

44. Ibid., 176.

45. Ibid., 172, emphasis in original.

46. See James Kyung-Jin Lee, *Urban Triage: Race and the Fictions of Multiculturalism* (Minneapolis: University of Minnesota Press, 2004), 64–99; Okihiro, *Margins and Mainstreams*, 31–63; and Clare Jean Kim, *Bitter Fruit: The Politics of Black–Korean Conflict in New York City* (New Haven, Conn.: Yale University Press, 2003), 14–52.

47. Lee, *Orientals*, 180–91.

3. American Anxiety and the Oriental City

1. http://www.google.com, April 19, 2010.

2. See, for instance, Mike Davis, "Chinatown, Part Two? The 'Internationalization' of Downtown Los Angeles," *New Left Review* 164 (1987): 65–86; Giuliana Bruno, "Ramble City: Postmodernism and Blade Runner," in *Alien Zone: Cultural Theory and Contemporary Science Fiction Cinema*, ed. Annette Kuhn (London: Verso, 1990), 183–95; Kaja Silverman, "Back to the Future," in *Camera Obscura* 27 (1991): 109–32; Scott Bukatman, *Blade Runner* (London: British Film Institute, 1997); Richard Dyer, *White* (London: Routledge, 1997), 213–16; and David Desser, "Race, Space and Class: The Politics of Cityscapes in Science-Fiction Films," in *Alien Zone II: The Spaces of Science Fiction Cinema*, ed. Annette Kuhn (London: Verso, 1999), 80–96.

3. See Stephen Neale, "Issues of Difference: Alien and Blade Runner," in *Fantasy and the Cinema: A Reader*, ed. Donald James (London: British Film Institute, 1989), 213–25; Brian Locke, "Three's a Crowd: The Racial Triangle of 'White,' 'Black,' and 'Asian' Men in Post–World War Two United States Culture" (Ph.D. diss., Brown

University, Providence, R.I., 1996); Robert G. Lee, *Orientals: Asian Americans in Popular Culture* (Philadelphia: Temple University Press, 1999), 191–96; and Charles Ramírez Berg, *Latino Images in Film: Stereotypes, Subversion, Resistance* (Austin: University of Texas Press, 2002), 171–82.

4. N. Kathryn Hayles, *How We Became Posthuman: Virtual Bodies in Cybernetics, Literature, and Informatics* (Chicago: University of Chicago Press, 1999), 160–63.

5. Richard Corliss, "His Dark Vision of the Future Is Now," *Time*, June 24, 2002, 63.

6. Robin Wood, *Hollywood from Vietnam to Reagan* (New York: Columbia University Press, 1986), 182–83.

7. Gwen Lee and Doris Elaine Sauter, eds., *What if Our World Is Their Heaven? The Final Conversations of Philip K. Dick* (Woodstock, N.Y.: Overlook Press, 2000), 32–33, emphasis in original.

8. Paul Sammon, *Future Noir: The Making of "Blade Runner"* (New York: HarperPrism, 1996), 66–67.

9. Geoff King, *New Hollywood Cinema: An Introduction* (New York: Columbia University Press, 2002), 112.

10. The Numbers: Box Office Data, Movie Stars, Idle Speculation, web site. For *Blade Runner* figures, see http://www.the-numbers.com/movies/1982/OBLRU.php. For *E.T.* figures, see http://www.the-numbers.com/movies/1982/OET.php.

11. Sammon, *Future Noir*, 322–25.

12. Rick Instrell, "Blade Runner: The Economic Shaping of a Film," in *Cinema and Fiction: New Modes of Adapting, 1950–1990*, ed. John Orr and Colin Nicholson (Edinburgh, Scotland: Edinburgh University Press, 1992), 164.

13. Richard Meyers, *The Great Science Fiction Films* (Secaucus, N.J.: Citadel Press, 1984), 242–44.

14. Daryl Miller, "Blade Runner: An Old Story in Fun, Futuristic Set," *The Arizona Daily Star,* June 29, 1982, quoted in William Kolb, "Blade Runner: An Annotated Bibliography," in *Retrofitting "Blade Runner": Issues in Ridley Scott's "Blade Runner" and Philip K. Dick's "Do Androids Dream of Electric Sheep?"* ed. Judith Kerman (Bowling Green, Ohio: Bowling Green University Press, 1991), 43.

15. "Do Disc Owners Dream of Letterboxed Sheep?" *Laser Disc Newsletter,* January 14, 1988, quoted in Kolb, "Blade Runner," 47.

16. Herb Lightman and Richard Patterson, "Blade Runner: Production Design and Photography," *American Cinematographer* (July 1982): 687, 715.

17. "Future Imperfect," *American Film* 8 (1983): 46–49, 75–76; Kolb, "Blade Runner," 32.

18. See Andrew Ross, *Strange Weather: Culture, Science, and Technology in the Age of Limits* (London: Verso, 1991), 144, 146.

19. Andrew Abbott, prod., "On the Edge of Blade Runner" (London: Channel 4 Television Corporation, 2000).

20. Sammon, *Future Noir,* 73.

21. Ibid., 71–75.

22. Nino Frank is credited with inventing the term "film noir" in 1946 and Jean Pierre Chartier with popularizing it later that year in his article in *La Revue du Cinema.* Alain Silver and Elizabeth Ward, *Film Noir: An Encyclopedia Reference to the American Style,* 3rd ed. (Woodstock, N.Y.: Overlook Press, 1992), 1–2.

23. Mike Davis, *City of Quartz: Excavating the Future in Los Angeles* (New York: Vintage Books, 1992), 40–41.

24. Pam Cook and Mieke Bernink, eds., *The Cinema Book,* 2nd ed. (London: BFI Publishing, 1999), 67–69, 186–88.

25. Silver and Ward, *Film Noir,* 2.

26. James Naremore, *More than Night: Film Noir in Its Contexts* (Berkeley: University of California Press, 1998), 225.

27. Lightman and Patterson, "Blade Runner," 720.

28. Ibid., 717.

29. Don Shay, "Blade Runner: 2020 Foresight," *Cinefex* (July 1982): 8.

30. Vincent La Brutto, *By Design: Interviews with Film Production Designers* (Westport, Conn.: Praeger, 1992), 170.

31. Shay, "Blade Runner," 6–7.

32. Bruno, "Ramble City," 186.

33. Lightman and Patterson, "Blade Runner," 687.

34. Sammon, *Future Noir,* 110.

35. Lightman and Patterson, "Blade Runner," 720.

36. Locke, "Three's a Crowd," 178–225.

37. Kevin McNamara, "Blade Runner's Post-Individual Worldspace," *Contemporary Literature* 38 (1997): 429.

38. Bruno, "Ramble City," 186.

39. Lee, *Orientals,* 194.

40. Bruno, "Ramble City," 186.

41. Bukatman, *Blade Runner,* 84–85.

42. See Sandra Liu, "When Dragon Ladies Die, Do They Come Back as Butterflies? Re-imagining Anna May Wong," in *Countervisions,* ed. Hamamoto and Liu, 23–39.

43. Berg, *Latino Images in Film,* 171–75.

44. Silverman, "Back to the Future," 115.

45. Locke, "Three's a Crowd," 147.

46. Ibid., 147–48.

47. Lee, *Orientals,* 194–96.

48. Bukatman, *Blade Runner*, 84.

49. Gina Marchetti, *Romance and the "Yellow Peril": Race, Sex, and Discursive Strategies in Hollywood Fiction* (Berkeley: University of California Press, 1993), 8.

50. Sammon, *Future Noir*, 113.

51. Ibid.

52. Ibid.

4. Oriental Buddies and the Disruption of Whiteness

1. Marshall McLuhan, "Television in a New Light," in *The Meaning of Commercial Television*, ed. Stanley Donner (Austin: University of Texas Press, 1966), 91.

2. Ibid., 93.

3. See Bob Keefe, "Children Get Wired into Tech Earlier," *Atlanta Journal–Constitution*, June 25, 2006; Laura Schreier, "Excessive Gaming Poses Dangers, Some Say," *Dallas Morning News*, June 26, 2006; Tamar Lewin, "The New Gender Divide," *New York Times*, July 9, 2006; and Leslie Brody, "Gaming Addiction Gets Serious Look," *Baltimore Sun*, August 31, 2006.

4. Karl Taro Greenfeld, *Speed Tribes: Days and Nights with Japan's Next Generation* (New York: HarperCollins, 1994), 274.

5. Susan Napier, *Anime from "Akira" to "Princess Mononoke": Experiencing Contemporary Japanese Animation* (New York: Palgrave, 2001), 254.

6. Gina Marchetti, *Romance and the "Yellow Peril": Race, Sex, and Discursive Strategies in Hollywood Fiction* (Berkeley: University of California Press, 1994), 202–21; Dorinne Kondo, *About Face: Performing Race in Fashion and Theater* (New York: Routledge, 1997), 240–51; and Robert G. Lee, *Orientals: Asian Americans in Popular Culture* (Philadelphia: Temple University Press, 1999), 196–203, 204–22.

7. Jane Iwamura, "The Oriental Monk in American Popular Culture," in *Religion and Popular Culture in America*, ed. Bruce Forbes and Jeffrey Mahan (Berkeley: University of California Press. 2005), 32.

8. Ibid., 33.

9. Ibid., 32.

10. Ibid., 32–33.

11. See Raymond William Stedman, *Shadows of the Indian: Stereotypes in American Culture* (Norman: University of Oklahoma Press, 1982); Philip Deloria, *Playing Indian* (New Haven, Conn.: Yale University Press, 1999); Jacquelyn Kilpatrick, *Celluloid Indians: Native Americans and Film* (Lincoln: University of Nebraska Press, 1999); and Shari Huhndorf, *Going Native: Indians in the American Cultural Imagination* (Ithaca, N.Y.: Cornell University Press, 2001).

12. Marchetti, *Romance and the "Yellow Peril*," 78–108.

13. Ibid., 89–91.

14. Gayatri Spivak, "Can the Subaltern Speak?" in *Marxism and the Interpretation of Culture*, ed. Cary Nelson and Lawrence Grossberg (Urbana: University of Illinois Press, 1988), 305.

15. Marchetti, *Romance and the "Yellow Peril,"* 91.

16. According to Chin and Chan, "The unacceptable model is unacceptable because he cannot be controlled by whites. The acceptable model is acceptable because he is tractable. There is racist hate and racist love. If the system works, the stereotypes assigned to the various races are accepted by the races themselves as reality, as fact, and racist love reigns." Frank Chin and Jeffrey Paul Chan, "Racist Love," in *Seeing through Shuck*, ed. Richard Kostelanetz (New York: Ballantine Books, 1972), 65.

17. Cynthia Sau-ling Wong, "Diverted Mothering: Representations of Caregivers of Color in the Age of 'Multiculturalism,'" in *Mothering: Ideology, Experience, and Agency*, ed. Evelyn Nakano Glenn, Grace Chang, and Linda Rennie Forcey (New York: Routledge, 1994), 70.

18. Ibid., 69.

19. Ibid., 69–71.

20. See Eugen Franklin Wong, *On Visual Media Racism: Asians in the American Motion Pictures* (New York: Arno Press, 1978), 95–108; Lee, *Orientals*, 113–17; Sheng-mei Ma, *The Deathly Embrace: Orientalism and Asian American Identity* (Minneapolis: University of Minnesota Press, 2000), 3–20; Jachinson Chan, *Chinese American Masculinities* (New York: Routledge, 2001), 27–50; and Daniel Kim, *Writing Manhood in Black and Yellow: Ralph Ellison, Frank Chin, and the Literary Politics of Identity* (Stanford, Calif.: Stanford University Press, 2005), 124–59.

21. David Morley and Kevin Robins, *Spaces of Identity: Global Media, Electronic Landscapes and Cultural Boundaries* (London: Routledge, 1995), 170, emphasis added.

22. Ed Guerrero, *Framing Blackness: The African American Image in Film* (Philadelphia: Temple University Press, 1993), 118.

23. Ibid., 128.

24. Yvonne Tasker, *Spectacular Bodies: Gender, Genre, and the Action Cinema* (New York: Routledge, 1993), 39.

25. Ibid., 45.

26. Hazel Carby, *Race Men* (Cambridge, Mass.: Harvard University Press, 1998), 169–71, 173–74.

27. Ibid., 171–76.

28. S. Craig Watkins, *Representing: Hip Hop Culture and the Production of Black Cinema* (Chicago: University of Chicago Press, 1998), 65–76.

29. Patricia Hill Collins, *Black Sexual Politics: African Americans, Gender, and the New Racism* (New York: Routledge, 2004), 158–59.

30. See Frantz Fanon, *Black Skin, White Masks,* trans. Charles Lam Markmann (New York: Grove Press, 1967), 109–40; Sander Gilman, *Difference and Pathology: Stereotypes of Sexuality, Race, and Madness* (Ithaca, N.Y.: Cornell University Press, 1985), 76–108, 131–49; Kobena Mercer, *Welcome to the Jungle: New Positions in Black Cultural Studies* (New York: Routledge, 1994), 131–70; and Thelma Bolden et al., *Black Male: Representations of Masculinity in Contemporary American Art* (New York: Whitney Museum of Art, 1995).

31. Toni Morrison, *Playing in the Dark: Whiteness and the Literary Imagination* (New York: Vintage, 1993), 66.

32. Eric Lott, *Love and Theft: Blackface Minstrelsy and the American Working Class* (New York: Oxford University Press, 1995), 38–62.

33. Ibid., 63–88. See also Noel Ignatiev, *How the Irish Became White* (New York: Routledge, 1995), and Michael Rogin, *Blackface, White Noise: Jewish Immigrants in the Hollywood Melting Pot* (Berkeley: University of California Press, 1996).

34. Collins, *Black Sexual Politics,* 153.

35. Ibid., 151–52.

36. Carby, *Race Men,* 183, emphasis added.

37. The handful of Hollywood movies featuring a white male lead and a black female lead include *Strange Days* (1995), *Eraser* (1997), *Mission Impossible II* (2000), *Monster's Ball* (2001), *Die Another Day* (2002), and *Something New* (2006). It is telling that of these, only one film features a dark-skinned black actress (Angela Bassett in *Strange Days*), and only two films end with the couple in a potentially permanent relationship.

38. Richard Fung, "Looking for My Penis: The Eroticized Asian in Gay Video Porn," in *How Do I Look: Queer Film and Video,* ed. Bad Object-Choices (Seattle, Wash.: Bay Press, 1991), 148.

39. David Eng, *Racial Castration: Managing Masculinity in Asian America* (Durham, N.C.: Duke University Press, 2001), 204–28.

40. See Audre Lorde, *Sister Outsider: Essays and Speeches* (Freedom, Calif.: Crossing Press, 1984), and Gloria Anzaldúa, *Borderlands/La Frontera: The New Mestiza* (San Francisco: Aunt Lute Books, 1987).

41. Frank Chin, Jeffery Paul Chan, Lawson Fusao Inada, and Shawn Wong, eds., *Aiiieeeee! An Anthology of Asian American Writers* (Seattle, Wash.: University of Washington Press, 1974), 3–15.

42. See Elaine Kim, *Asian American Literature: An Introduction to the Writings and Their Social Context* (Philadelphia: Temple University Press, 1984), 173–213, and King-Kok Cheung, *Interethnic Companion to Asian American Literary Studies* (New York: Cambridge University Press, 1996), 1–38.

43. James Kyung-Jin Lee, "Asian American," in *The Cambridge Companion to Modern American Culture,* ed. Christopher Bigsby (New York: Cambridge University Press, 2006), 186–87.

44. Fung, "Looking for My Penis," 148–60.

45. See Russell Leong, ed., *Asian American Sexualities: Dimensions of the Gay and Lesbian Experience* (New York: Routledge, 1996); David L. Eng and Alice Y. Hom, eds., *Q & A: Queer in Asian America* (Philadelphia: Temple University Press, 1998); Chan, *Chinese American Masculinities;* Kim, *Writing Manhood in Black and Yellow;* Darrell Hamamoto, "The Joy Fuck Club: Prolegomenon to an Asian American Porno Practice," in *Countervisions: Asian American Film Criticism,* ed. Darrell Hamamoto and Sandra Liu (Philadelphia: Temple University Press, 2000), 59–89.

46. See, for instance, Vijay Prashad, *Everybody Was Kung Fu Fighting: Afro-Asian Connections and the Myth of Cultural Purity* (New York: Beacon Press, 2002); Bill Mullen, *Afro Orientalism* (Minneapolis: University of Minnesota Press, 2004); Mae Ngai, *Impossible Subjects: Illegal Aliens and the Making of Modern America* (Princeton, N.J.: Princeton University Press, 2005); and Vijay Prashad, The *Darker Nations: A People's History of the Third World* (New York: New Press, 2008).

47. Clare Jean Kim, *Bitter Fruit: The Politics of Black–Korean Conflict in New York City* (New Haven, Conn.: Yale University Press, 2003), 9–10.

48. Kondo, *About Face,* 10, 78–85, 165–66.

49. *The Way of The Karate Kid: Part 2,* dir. Michael Gillis, *The Karate Kid* DVD (Culver City, Calif.: Columbia Pictures Corporation; Dallas, Tex.: Delphi Films).

50. *The Way of The Karate Kid: Part 1,* dir. Michael Gillis, *The Karate Kid* DVD (Culver City, Calif.: Columbia Pictures Corporation; Dallas, Tex.: Delphi Films).

51. Other actors include Jackie Chan, Sessue Hayakawa, Philip Ahn, Bruce Lee, Mako, Sabu, George Takei, and Anna May Wong.

52. Jon Thurber, "Pat Morita, 73: Actor Starred in 'Karate Kid' Movie Series," obituary, *Los Angeles Times,* November 26, 2005, 16.

53. Patricia Sullivan, "Noriyuki 'Pat' Morita, 73: Played 'Karate Kid' Teacher," obituary, *Washington Post,* November 26, 2005, B04.

54. Thurber, "Pat Morita," 16.

55. Lawrence Downes, "Goodbye to Pat Morita, Best Supporting Asian," obituary, *New York Times,* November 29, 2005, 26.

56. Mike Lipton and Howard Breuer, *People* 64 (December 12, 2005): 79.

57. *The Way of The Karate Kid: Part 1.* Italicized words spoken in character.

58. Ibid.

59. Ibid.

60. Vincent Canby, "Banzai Detroit," *New York Times,* March 14, 1986.

61. Chris Hicks, "Youthful-Looking Ogden Native Enjoys Career as Character Actor," *Salt Lake City Deseret Morning News,* February 11, 2005.

62. Erik Fong, "What's a-Happenin', Hot Stuff?" *Wave Magazine* 3 (August 14–27, 2003), available at http://www.thewavemag.com.

63. Rita Kempley, "'Gung Ho': Auto Manifesto," *Washington Post*, March 14, 1986, 27.

64. Jim Naureckas, "Gung Ho," *Cineaste* 15 (1986): 44.

65. Sony bought Columbia Pictures for $3.4 billion; Matsushita bought MCA/Universal for $6 billion. Janet Wasko, *Hollywood in the Information Age: Beyond the Silver Screen* (Austin: University of Texas Press, 1995), 149.

66. Joseph Nye, "Soft Power," *Foreign Policy* 80 (Fall 1990): 153–72.

67. Wasko, *Hollywood in the Information Age*, 67.

68. Ibid.

69. Aljean Harmetz, "2 movies called 'Black Rain,'" *New York Times*, September 27, 1989, C17.

70. Vincent Canby, "Police Chase a Gangster in a Bright, Menacing Japan," *New York Times*, September 22, 1989, 12.

71. J. Hayward, "A Question of Power or Honor," *Nationwide News*, January 16, 1990.

72. Donald Chase, "In 'Black Rain,' East Meets West with a Bang! Bang!" *New York Times*, September 17, 1989, 20.

73. Ibid.

74. Hayward, "A Question of Power or Honor."

75. Kevin Thomas, "Black Rain Star Finds His Place in the Sun," *Toronto Star*, October 16, 1989, C5.

76. P. Wilson, "Accuracy Scores a Hit in Japan," *Nationwide News*, February 2, 1990, 5.

77. Hayward, "A Question of Power or Honor."

78. Susan Chira, "Japan's New Screen Image: Economic Toughie," *New York Times*, November 19, 1989, 17.

79. Rita Kempley, "'Black Rain': All Guts, No Story," *Washington Post*, September 22, 1989, B1.

80. Greenfeld, *Speed Tribes*, 22.

81. Pat Dowell, "Black Rain: Hollywood Goes Japan Bashing," *Cineaste* 17 (1990): 8–10.

82. Ibid., 9.

83. See Kempley, "'Black Rain,'" and Dowell, "Black Rain."

5. Martial Arts as Oriental Style

1. The film grossed $135,265,915 domestically and $66,700,000 overseas, earning a total of $201,965,915. http://www.boxofficemojo.com.

2. Marsha Kinder, *Playing with Power in Movies, Television, and Video Games: From Muppet Babies to Teenage Mutant Ninja Turtles* (Berkeley: University of California Press, 1991), 121–22.

3. Ibid., 134–35.

4. Ibid., 152.

5. Ibid.

6. Toby Miller, Nitlin Govil, John McMurria, and Richard Maxwell, *Global Hollywood* (London: British Film Institute, 2001), 1–43.

7. William Strauss and Neil Howe, *Generations: The History of America's Future, 1584–2069* (New York: Morrow, 1991), 317.

8. Marshall McLuhan, "Television in a New Light," in *The Meaning of Commercial Television*, ed. Stanley Donner (Austin: University of Texas Press, 1966), 92.

9. See Danae Clark, "Commodity Lesbianism," in *The Lesbian and Gay Studies Reader*, ed. Henry Abelove, Michèle Aina Barale, and David M. Halpern (New York: Routledge, 1993), 186–201, and Marilyn Halter, *Shopping for Identity: The Marketing of Ethnicity* (New York: Schocken, 2000).

10. Douglas Coupland, "Douglas Coupland Commits Gen-X-cide," *Details* 14 (1995): 72.

11. Rob Owen, *Gen X TV: The Brady Bunch to Melrose Place* (Syracuse, N.Y.: Syracuse University Press, 1997), 5.

12. Todd Gitlin, "Postmodernism: Roots and Politics," in *Cultural Politics*, ed. Ian Angus and Sut Jhally (New York: Routledge, 1989), 350.

13. Glenn Omatsu, "Fists of Legend and Fury: What Asian American College Students Can Learn from Jet Li and Bruce Lee," *Pacific Ties* (1998): 231–32.

14. Made for $90 million, *Rush Hour 2* grossed $226,164,286 domestically and $121,161,516 overseas for a total box office of $347,325,802. http://www.boxoffice mojo.com.

15. Pamela McClintock, "'Forbidden Kingdom' Lures Lionsgate: Martial-Arts Film Pairs Chan, Li, *Variety*, April 10, 2007, http://www.variety.com.

16. David Desser, "The Kung Fu Craze: Hong Kong Cinema's First American Reception," in *The Cinema of Hong Kong: History, Arts, Identity*, ed. Poshek Fu and David Desser (New York: Cambridge University Press, 2000), 20.

17. Guerrero, *Framing Blackness*, 69–112.

18. Desser, "The Kung Fu Craze," 25.

19. See Meaghan Morris, "Transnational Imagination in Action Cinema: Hong Kong and the Making of a Global Popular Culture," *Inter-Asia Cultural Studies* 5 (2004): 181–99.

20. David Bordwell, *Planet Hong Kong: Popular Cinema and the Art of Entertainment* (Cambridge, Mass.: Harvard University Press, 2000), 90–91.

21. Esther Yau, "Introduction," in *At Full Speed: Hong Kong Cinema in a Borderless World*, ed. Esther Yau (Minneapolis: University of Minnesota Press, 2001), 8.

22. Bordwell, *Planet Hong Kong*, 7–17.

23. Ibid., 10–12, 149–53.

24. Vijay Prashad, *Everybody Was Kung Fu Fighting: Afro-Asian Connections and the Myth of Cultural Purity* (New York: Beacon Press, 2002), 126–49.

25. Kwai-cheung Lo, "Transnationalization of the Local in Hong Kong Cinema of the 1990s," in *At Full Speed*, 261, emphasis added.

26. Ibid., 264.

27. Koichi Iwabuchi, *Recentering Globalization: Popular Culture and Japanese Transnationalism* (Durham, N.C.: Duke University Press, 2002), 27–28.

28. Kenneth Chan, "The Global Return of the Wu Xia Pian (Chinese Sword-Fighting Movie): Ang Lee's Crouching Tiger, Hidden Dragon," *Cinema Journal* 43 (2004): 5.

29. Kenneth Hall, *John Woo: The Films* (Jefferson, N.C.: McFarland), 13.

30. "John Woo Movie Is China's Biggest Ever Seller," *World Entertainment News Network* (August 12, 2008), www.wenn.com.

31. Christina Klein, "Crouching Tiger, Hidden Dragon: A Diasporic Reading," *Cinema Journal* 43 (2004): 23.

32. Ibid., 18.

33. S. Craig Watkins, *Representing· Hip Hop Culture and the Production of Black Cinema* (Chicago: University of Chicago Press, 1998), 65–70.

34. See Yvonne Tasker, "Fists of Fury: Discourses of Race and Masculinity in the Martial Arts Cinema," in *Race and the Subject of Masculinities*, ed. Harry Stecopoulos and Michael Uebel (Durham, N.C.: Duke University Press, 1997); Prashad, *Everybody Was Kung Fu Fighting*, 126–49; and Amy Onigiri, "'He Wanted to Be Just Like Bruce Lee': African Americans, Kung Fu Theater and Cultural Exchange at the Margins," *Journal of Asian American Studies* 5 (February 2002): 31–40.

35. Bill Mullen, *Afro Orientalism* (Minneapolis: University of Minnesota Press, 2004), xi–xx.

36. See Oliver Wang's "These Are the Breaks: Hip-Hop and AfroAsian Cultural (Dis)Connections," in *AfroAsian Encounters: Culture, History, Politics*, ed. Heike Raphael-Hernandez and Shannon Steen (New York: New York University Press, 2006), 146–66.

37. Derek Elley, "Asia to 'Tiger': Kung-Fooey," *Variety*, February 7, 2001.

38. Anya Kamenetz, "Extreme Makeovers: The Fine Art of Picking a Shtick," *Village Voice*, August 27–September 2, 2003, http://www.villagevoice.com.

39. Antonia Levi, *Samurai from Outer Space: Understanding Japanese Animation* (Chicago: Open Court, 1999), 1.

40. Shinobu Price, "Cartoons from Another Planet: Japanese Animation as Cross-Cultural Communication," *Journal of American & Comparative Cultures*, Spring–Summer 2001, 153–70.

41. Napier, *Anime from "Akira" to "Princess Mononoke,"* 33.

42. Douglas McGray, "Japan's Gross National Cool," *Foreign Policy*, May 2002, 53.

43. Napier, *Anime from "Akira" to "Princess Mononoke,"* 249–55.

44. See Annalee Newitz, "Anime Otaku: Japanese Animation Fans Outside Japan," *Bad Subjects* 13 (1994): 1–12, and Matt Hills, "Transnational Otaku: Japanese Representations of Fandom and Representations of Japan in Anime/Manga Fan Cultures," paper presented at the Media in Transition 2 International Conference, Boston, May 11, 2002 (MIT2: Globalization and Convergence), http://cms.mit.edu/conf/mit2/Papers.html.

45. Jonathan Clements and Helen McCarthy, *The Anime Encyclopedia: A Guide to Japanese Animation since 1917* (Berkeley, Calif.: Stone Bridge Press, 2001), 21, 370, 29–30, 435, 409.

46. Levi, *Samurai from Outer Space,* 9.

47. Ibid., 9–15

48. Anne Allison, "A Challenge to Hollywood? Japanese Character Goods Hit the US," *Japanese Studies* 20 (2000): 67–88.

49. Napier, *Anime from "Akira" to "Princess Mononoke,"* 85–116.

50. *Volcano High* was a Korean film taken up by MTV and redubbed for U.S. distribution, with a multicultural cast and hip-hop soundtrack featuring rap artists such as Snoop Dogg, Andre 3000, Big Boi, and Method Man doing the voices.

51. Mita Banerjee, "The Rush Hour of Black/Asian Coalitions? Jackie Chan and Blackface Minstrelsy," in *AfroAsian Encounters,* ed. Raphael-Hernandez and Steen, 204, and LeiLani Nishime, "'I'm Blackanese': Buddy-Cop Films, Rush Hour, and Asian American and African American Cross-racial Identification," in *Asian North American Identities beyond the Hyphen,* ed. Eleanor Ty and Donald C. Goellnicht (Bloomington: Indiana University Press. 2004), 48.

52. Banerjee, "The Rush Hour of Black/Asian Coalitions?" 209.

53. As Gates puts it, "The black tradition is double-voiced. The trope of the Talking Book, of double-voiced texts that talk to other texts, is the unifying metaphor within this book. Signfiyin' is the figure of the double-voiced, epitomized by Esu's (Yoruban trickster deity) depictions in sculpture as possessing two mouths." Henry Louis Gates Jr., *The Signifying Monkey: A Theory of Afro-American Literary Criticism* (New York: Oxford University Press, 1988), xxv.

54. Roger Ebert, "What a Pair: Fast-Paced 'Cradle' Worth a Look," *Chicago Sun-Times,* February 28, 2003, 27.

55. See Stephen Holden, "When Kung-Fu Overcomes Chest-Beating Hip-Hop," *New York Times,* February 28, 2003, 17; Janice Page, "High-Octane 'Cradle 2 the Grave' is Unapologetically Overblown," *Boston Globe,* February 28, 2003, C5; and Paul Sherman, "The Fists and the Furious: All Action and No Plot Make a 'Grave' Error," *Boston Herald,* February 28, 2003, S11.

56. Peter Biskind, *Down and Dirty Pictures: Miramax, Sundance, and the Rise of Independent Film* (New York: Simon & Schuster, 2004): 185–215.

57. Richard Corliss, "Samurai Cineaste," *Time*, March 13, 2000, 82.

58. See Don Groves, "Asia: Int'l Auds' Appetite for Local films Has Risen," *Variety*, October 27, 2002; Yeh Yueh-Yu and Darrell William Davis, "Japan Hongscreen: Pan-Asian Cinemas and Flexible Accumulation," *Historical Journal of Film, Radio & Television* 22 (March 2002): 61–83; and "Bringing Asian Cinema into Focus," *Cineaste* 30 (Spring 2005): 1.

59. Derek Elley, "Remake Fever Hits Pusan Fest," *Variety*, December 1, 2002.

60. Miller et al., *Global Hollywood*, 8.

6. The Virtual Orient

1. The Numbers: Box Office Data, Movie Stars, Idle Speculation, web site. For *Matrix* figures, see http://www.the-numbers.com/movies/1999/MATRIX.php.

2. See Lisa Nakamura, *Cybertypes: Race, Ethnicity, and Identity on the Internet* (New York: Routledge, 2002), 61–86; Pat Mellencamp, "The Zen of Masculinity—Rituals of Heroism in The Matrix," *The End of Cinema as We Know It: American Film in the Nineties*, ed. Jon Lewis (New York: New York University Press, 2001), 83–94; Peter Feng, "False and Double Consciousness: Race, Virtual Reality and the Assimilation of Hong Kong Action Cinema in The Matrix," in *Aliens R Us: The Other in Science Fiction Cinema*, ed. Ziauddin Sardar and Sean Cubitt (London: Pluto Press, 2002), 149–63; William Irwin, ed., *The Matrix and Philosophy: Welcome to the Desert of the Real* (Chicago: Open Court, 2002); Kim Hester-Williams, "NeoSlaves: Slavery, Freedom, and African American Apotheosis in Candyman, The Matrix, and The Green Mile," *Genders* 40 (2004), http://www.genders.org; Stacy Gillis, ed., *The Matrix Trilogy: Cyberpunk Reloaded* (London: Wallflower Press, 2005); Myriam Diocaretz and Stefan Herbrechter, eds., *The Matrix in Theory* (Amsterdam: Rodropi, 2006); Stacy Gillis, ed., *The Matrix Trilogy: Cyberpunk Reloaded* (London: Wallflower Press, 2005).

3. Todd Gitlin, *Media Unlimited: How the Torrent of Images and Sounds Overwhelms Our Lives* (New York: Henry Holt, 2002), 15–24, 176–210.

4. See Sherry Turkle, *Life on the Screen: Identity in the Age of the Internet* (New York: Touchstone, 1997); Jean Baudrillard, *Selected Writings*, ed. Mark Poster (Stanford, Calif.: Stanford University Press, 1998); and Lev Manovich, *The Language of the New Media* (Cambridge, Mass.: MIT Press, 2001).

5. Benjamin Woolley, *Virtual Worlds: A Journey in Hype and Hyperreality* (London: Penguin Books, 1992), 60.

6. Ibid., 68–69.

7. Carlos Fernández, "Testimony of the Association of MultiEthnic Americans before the Subcommittee on Census, Statistics, and Postal Personnel of the U.S. House of Representatives," in *American Mixed Race: The Culture of Microdiversity*, ed. Naomi Zack (Landham, Md.: Rowman & Littlefield, 1995), 192.

8. Mary Beltrán, "The New Hollywood Racelessness: Only the Fast, Furious (and Multiracial) Will Survive," *Cinema Journal* 44 (2): 55.

9. Susan Courtney, *Hollywood Fears of Miscegenation: Spectacular Narratives of Gender and Race, 1903–1967* (Princeton, N.J.: Princeton University Press, 2005), 5.

10. The practice is complicated by that of nonwhite performers' playing characters of nonwhite groups other than their own. Examples include Juanita Hall (black), Anthony Quinn (Chicano), and Rita Moreno (Chicana) who have played Asian and Pacific Islander, Arab, and Native American characters. This kind of intraracial performance presents another set of power relations that should be explored further in future research.

11. Freda Scott Giles, "From Melodrama to the Movies: The Tragic Mulatto as a Type Character," in *American Mixed Race*, ed. Zack, 63–64.

12. See Gayle Wald, *Crossing the Line: Racial Passing in Twentieth-Century U.S. Literature and Culture* (Durham, N.C.: Duke University Press, 2000), and Jane Gaines, *Fire and Desire: Mixed-Race Movies in the Silent Era* (Chicago: University of Chicago Press, 2001).

13. Teresa Kay Williams, "Race-ing and Being Raced," *Amerasia Journal* 23 (1997): 63.

14. Census 2000 PHC-T-6, "Population by Race and Hispanic or Latino Origin for the United States, Regions, Divisions, States, Puerto Rico, and Places of 100,000 or More Population," released on the Internet April 2, 2001, http://www.census.gov/population/www/cen2000/briefs/phc-t6/index-html.

15. See Lauren Berlant, *The Queen of America Goes to Washington City: Essays on Sex and Citizenship* (Durham, N.C.: Duke University Press, 1997); Donna Haraway, *Modest_Witness@Second_Millennium.FemaleMan©Meets_OncoMouseTM: Feminism and Technoscience* (New York: Routledge, 1997); and Jeffrey J. Santa Ana, "Affect-Identity: The Emotions of Assimilation, Multiraciality, and Asian American Subjectivity," in *Asian North American Identities: Beyond the Hyphen,* ed. Eleanor Ty and Donald Goellnicht (Bloomington: Indiana University Press, 2004), 15–42.

16. Some examples from television include Clark Kent (Dean Cain) in *Lois & Clark: The New Adventures of Superman* (1993–97), adventurer Sydney Fox (Tia Carrere) in *Relic Hunter* (1999–2002), cyborgian military weapon Max (Jessica Alba) in *Dark Angel* (2000–2002), and Superman's love interest, Lana Lang (Kristin Kreuk), in *Smallville* (2000–present).

17. Gloria Anzaldúa, *Borderlands/La Frontera: The New Mestiza* (San Francisco: Aunt Lute Books, 1987), 79–80.

18. Jane Park, "Virtual Race: The Racially Ambiguous Action Hero in *The Matrix* and *Pitch Black*," in *Mixed Race Hollywood*, ed. Mary Beltrán and Camilla Fojas (New York: New York University Press, 2008), 182–202.

19. Yvonne Tasker, *Spectacular Bodies: Gender, Genre, and the Action Cinema* (New York: Routledge, 1993), 35.

20. Vivian Sobchack, *Screening Space: The American Science Fiction Film*, 2nd ed. (New Brunswick, N.J.: Rutgers University Press, 2001), and Scott Bukatman, *Terminal Identity: The Virtual Subject in Postmodern Science Fiction* (Durham, N.C.: Duke University Press, 1993).

21. Janet Maslin, "The Reality Is All Virtual, and Densely Complicated," *New York Times,* March 31, 1999.

22. Ibid.

23. Richard Corliss and Jeffrey Ressner, "Popular Metaphysics: In the Matrix, the Wachowskis Make a Hit Film out of the Bible, Cyberpunk, and Higher Math," *Time* 153 (April 19, 1999): 75–76.

24. N'gai Croal and Devin Gordon, "The Matrix Makers," *Newsweek,* December 30, 2002, 64.

25. "What Is the Matrix?" the official *Matrix* web site, http://www.whatisthema trix.com.

26. N'gai Croal, "Synergy: Attacking on All Fronts: Team 'Matrix' Is Launching Not Only Two Sequels, but a Multimedia Offensive with Videogames and Anime," *Newsweek,* December 30, 2002, 89.

27. Napier, *Anime from "Akira" to "Princess Mononoke,"* 105.

28. Feng, "False and Double Consciousness"; LeiLani Nishime, "Is Keanu Reeves a Cyborg? APAs at the Century's End," paper delivered at the Society for Cinema Studies Annual Conference, Philadelphia, 2001, and William Wu, *Yellow: Race in America beyond Black and White* (New York: Basic Books, 2002).

29. Wu, *Yellow,* 296.

30. Nishime, "Is Keanu Reeves a Cyborg?" 3.

31. Mary Kittleson, "The New American Hero: Made in Japan," in The *Soul of Popular Culture: Looking at Contemporary Heroes, Myths, and Monsters,* ed. Mary Kittleson (Chicago: Open Court, 1998), 72.

32. Ibid.

33. Larry and Andy Wachowski, "The Matrix: Shooting Script, August 12, 1998," in *The Art of the Matrix* (New York: Newmarket Productions, 2000), 281. Hereafter cited as "Shooting Script."

34. Ibid., 296.

35. Samuel A. Kimball, "Not Begetting the Future: Technological Autochtony, Sexual Reproduction, and the Mythic Structure of the Matrix," *Journal of Popular Culture* 35 (Winter 2001): 13.

36. Dorinne Kondo, *About Face: Performing Race in Fashion and Theater* (New York: Routledge, 1997), 131.

37. "Shooting Script," 292.

38. Richard Dyer, *White* (London: Routledge, 1997), 28.

39. "Shooting Script," 185–86.

40. Ibid., 300.

41. Ibid., 317.

42. Ibid., 318.

43. Robert G. Lee, *Orientals: Asian Americans in Popular Culture* (Philadelphia: Temple University Press, 1999), 2, emphasis added.

44. Joseph Won, "Yellowface Minstrelsy: Asian Martial Arts and the American Popular Imaginary," Ph. D. diss., University of Michigan, Ann Arbor 1996, and Jeffrey Ow, "The Revenge of the Yellowfaced Cyborg Terminator: The Rape of Digital Geishas and the Colonization of Cyber-Coolies in 3D Realms' *Shadow Warrior*," in *Asian America.Net: Ethnicity, Nationalism, and Cyberspace*, ed. Rachel C. Lee and Sau-ling Cynthia Wong (New York: Routledge, 2003), 249–66.

45. "Shooting Script," 381.

46. Ibid., 381, emphasis in original.

47. Ibid., 382.

48. Ibid.

49. Ibid., 391.

50. Ibid.

51. Ibid.

Afterword

1. For an engaging analysis of crossover in Asian American independent media, see Kent A. Ono and Vincent Pham, *Asian Americans and the Media* (London: Polity Press, 2008), 124–39.

2. Lisa Lowe, "Heterogeneity, Hybridity, Multiplicity: Marking Asian American Differences," in *Contemporary Asian America: A Multidisciplinary Reader*, ed. Min Zhou and James Gatewood (New York: New York University Press, 2000), 677–97; David Eng, *Racial Castration: Managing Masculinity in Asian America* (Durham, N.C.: Duke University Press, 2001), 204–28; and Rachel C. Lee and Sau-ling Cynthia Wong, *AsianAmerica.Net: Ethnicity, Nationalism, and Cyberspace* (New York: Routledge, 2003), xiii–2.

3. Lowe, "Heterogeneity, Hybridity, Multiplicity," 680–85.

4. Benedict Anderson, *Imagined Communities: Reflections on the Origin and Spread of Nationalism* (London: Verso, 1991) 7, 24–26.

Index

Abbott, Andrew, 214n.19
Abercrombie & Fitch, 190
accumulated progress: notion of, 61
action films: emphasis on physicality
    and nonwhite characters and motifs
    in, 171
action heroes: Neo's divergence in *The
    Matrix* from, 179–80
Adams, Brooks, 7
addiction in *Neuromancer*, 12
*Adventures of Priscilla, Queen of the
    Desert, The*, xiv
affirmative action initiatives, 169
African Americans: authenticity
    attached to, 93–94, 98, 100; in
    Batman Begins, 32; in cyberpunk,
    13; masculinity, 98, 100, 122; racial
    triangulation and, 40, 95. *See also*
    blackness; black/white binary; race
"Afro-Asian" films, xi, xiii, 19. *See also*
    hip-hop kung fu
Afro Orientalism, 19, 136
Ahmed, Sara, 15, 206n.6, 208n.39,
    209n.60
Ahn, Philip, 218n.51
*Aiiieeeee! An Anthology of Asian
    American Writers* (Chin et al.):
    introductory essay in, 98–99
Akira (1986), 174
Alba, Jessica, 224n.16
Alexie, Sherman, 197

Alias (2001–6), 153
Alien (1979), 56, 58, 182
alienation effect *(Verfremudungs effekt)*,
    35
Allison, Anne, 222n.48
All the Invisible Children (2005), 133
Altman, Robert, 34
American Africanism, 93
American Dragon: Jake Long (2005–7),
    141
American exceptionalism, 88
American Orientalism, 4, 33, 38–42;
    Cold War, 41, 44; contradictory faces
    of, 65–75; divergences from
    European Orientalism, 38–39, 41
Ana, Jeffrey J. Santa, 224n.15
Anderson, Benedict, 200, 206n.13,
    226n.4
Ang, Ien, 209n.52
Animatrix, The (2003), 163, 174
anime (Japanese animation), xiii, 139–
    43; as cinema of de-assurance, 139–
    40; distributors, 141; as Hollywood's
    aesthetic and narrative other, 140;
    influence of *Blade Runner* on
    Japanese animators, 175; influence
    on *The Matrix*, 174, 179; *mecha*,
    141–43, 174; mise-en-scène in, role
    of, 140; narrative characteristics of,
    139–40; *otaku* label as badge of
    honor among hard-core U.S. anime

227

Lowe, Lisa, 2, 46, 47, 199–200, 206n.3, 211n.16, 226n.2
Loy, Myrna, 73, 78
Lucas, George, 34, 163
Lust, Caution (2008), 135
Lye, Colleen, 29, 42, 206n.8, 211n.23

Ma, Sheng-mei, 206n.8
Ma, Tzi, 144
McCarran Walters Act (1952), 44, 45
McCarthy, Helen, 222n.45
Macchio, Ralph, 101, 104, 106, 107, 108. *See also Karate Kid, The* (1984)
McClintock, Pamela, 220n.15
McClory, Belinda, 177
McG, 127, 174
McGray, Douglas, 140, 221n.42
machines: Asian American men perceived as, 98; *mecha* body, 142; *otaku* as symbiosis of man and, 84, 90. *See also* replicants in *Blade Runner;* technology(ies)
McKinley, William, 7
McLuhan, Marshall, 83, 85, 126, 215n.1, 220n.8
McMurria, John, 220n.6
McNamara, Kevin, 64, 65, 214n.37
Madama Butterfly, 87
Magnuson Act (1943), 44
Mako, 218n.51
Malick, Terrence, 156
Malthusian population studies, 7
Manchurian Candidate, The (1962), 60, 128
manga (Japanese comics), 141–42
Manifest Destiny narrative of "going West" in *The Karate Kid,* 104
Manovich, Lev, 223n.4
Marchetti, Gina, ix, 77, 85, 87–88, 205n.2, 215n.6, 215n.49

marginality of subordinate group: as necessary condition for representation in dominant culture, 22–23
marketing strategy: for blockbusters, 36, 37, 163; "supersystem" of media and consumer products around *Teenage Mutant Ninja Turtles* concept, 125–26
martial arts as oriental style, x, 125–62; anime and, xiii, 84, 139–43, 174, 179; in *Cradle 2 the Grave,* xiii, 128, 137, 143, 151–53, 159; in *Ghost Dog,* xiii, 136, 137, 143, 157–59; hip-hop kung fu, 143–59; in *Kill Bill* dyad, viii, xiii, 137, 143, 153–57, 159; martial arts training in *The Karate Kid,* 106; in *The Matrix,* 143, 174; mechanical moves transcending limits of physical body in, 142; modes of representing East Asian Orient in Hollywood, 132–39; reception of Hong Kong films in United States, 128–32; in *Rush Hour* movies, viii, ix, xiii, 143–51, 159; special effects and, 173–74
masculinity: African American, 98, 100, 122; alternative modes of, posited in *Rush Hour,* 148; Asian Americans perceived as sexually passive and inauthentic, 97–100; black, 18, 92–93, 94, 98, 100, 122; external castrating forces threatening, 178–79; foreign Asian, perceived authenticity of, x, 97; hero as feminized infant in *The Matrix,* 178–86; mechanistic, marginalized, in Vapor's "Turning Japanese," 85; of oriental buddy, 97–100; orientalist vs. techno-orientalist, 12; racial ordering of American

nuclear family: absence and/or
dysfunction of Anglo-American,
need for surrogate oriental other
and, 86, 104–8, 109, 118, 119–20,
123; impulse to restore, in *Rush
Hour,* 146–47
Nye, Joseph, 114, 219n.66

Oh, Sandra, x
Ohara (1987), 102
oil crisis: economic depression
following 1973, 43
Okazaki, Robert, 67
Okihiro, Gary, 18, 208n.50, 210n.10,
212n.46
Oldboy (2003/2005), 198
Oldenziel, Ruth, 208n.47
Olmos, Edward James, 68, 79–80
Omatsu, Glenn, 128, 211n.20, 220n.13
Omi, Michael, 14, 208n.37
Once upon a Time in China (1991), 128
One, The (video game, 2005), 163
one-drop rule, 168
180-degree rule, 35, 210n.1
Ong, Aiwa, 5–6, 206n.11
Ong, Paul, 211n.33, 212n.37
Ong-bak (2003/2004), 198
Onigiri, Amy, 221n.34
Only the Brave (2005), 103
Ono, Kent A., ix, 226n.1
Open Door Policy, 38
Ophuls, Max, 60
Oren, Tasha, 206n.8
Orient: in *Blade Runner,* as consumable
style, 65, 71–75; in *Blade Runner,* as
invisible worker, 66–70; in *Blade
Runner,* as raced replicant, 76–78;
category of, from period of the
Enlightenment, 2; representation in
film noir, 60

oriental buddy, 90–100; Takakura in
Black Rain, 100, 115, 116, 119–22;
Watanabe in *Gung Ho,* 100, 110–13.
See also buddy films
Oriental city, American anxiety and,
51–81; vision of Los Angeles in *Blade
Runner* and, 51–53, 61–63. *See also
Blade Runner* (1982)
oriental imagery: hypervisible fêted and
invisible abject, vii, viii, ix. *See also*
oriental style
Orientalism, xii; Afro Orientalism, 19,
136; alternate model for exploring
ambivalences in identity and
community construction in, 161–62;
American, 4, 33, 38–42; American,
contradictory faces of, 65–75;
American, divergences between
European and, 38–39, 41; coining of
term, 2; commercial, 39; differences
between techno-orientalism and,
11–12; eminent marketability of,
195; in film noir, 60; as gendered, 3;
high-tech, in cyberpunk and
cyberspace, 10–14; hybridized, 109,
113, 123; inherent virtuality of, as a
western fantasy of Asia, 11; modes
of expression in Hollywood, 195;
Pacific Rim discourse and, 44;
patrician, 39, 41; postmodern, 125–
26; productiveness of, 3; redux in *The
Matrix,* 174–76; reworking, 2–6;
Said's model of, challenge to, 126;
shaping futuristic world of *Blade
Runner,* 53
Orientalism (Said), 2, 3, 4
orientalized woman in *Blade Runner,*
71–75
Oriental Monk, 86–87, 88, 89, 95, 96;
caregiver of color as variation of,

special effects and martial arts,
combination of, 173–74. *See also*
martial arts as oriental style
spectacle: mass fantasies communicated
in cinema indirectly through, 23–24;
narrative in cinema privileged over,
24; nonwhite bodies and cultures
rendered as, 24
Speed Racer (TV, 1967), 127, 140
Spiegelman, Art, 54
Spielberg, Steven, 34, 57
Spirited Away (2002), 141
Spivak, Gayatri, 87–88, 206n.6,
216n.14
Stallone, Sylvester, 179
Stam, Robert, 206n.12
Stand and Deliver (1988), 96
Star Wars (1977), 36, 56, 190
Star Wars I: The Phantom Menace
(1999), 163
Stedman, Raymond William, 215n.11
Stephenson, Neale, 13
stereotype(s): alternative modes of
masculinity in *Rush Hour* movies,
148; Asian American actors playing
to, 103, 110; Asian American protest
against release of *Rush Hour* for,
144–45; Asian Pocahontas, 87–89, 95,
96; Asiatic, in Hollywood, xi, 86–100,
205n.2; of Asiatic men, 97–100;
Bhabha's definition of, 15–16; as
fixed and arrested image of group,
16; Generation X, 126, 127; from
hip-hop and martial arts cultures, as
commodified types, 159; of Japanese,
7–8; learning to be racist through,
15; Lotus Blossom, 78; masculine, in
Cradle 2 the Grave, 152; model of
normative visibility and, 23; negative,
159; Oriental Monk, 86–87, 88, 89;

primitivist, of African Americans, 94;
as racialized fetish, 16; racist, viii, xi;
technologized, of Asians and Asian
Americans in 1980s, 42; techno-
orientalist, 194. *See also* model
minority; techno-oriental other
Sterling, Bruce, 10
Stoddard, Lothrop, 7
Stone, Allucquère Rosanne, 208n.36
Strange Days (1995), 53, 217n.37
Stranglehold (video game, 2007), 134
Strauss, William, 220n.7
structural unemployment, 43
studio system: demise of, 33, 34; film as
finished, unified product in, 36;
Paramount decree (1948) ending
vertical integration of, 34
Styx, 84
subcultural cinema, 130
subject-as-mind/object-as-body split: in
Dyer's study of whiteness in visual
culture, 17; enacted by and through
normalizing gaze, 3, 16; race kept
real by anxiety based on, 17
subjectivity, multiracial, 169–70
suburbanization, 34
Sullivan, Patricia, 218n.53
Sundance Institute and Film Festival,
157
Super Fly (1972), 129
Suzuki, Seijun, 62

Tajima, Renee, 211n.21
Taka, Miiko, 78
Takakura, Ken, 100, 115, 116, 119–22
Takei, George, 218n.51
Talking Book trope, 222n.53
Tandem Productions, 56
Tarantino, Quentin, xi, 127, 137, 143,
153, 154, 156–57, 174, 196

Tasker, Yvonne, 91, 171, 216n.24,
  221n.34, 224n.19
Taxi Driver (1976), 34
Taylor, Robert, 193
Tchen, John Kuo-Wei, 39, 41, 206n.8,
  210n.11
Teahouse of the August Moon (1956), 77
*Technologies of Gender: Essays on
  Theory, Film, and Fiction* (de
  Lauretis), 25
"Technologizing the Self: A Future
  Anterior for Cultural Studies"
  (Probyn), 26
technology(ies): associated with the
  Orient, in *Batman Begins,* 32–33;
  Neo's relationship in *The Matrix* to,
  180–83; race and, in *The Matrix,*
  186–88
techno-orientalism, xii, xiii, 6–8, 161;
  blended martial arts cinema and
  mecha anime as "authentic" examples
  of, 142–43; coining of term, 6;
  differences between Orientalism and,
  11–12; in near-future settings of
  cyberpunk narratives, 9–10; resent-
  ment of nonwhite appropriators of
  Western technology, 8; stereotypes
  associated with Asian Americans,
  194
techno-oriental other, xii, 89–90; of
  Japanese corporate culture in *Gung
  Ho,* 111, 112–13; of Kreese and
  Cobra Kai in *The Karate Kid,* 106,
  117; movement from background to
  foreground in biracial buddy films of
  1980s, xiii; of Sato in *Black Rain,* 117,
  118
technophilic style, 10
Teenage Mutant Ninja Turtles (1990),
  87, 89, 125–26, 127, 129

television, 87, 127, 128, 154; advent of,
  34; cartoons or *terebi manga,* 140;
  martial arts as theme and trope on,
  129; Morita's career in, 102; oriental
  buddies in, 91
"television child": McLuhan on, 83–84,
  85, 126
terebi manga (cartoons), 140
Terminator series (1984, 1991, 2003), 53
Territories, 21
Thing from Another World, The (1951),
  171
Thomas, Kevin, 219n.75
Thompson, Richard, 7, 207n.16
Thoroughly Modern Millie (1967), 102
Three Stigmata of Palmer Eldritch, The
  (Dick), 54
Three the Hard Way (1974), 129
Thurber, Jon, 218n.52
Thurman, Uma, 153, 154
Time magazine, 169; review of *The
  Matrix,* 172, 173
Titanic (1997), 34
Toei Film Company, 119
Tokyo Drifter (1966), 62
Tong, Stanley, 130, 173
Total Recall (1990), 54
"tragic mulatto" narrative, 167–68
Transformers (TV, 1985), 140
transnational citizens, 5–6
transnational corporations (TNCs), 36
transnationalism, 199; postmodern
  transnational system of cultural
  exchange, 200
transnationalization of "Asian
  America," 4, 5
transnational narratives, 131–43;
  anime, xiii, 84, 139–43, 174, 179;
  modes of representing East Asian
  Orient in Hollywood, 132–39;

Watanabe, Gedde, xi, 100, 110, 110–13
Watanabe, Ken, 30
Watkins, S. Craig, 92, 216n.28, 221n.33
Wayne, John, 68
Weaving, Hugo, xiv, 164, 183, 184, 193
Wedding Banquet, The (1993), 134
Weinstein Company, 128
Weintraub, Jerry and Evelyn, 103
Weller, Peter, 17
Westmore, Marvin, 63, 80
Whitaker, Forest, 157
white consumer subject/nonwhite
  consumed object binary, 19–24
White (Dyer), 17, 184–85
whiteface, Asian, 137
white male privilege: anxiety over,
  50; Asian Pocahontas icon and, 88;
  cultural and emotional lack linked to
  excessive capitalist consumption in
  The Karate Kid, 105–7; in cyberpunk,
  13, 17; in perspectives and fantasies
  in contemporary Hollywood cinema,
  37–38; white male as invisible
  standard in racialized hierarchy of
  masculinity, 100
white male protagonist: Asiatic
  characters and motifs as devices
  aiding development of, 85, 88, 90;
  geeky orientalized, in *The Karate Kid,*
  104; as "imperial subject" vs. "console
  cowboy," 11–12; masculinity of, in
  Black Rain, 118, 119, 120–22, 123;
  oriental buddy of, 90–100
whiteness: defamiliarized in Jarmusch's
  Dead Man and *Ghost Dog,* 158; as
  default mode, 176; fissures in
  paradigms of normative, in Reagan
  era, 86; friendships between white
  protagonists and nonwhite sidekicks
  in U.S. popular culture, 90–100;

performance of, through possession
  of class and cultural capital, 77; as
  racial and cultural norm, orientalist
  misrepresentations of East Asia used
  to secure tenuous centrality of,
  84–85; as universal signifier for
  humanity, 185; unpopularity and
  blandness in era of ethnic
  resurgence, 20–21; in visual culture,
  sense of absence in, 17, 21
Who Killed Vincent Chin (1989), 211n.21
Wicked City, The (1992), 174
Wiegman, Robyn, 209n.52
Wild Bunch, The (1969), 75
Wilder, Billy, 60
Wilkinson, Tom, 144
William II, Kaiser, 7
Williams, Patricia, 209n.60
Williams, Teresa Kay, 168, 224n.13
Willis, Bruce, 179
Wilson, P., 219n.76
Winant, Howard, 14, 208n.37, 209n.60
Windtalkers (2002), 95, 133
women: assimilated Asian American
  woman, 95–96; orientalized martial
  arts heroine of *Kill Bill* dyad, 153–
  57; representations of violent
  femininity, 153; role of alleviating
  homoeroticism between buddies,
  147–48; Trinity's tough, controlled,
  and empowered woman in *The
  Matrix,* 180
Won, Joseph, 190, 226n.44
Wong, Anna May, 73, 78, 218n.51
Wong, Cynthia Sau-Ling, 88, 105, 199,
  207n.26, 216n.17, 226n.2
Wong, Eugene Franklin, ix, 205n.2,
  216n.20
Wong, Russell, x
Wong, Shawn, 98, 217n.41

JANE CHI HYUN PARK is lecturer in the Department of Gender and Cultural Studies at the University of Sydney in Australia.